# THE ETHOS OF THE HONG KONG CHINESE

# THE *ETHOS* OF THE HONG KONG CHINESE

LAU SIU-KAI ▪ KUAN HSIN-CHI

The Chinese University Press

ISBN 962–201–431–3

First edition 1988
*Second printing* 1989
*Third printing* 1991

**The Chinese University Press**
The Chinese University of Hong Kong
SHATIN, N. T., HONG KONG

Printed in Hong Kong by Nam Fung Printing Co., Ltd.

To the Hong Kong and Chinese People

# Contents

## TABLES

# Preface

The eruption of the question of Hong Kong's future as a momentous issue in the early 1980s has irrevocably altered the political landscape of this once tranquil British colony. Many Hong Kong Chinese have been awakened from their political hibernation to become more aware of changes in their political environment. Yet, true to the label of "political apathetic" which has long been used pejoratively to designate them, the Hong Kong Chinese, though gripped by anxieties, uncertainties and fear, have not been roused to overt political actions. The small-scale democratic movement which came hard on the heels of the Sino-British negotiation over the future of Hong Kong is still the game of a small group of political activists who enjoy limited following.

The 1997 "shock" came in the wake of stepped-up contacts between Hong Kong and China that have grown since the mid-1970s. Before then, the identity of Hongkongese was largely a non-issue. Sudden and dramatic confrontation with one's fellow "compatriots" who differed from oneself in many significant ways willy-nilly forced one to ask the soul-searching question of "Who am I?" If there is any virtue in the heated but rather prosaic debates on Hong Kong's future that have been going on since 1981 and that have galvanized the attention of a small attentive public, it is that the Hong Kong Chinese are made more conscious of their distinct identity when placed in juxtaposition with the mainland Chinese people. In fact, the primary purpose of both the Sino-British Joint Declaration, signed in 1984, and the Basic Law, to be promulgated by the National People's Congress in 1990, is to design the necessary measures so that the distinctiveness of Hong Kong can be maintained under the formula "one country, two systems" for another fifty years after 1997. Whether this gargantuan undertaking will bear fruit in the future is difficult to say at the present. But from the point of view of social scientists, the distinctive Hong Kong identity and all that it embodies is already a tremendously challenging task. It is this challenge that we take up in this book. It goes without saying that we hope to make a modest contribution to the future development of Hong Kong by trying to clarify the Hong Kong identity and how it comes about. Only when these questions are adequately answered can we proceed to deal with the issues.

The data collected in two questionnaire surveys form the bulk of the data base of the book, particularly the survey conducted in 1985. We are deeply grateful to the Hong Kong Television Broadcasts Limited for generously funding this survey. The 1986 survey represents the pilot study of the long-term Social Indicator Project, and part of its findings have been incorporated in the book. We have to thank the Institute of Social Studies and the Centre for Hong Kong Studies at The Chinese University of Hong Kong for their financial support.

Mr. Peter T. Y. Cheung, Ms. Elaine Chan and Ms. Wan Po-san were our research assistants at different stages of our study. We owe them a lot for their dedication, competence and conscientiousness.

Needless to say, we are solely responsible for the shortcomings in the book.

Lau Siu-kai
Kuan Hsin-chi
October 1987

# 1

# Hong Kong as a Chinese Society

Hong Kong is geographically a part of China, but for more than a century and a half it has developed apart from China as an increasingly distinctive social entity. Under British colonial rule, this predominantly Chinese-populated society has developed into a prosperous and vibrant capitalist metropolis, which is a stark contrast with the essentially slow-moving command economy of Socialist China. Unlike China, which until recently pursued a strategy of autarkic development, Hong Kong's export-oriented industrialization ineluctably exposes it to international economic risks and fluctuations. The socialist state in China has played a dominant role in restructuring Chinese society through a combination of mass mobilization and ideological inculcation, while simultaneously warding off alien cultural influence by various thought control measures. The Hong Kong government has a much more limited conception of its role and thus makes it possible for the people to enjoy substantial measures of social, economic and cultural freedom. Economic growth and the ensuing rise in the standard of living in Hong Kong in turn fuel the inexorable processes of Westernization and modernization, the pervasive effects of which are evident in almost all spheres of social life. These effects are discernible even among people in the lower strata, thus testifying to their penetrative potency.

From the late 1960s to the late 1970s, the divergence in the paths of development between Hong Kong and China intensified. In this crucial decade, the pace of development of Hong Kong accelerated, producing enormous changes in the social landscape. In the same period, China turned even more vigorously to an introverted mode of development with primary emphasis upon the creation of the "new socialist man," "revolutionizing" state structures, social leveling and Maoist indoctrination. In this period of political and social upheaval, the economy was in chaos and the standard of living declined. Exerting arduous effort at ideological purity, China, in this crucial decade, was almost totally shut off from foreign cultural influences. If the normative orientations, life-style and mental outlook of the Hong Kong Chinese and the Chinese on the Mainland were already quite different by the late 1960s, they became wide apart in the late 1970s.

Even though no hard evidence is available, it might not be unreasonable to characterize the basic identity of the Hong Kong Chinese before the 1960s as "Chinese," with this "Chineseness" based more on social and cultural factors than on economic or political factors. Gradually, this "Chinese identity" has undergone slow and subtle changes. In our 1985 survey,[1] an astonishingly large proportion of respondents (59.5 percent) identified themselves as "Hongkongese" (*Xianggang ren* 香港人 ) when they were asked to choose between it and "Chinese." This Hong Kong identity, though not implying rejection of China or the Chinese people, necessarily takes China or the Chinese people as the reference group and marks out the Hong Kong Chinese as a distinctive group of Chinese. This group is perceived as one with a separate subculture which is more "advanced" than the dominant culture in contemporary China or the so often touted traditional Chinese culture. This Hong Kong identity does not entail much political overtones in terms of "Hong Kong nationalism" or the desire for political independence, thus indicating the lingering dominance of the unitary political ideology (*da yitong* 大一統 ) which is probably the fundamental principle in the Chinese political heritage.

The major features of this Hong Kong identity are what we shall explore in this book, and in doing so we have confined ourselves primarily to the social, economic, legal and political realms. We approach the subject by starting with the not unreasonable assumption that the Hong Kong ethos represents a mixture of traditional Chinese culture and modern cultural traits fostered by the particular nature of the Hong Kong society itself and the changes it has experienced in the past, particularly since the Second World War. Nonetheless, this overly simplistic assumption, which forms the cornerstone of our study, has to be qualified. In addition, some caveats have to be made in order to obtain a more balanced appreciation of the arguments in subsequent discussions. Firstly, the mixture of traditional Chinese and modern Hong Kong cultural elements has to be seen in the dynamic sense of interaction between different cultural features. There is no presumption that the traditional and modern elements are mutually exclusive or that the former are destined to ultimately disappear upon the onslaught of the latter. Instead, we expect a continuous and changing relationship between the two, which might encompass erosion of modern elements by traditional concerns, reinvigoration of particular traditional elements, preservation of traditional forms but with inclusion of modern content and enduring conflict between the traditional and the modern, among other possibilities. Secondly, there is always the risk that what is considered traditional in this discourse might turn out to be largely a straw-man assembled through subjective judgments and with dubious, scattered pieces of evidence. For our purpose of studying the popular ethos of the Chinese people, it is quite unfortunate that we cannot base our comparisons on systematic empirical data of the traditional values of the common Chinese people in the past. What are generally classified as traditional Chinese values are in many cases popular values found in rural China in the last two centuries when the West made inroads into China. Traditional Chinese values have also been drawn from the classics, the exhortatory statements of the scholar-officials, and the quite impressive amount of disparate studies on specific social phenomena in China. Accordingly, we have no choice but to treat as basically traditional values those receiving more or less consensual agreement in the literature. This unavoidably leaves open the possibility of misclassification or misunderstanding, but this is the risk we have to take. Lastly, it is generally agreed among scholars and observers that many so-called modern values structures already existed in traditional China, though in embryonic or primitive forms, such as the rationalized bureaucracy and the idea of equality of opportunity in civil service examinations. As such, the boundary between traditional and modern becomes blurred in particular cases. Upon encountering these situations, we will try to tone down the supposed contrast between the two and hopefully redress the balance in the process. Lastly, throughout the discussion we shall argue as though the Chinese and Hong Kong ethos were the causal product of social structural factors. We do so only for the sake of convenience of presentation, without making any claim of a structural determination of value and behavior. Yet, in view of the lack of suitable data and the insurmountable methodological hurdles involved, we are not able to prove the relationships, which we contend exist, between structural factors and values. What we aim at is modest. By providing a structural context within which the traditional Chinese values are transformed and the modern values take root, we hope to set up an interpretive scheme to make sense of the process of value change and the reconstruction of the distinctive ethos of the Hong Kong Chinese.

## The Traditional Chinese Social Order

The traditional Chinese social order and the homologous cosmic order in which it was a part were basically Confucian in nature. Nevertheless, in its tortuous history of development, Confucianism had incorporated a substantial amount of the tenets of Legalism and included certain Taoist and Buddhist doctrines as well. The elevation of Confucianism to the status of a state religion also had the effect of bureaucratizing it and shearing it of its anti-authority and populist pretensions. In its preoccupation with human affairs and the secular, it was more likely that the cosmic order, as conceived by Confucianism, was mimicked on the social level by generalizing the social order into the cosmic order. As the social order was understood as essentially a moral or ethical order, so was the cosmic order. By reversing the sequence of argumentation, the moral cosmic order was, in turn, evoked to legitimize the social order.

The Confucian social order was based upon a conception of human nature which allowed for the natural or theoretical equality of man but, at the same time, Confucianism rationalized a hierarchical order of status and roles. The status order was founded on the criterion of moral cultivation, with knowledge as either of secondary importance or the direct reflection of moral achievement. As Munro describes it,

> Three related elements are included in the early Confucian vision of the "social order," and it can be argued that a basis for each of the three exists in nature. The first element is a collection of occupational positions, every one having its own "job description." Second, there is a hierarchical relationship between these positions. Third, a formalized code of behavior, variously affecting the occupants of each place in the hierarchy, ties the whole together; the social virtues are realized by individuals who abide with this code. The social norms set the standard for distinguishing the noble from the

> base (as between any two social positions) and right from wrong (as regards acts). These two standards are interrelated, and what is right or wrong in the case of an act frequently varies with the relative status of the person affected by the act.[2]

Within the Confucian social order, the superior and superordinate component was the government, which was composed of the emperor and the imperial bureaucracy staffed by scholar-officials. The government would excel in moral performance, and act as the exemplar of moral deeds and the inculcator of moral ideals. Primarily by virtue of the moral competence of the ruler and his subordinates social harmony and *pari passu* cosmic harmony would be maintained. As a matter of fact, harmony was upheld as the normal state in the social order as well as the ideal to be attained.

Even though the emperor's right to rule was legitimized by a variety of myths, dogmas, beliefs and traditions, the legitimacy of the government in traditional China was not contingent upon the consent of another higher institution, such as the Catholic Church in medieval Europe. In traditional China, the government *was* the political institution, and politics was nothing other than *politics within the government.* All other social groups and institutions were subject to the government, and there were no institutional or legal limits upon the power of the state. As a result, the civil society was vulnerable to encroachment by the state. This unlimited conception of the scope of political power sets the stage for the emergence of the so-called "totalistic politics" which Tang Tsou found in Socialist China. "Totalistic politics" denotes "a particular form of relationship between politics and society; it leaves open the question of the nature of political institutions or organizational structures within society. 'Totalism' simply indicates a guiding doctrine that the power of political organizations may penetrate into and control every level and every sphere of society at any time and without any limitation."[3]

Despite the theoretical all-powerfulness of the traditional government, its right to rule seemed to rest on less than solid ground. In general, all the important legitimizing principles in traditional China could be subsumed under the notion of Mandate of Heaven (*tian ming* 天命 ), which in essence provided the *post facto* rationale for the continuous rule of a government that could preserve social and cosmic harmony as well as promote the well-being of its subjects. When political legitimacy was conceptualized in such a way, whether the ruler was entitled to rule or not would always be a controversial matter, with the intensity of the controversy rising and subsiding with the incidence or absence of politically significant events. Consequently, the Mandate of Heaven was something that "one must gain and maintain by constant virtue and effort."[4]

The relatively insecure basis of legitimacy provided by the Mandate of Heaven doctrine might further reinforce the paternalistic tendency of the Chinese ruler, but, at the same time, it might contribute to the suspicious and repressive disposition of the government, making it doubly intolerant of challenges to its authority from the civil society, and straining the state-society relationship.

Still, the power of the traditional government was supreme and unchecked until the situation was so serious that peasant rebellions toppled it and made way for its replacement. The government was not only unhampered by any forces from the civil society, it was not even effectively checked by moral forces, despite the doctrinal equivalence between ethics and government. As Nathan elaborates,

> For the Confucians, [the moral order was] created by humans, not nature. Moreover, their moral order differed in content from that which underlay modern Western theories of natural law such as those of Hobbes, Locke, and Rousseau. Confucians did not see the moral order as limiting the powers of the ruler. Instead, they saw it as calling for the fulfillment of the ruler's and the people's innate promptings as social beings. . . .[5]

The preoccupation with social harmony and the responsibility of the autonomous state to achieve it were closely tied to the way the Chinese socio-political order was formed. Its development took place over an extended period through the continuous assimilation of foreign elements into a unitary whole. To borrow the term used by Kamishima Jiro to characterize Japan,[6] traditional China was an "assimilating unitary society." The absence of the concepts of individualism and individuality in traditional China strengthened the collectivistic orientation innate in this particular kind of social formation. The relative geographical isolation of China and the ease with which neighboring barbarian tribes were assimilated into the Chinese civilization relieved traditional China from the need to change this basic predisposition. The fact that traditional Chinese society had been subjected to long periods of centralized bureaucratic rule, which had the effect of homogenizing society and reducing social differences, further provided the dogma of harmony with solid structural support.

Not surprisingly, social harmony was the preponderant theme in the vast literature of Chinese philosophical writings and the *leitmotif* of political actions.

To attain harmony and to equate this with "public interest" *par excellence* has had momentous implications for the relationship between state and society in traditional China. The penchant for harmony and stability elevated public interest high above selfish and potentially disruptive "private interest." The state, as the guardian and embodiment of all-important public interest, had the right to dominate and control the civil society, the domain of private interests. This line of reasoning often went so far as to deny the rightful existence of private interests. At the very least, conflicts between private interests, or between private interests and the state-represented public interest, were not only frowned upon, they were not even allowed to occur. It was the responsibility of the state to suppress private interest in order to restore the cherished aim of harmony. Accompanying the denigration of private interests was the failure to recognize any concept of individual rights or the rights of particular groups in society. If any such rights or privileges were found in traditional China, they were enjoyed either because of the tolerance of the state or because of it lacked sufficient power to curb them. In neither case was there any concept of their inviolability. All in all, there were no ideas of natural rights, no sense of social conflict as a natural thing, and no idea of a contract between the state and people; none of these concepts could be found in traditional China.

As our interests in this study are the social, economic, political and legal aspects of the ethos of the Hong Kong Chinese, there is a need to briefly describe the relevance of the traditional Chinese social order to these themes. These discussions can then lay the groundwork for assessing the content and magnitude of value change which the Hong Kong Chinese have undergone.

Firstly, the dominance of the state over civil society in traditional China meant that it was the prerogative of the state to mold society in such a manner that a favorable social environment could be created. This would enable personal moral cultivation, which would eventually promote social harmony, to take place. The role of the state *vis-à-vis* society was that of the *paterfamilias* (as the social order was conceived of as one big family), educator, leader, governor and controller combined. Among the governmental functions of the state, the pedagogical one was essential. Based on a theory of the plasticity of human beings, Confucian officials (including the ruler) were to serve as models for the people. To achieve this pedagogical end, there was no limit to social interventionism by the state, except for its actual capability. In fact, the state would devise a variety of institutional arrangements and administrative practices as the means to mold society.[7] Concomitant with this was the state's reluctance to recognize the autonomy of the natural or secondary groups that abounded in traditional China, for fear that they would then become entrenched interests withstanding state intervention. The role of private groups in traditional China as described by Fewsmith is revealing:

> In practice the Confucian monopoly on moral knowledge and legitimate political action was institutionalized in a bureaucracy which, through the law of avoidance, attempted to insulate itself from society. In a constant effort to maintain the centralization of authority, the government relied on a relatively small bureaucracy whose officials were regularly rotated. To expand the bureaucracy to further "penetrate" the society or to choose officials from the local areas, as some writers in the "feudal" (*fengjian* 封建 ) tradition desired, risked the "capture" of the bureaucracy by society and the consequent overwhelming of centripetal forces by centrifugal pulls. The bureaucracy monopolized communication to the throne and hence could dominate without penetrating.
>
> The low degree of bureaucratic penetration left ample political space on the local level, which was filled by voluntary and ascriptive associations of one type or another: clan, secret society, guild, and so on. Such extrabureaucratic "private" associations . . . were forbidden, and secret societies were strictly, if not effectively, prohibited. Clan organizations, normally co-opted to maintain local order, became suspect if they grew too large or too powerful. Guilds were important for the regulation of the economy but had no foundation in law. One senses a contradiction between the *de facto* organization of local society and the lack of legitimacy of such organization. Existing on the boundary between *gong* 公 and *si* 私 , they often pursued *si* while the state pretended they were *gong*. A game of words perhaps, but one with important ramifications for the legitimacy of the state and the role of local associations.[8]

In fact, this doctrine of the prerogative of the state to legitimize private organizations was so pervasive that traditionally, "local elites, like guild organizations, had accepted the fiction that they performed functions delegated by the state. The authority was derivative, not primary."[9]

Both the moralizing function of the state and the lack of institutional autonomy of civil society in traditional China legitimized the social interventionism of the state, which felt free to create social organizations as well as change or suppress existing ones.

In the political realm, the relationship between the rulers and the ruled in traditional China was quite a complicated one. Unlike traditional Japan, where the emperor might reign (but not always so) but not rule, the combination of the functions of reigning as well as ruling in the person of the Chinese emperor made it inevitable that he had to involve himself in a potentially conflictive relationship with his subjects. Despite stated ideals, the relationship between the people and their government in traditional China was an ambivalent one of approach-avoidance. The domineering role of the government was to extract resources (human and material) from society. But the government was not to be held accountable or effectively checked; this inevitably engendered grievances. As a result, the Chinese *citizen* "combined readiness to appeal to the government to intervene in any aspect of life in order to protect his interests or opinions, with a fierce resentment of government interference when applied to himself, and infinite resource in evading his obligations."[10] This simultaneous dependence upon government authority and resentment of its interference was likely to be an inevitable result of the need for public authority in a complex agrarian society where small-scale agricultural production centering upon the household was the norm. In this sense, the traditional Chinese was not alone.

> Like other nations, the Chinese people have long displayed ambivalent attitudes towards their rulers. Basically, the latter are expected to show the minimum of organizational virtues which will make regular food-crop cultivation possible. In the absence of natural or man-made calamities—and provided it performs its symbolic functions—a weak central authority will receive the deferential "filial" treatment stronger regimes outside of China would find necessary to demand forcibly. . . . This does not detract from the vital character of the role ascribed to the supreme ruler or leader: he is and must remain a life-giving unifier, or in other words, the man capable through presence, example, suasion or action, of

maintaining in a normal state of repair the social organization that ensures the livelihood of the Chinese people.[11]

Traditional Chinese generally lacked an abstract concept of government as a structural entity. On the contrary, government was personified, and this tendency was reinforced by the disposition of officials to act as father-figures to their charges. Paternalism in traditional China was therefore not something to be deplored, but a political ideal upheld by both officials and people.[12] The generally accepted superordinate-subordinate relationship between officials and people was converted in actual contacts between them into deference from the former and haughtiness from the latter. Whether dependence on authority was produced by the structural context of traditional China or, is a derivative of the particular mode of childhood socialization in an authoritarian family setting is immaterial here,[13] the upshot is that traditional Chinese were at the mercy of their parent-officials if by chance they got involved with them.

> The Chinese, with his pattern of mutual dependence, maintains strong ties with his family, kin, and local group that necessarily overshadow all his relationships with the wider society. He has, therefore, little reason to look for his social and emotional security among personalities and objects in the wider world. However, should contact with government become necessary, as when he is involved in legal action or seeks a place in officialdom, the Chinese cannot, naturally, conceive of such contacts other than in that frame of mutual dependence experienced with his seniors. He expects financial benefits, but he asks for them in terms of his superior's generosity. He hopes to win a lawsuit, but he phrases that hope in terms of the official's good graces. For the officials possess the law and he, one of the common people, can gain only by subordination.[14]

The normally unpleasant and demeaning official-people encounters naturally instilled an attitude of avoidance toward the government. However, the indispensability of the government in the social order and the enormous status-granting power at its disposal, derived from its monopoly of political power, inevitably rendered this avoidance stance also an ambivalent stance. This point can be made clearer by looking at the role played by the gentry in the lineages in rural China. They were the link between state and society. The clan rules in traditional China sought to keep the state at arm's length by paying taxes to the government on time and settling disputes within the clan without resorting to litigation.[15] Popular attitude toward the gentry, however, was to embrace them but to remain fully aware of the threats involved. This dilemma is brought out vividly by Freedman:

> It is precisely in the ambivalence towards the state that we see the crucial position of those lineage members who were also members of the gentry. They could act to moderate and restrain open hostility; they could mediate and soften the demands for taxes and reprisals made by the state upon their communities; they could bring the prestige of the bureaucratic system into their lineages and yet strengthen them against the system. The differentiated lineage was not autonomous, not simply because it was part of a centralized polity, but also because actual and potential agents of bureaucratic control were incorporated into its community. The ideas and authority represented by the lineage gentry might be resisted, but the gentry were at the same time sources of general benefit. Acts of defiance by the lineage directed against the state in one sense weakened the lineage gentry; yet in another sense these acts enhanced their strength, for the protection which they could afford had in the long run to be called into play.[16]

Without question, the role of the middleman or intermediary played by the gentry and other forms of social leaders (e.g., guild officers, clan elders and village heads) was crucial in the avoidance-approach syndrome of the traditional Chinese orientation to politics.[17] Nevertheless, that does not mean that traditional Chinese were totally at the mercy of the unchecked and arbitrary power of the government. Aside from the consideration that there were built into the traditional political system some sorts of checks and balances (such as the censorial system) that, to a certain extent, reined in blatant abuse of power by officials (including the emperor),[18] opportunities were available to traditional Chinese to restrain official power. In the first place were the more passive maneuvers.

> [T]he Chinese people, for their part, have protected themselves (a) by a system of negative checks through which they settle their own disputes and limit the government's power to that approved by custom and tradition, and (b) by a system of nepotism and favors through which the individual seeks to

> join the ranks of the elite or at least free himself from the burden of extralegal levies or other miscarriages of justice.[19]

Secondly, there was always the perennial threat of rebellion or symptoms that rebellions were in the offing. But, of most importance, must be the "less than given"nature of Chinese political authority based on the doctrine of the Mandate of Heaven. This doctrine subjected the legitimacy of the rulers to a standard, the measurement of which was somewhat obscure but included such things as peace and prosperity in the empire. This point can be clarified by comparing political authority in traditional China and traditional Japan. In both societies, by and large, political authority was considered as "given,"taken for granted and *a priori* in nature. This concept of "givenness" was apparently a result of the "remarkable similarity in patterns of authority, that is to say, in the ways that superordination and subordination are organized and exercised in both governmental and nongovernmental contexts."[20] In fact, the hierarchical authority pattern was embedded in the state and in the disparate groups in civil society: family, clan, village, guilds, secret societies and religious organizations. Furthermore, both traditional China and traditional Japan had been long immunized from encounters with other systems of authority in their historical development. This uncontaminated single experience with authority bolstered the sacrosanct character of political authority. As Koschmann explains,

> In order for man to develop a clear conception of political authority in terms of its essential components, and thereby to demystify it, he must come in contact with more than one system of authority. He must encounter political phenomena in a variety of contexts, where they are identical in essence but differ in detail. Only then can he discriminate essential aspects from nonessential ones. And only then can he finally learn that political authority depends upon his respect and is a product of his consent.
>
> In Japan, while unchanging authority was translated into real power by a succession of military and bureaucratic rulers, alternative examples of political authority itself were rarely if ever available to a large number of people. Never conquered by or directly confronted with external forms of political rule, they remained unaware of the potentially relative, fallible nature of all authority. Authority was a "given," taken for granted as an inalienable part of the natural order.[21]

While the similarities between traditional China and traditional Japan are impressive and most important, there is a significant difference between the two. In contrast with the more "insecure," posterior nature of the legitimacy of authority in traditional China, the legitimation of the authority of the Japanese emperor was of an anterior nature and hence more secure. And the *a priori* nature of this authority was protected by the fact that the emperor normally reigned but did not rule.

> Whether or not the legendary and semilegendary emperors are included in the reckoning, it is easily the world's longest royal dynasty. The present emperor is the 124th of his line, which traces its descent from Amaterasu, the sun goddess. . . . Alone among Japanese families, the imperial family bears no surname and to it alone is forbidden the otherwise common practice of adoption. . . .
>
> Given the nature of the claim to the throne, usurpation is simply not possible, for it is occupied not by divine right or the Mandate of Heaven, but by virtue of authentic genealogical descent from the divine founder of the line. Indeed, the Japanese imperial house advances the rather unusual and possibly unique claim of being able to trace its ancestry back in cosmic time before the establishment of the state over which it was to exercise sovereignty. Yet these divine kings were divested of political, secular power for a full seven hundred years between the inception of warrior rule with the founding of the Kamakura shogunate in 1185 and the Meiji Restoration of 1868. Why, then, did the institution persist, and why does it still exist? The answer lies, I think, in its very long and complete uncoupling from the exercise of secular, political power and its role as the ultimate source of legitimacy for those who sought to wield that power in its name.[22]

The less-than-given nature of Chinese political authority might be related to some salient political phenomena in traditional China: frequent succession of ruling dynasties; the incessant temptations to challenge authority by the politically ambitious; the lack of emotional involvement of the people with their rulers, which created a distance between them (this distance permitted the emperor to be autocratic but never totalitarian);[23] the concept of equality of opportunity in obtaining the right to rule (the Mandate of Heaven); the lack of total loyalty to the emperor or total allegiance to the regime; the instrumental conception of authority-self relationship and the proclivity to be suspicious of, to castigate and even to betray authority when it was in trouble or when it fell below popular expectations.[24] All this most probably produced an environment which compelled the rulers to resort to "soft" rather than "hard" authoritarian rule.

Like the social and political spheres, the legal sphere in traditional China was also dominated by the state. State dominance was expressed principally in the absence of an autonomous legal institution and in the status of law as the administrative tool of the government. The judiciary was an integral part of the administrative apparatus, whose functionaries were state employees, liable to dismissal and transferal, and loyal to the emperor. At the national level, there was a division of labor between the judicial branch and other administrative functions. In the localities, the county magistrate combined the roles of the executive, the legislator and the judge. As the administrative tool of the state, the functions of law were to uphold the social order and its status hierarchies, control and punish offences against the state (hence the prominence of criminal law in traditional China), inculcate social values and moral norms and, less importantly, facilitate the resolution of conflicts between private parties in civil society. The elevation of state interests to the neglect of private interests and the abhorrence of conflict were reasons for the nonexistence of such principles as *voluntas ius suum cuique* (rendering to each his due) and *nullum crimen sine lege* (no crime except in accordance with the law) that we find in Roman Law. In fact, law was considered a necessary evil which would be appealed to only as a last resort. The very occasion in which law had to be applied was usually a lamentable one as it implied the breakdown of moral norms or the ineffectiveness of reconciliation. Because of this negative attitude toward law, and the costliness of operating the legal machinery, the legal institutions were so designed as to deter people from using them.[25]

As law was used as a means to achieve the ends defined by the moral code and by the state, it had no autonomous function. Consequently, Chinese law did not exist as a system of codified rules that could be applied universally and predictably. Though it might be fair to say that the legal system in traditional China did function with a certain degree of rationality,[26] it must be stressed that it was permeable to the intrusion of moralistic and political considerations. Since political interests were variegated and forever changing and morality in traditional China was situationally oriented,[27] the application of law was always plagued by arbitrariness, though occasionally this "arbitrariness" did enable the judicial process to fit better with the idiosyncratic social realities. Still, we cannot avoid the conclusion that the legal institution in traditional China markedly emphasized the moral and political duties of the people to the detriment of their civil rights, particularly rights against the omnipotent state.

State domination of the economic sphere in traditional China is equally striking, even though the degree of domination decreased with time. In the Ming and Qing dynasties, the expansion of commerce led to the elevation of the status of the formerly despised merchants, who with their wealth, were able to buy into the ranks of the scholar-officials or to facilitate the entry of their progeny into this coveted stratum. At the same time the scholar-officials had no qualms about engaging in commercial pursuits.[28] Even so, the heavy hand of the state was felt by those with wealth.

The relationship between economic power and political power in traditional China was always a complicated and messy one. As a highly developed traditional society which could generate the necessary surplus resources for the support of a large-scale bureaucratic state, China could not do without commerce and trade. The dynamic character of the traditional Chinese economy and the role played by the state in it can be gleaned from the following descriptions of the Qing economy:

> While still premodern, however, the Chinese pattern of production and exchange had numerous modern elements: the widespread use of money; long-established and widely accepted legal behavior and institutions that encouraged rational choice by organizers of production and commerce; the widespread use of contracts to minimize risk and uncertainty; highly competitive markets characterized by ease of entry and exit, numerous suppliers and buyers, and little product differentiation. Individuals with family support readily contemplated occupational change and social mobility. Few obstacles hindered transactions in land, labor and commodities. Under these conditions, individual households allocated their resources to the highest paid users in order to satisfy their desired goals.[29]

Rozman goes on to say:

> China was unusual in its key organizational underpinnings, which permitted the private sector to operate relatively unfettered. Among them were the practices of customary law

> and the flexible policies of state organizations themselves. Households continually entered into exchanges with each other or shared resources, and customary law agreements, especially when formalized in written contracts, made promises fairly binding and minimized uncertainty. Households also combined to form economic organizations like merchant partnerships, guilds, and irrigation associations. The ability of households to work together for certain common goals and still produce benefits and rewards for each household in the collectivity greatly depended upon their compliance to common law. The state, on the other hand, left many decisions and transactions to the private sector and did not itself engage in costly intervention and regulation. Yet state organizations helped to offset occasional, critical scarcities within the private sector by maintaining flood control projects, distributing grain when necessary, and expanding the money supply to meet demand. Low taxes gave local areas more flexibility in using their own surplus resources.[30]

But economic power posed an endemic threat to political power. The survival of the state depended on the extraction of economic surplus from the traditional economy, and a static, zero-sum view of economic resources,[31] so common in traditional societies, would inevitably lead to seeing the wealthy as undercutting the foundation of the state. "In all Asian societies, including Japan, there has been ambivalence about the relationship between wealth and power. The general view was usually one in which wealth should not properly lead to power."[32] Because of the relatively small material resource base of traditional China, almost all political philosophers (including the Confucians and the Legalists) called for equitable distribution of wealth so that no section of population would be so impoverished as to become a source of political discontent in the system. The state was specifically charged the responsibility of nourishing the people (*yang min* 養民). To Confucius, for instance, the course to be followed in nourishing the people was simple and direct. "[I]n the main it does not go beyond enriching the people's livelihood, keeping taxes and imposts light, limiting labor service exactions, and restricting fiscal expenditures. . . . Moreover, the standard of plenty, as Confucius saw it, apparently had nothing to do with the absolute quantity of production, but merely with relative equality of distribution."[33] The call of Mencius to revive the abandoned "well-field" system (*jing-tian zhi* 井田制) put the same emphasis on distribution and redistribution rather than on production. Chinese philosophers would even countenance confiscation of the wealth of the rich by the state for distributive purposes if the need justified it.

The state's suspicion of private wealth was expressed in its hostility to the merchants. Merchants were usually condemned for being selfish, corrupt, immoral and despicable. They were accused of depriving peasants of their land, undermining the tax and corvée base of the state, luring peasants away from the farm, accumulating filthy lucre, disseminating dissoluteness and debauchery, displaying conspicuous consumption, shirking public duties, disrupting the economy and other sins *ad infinitum*. The penchant of the state for controlling the threatening private economic power explained many of the salient social-economic phenomena in traditional China: the violability of private property (it existed at the sufferance of the state); the not too infrequent expropriation of private possessions by the state; the *de jure* (not necessary *de facto*) lowly status of the merchants and their offsprings; the deprivation of merchants' rights (e.g., they and their sons were not allowed to take the civil service examinations, they were forbidden to wear gorgeous clothing in public); the merchants' perduring efforts to emulate the scholar-officials in thinking and comportment so as to mold themselves into "gentry-merchants" (*ru shang* 儒商 ); the reluctance of traditional Chinese to enter into trade and commerce; the goal of the merchants to ultimately leave their business; and the lackluster merchant-based or commerce-based urban culture in traditional China. Intent on controlling commerce and the merchants, the Chinese state was economically interventionist, so much so that it might even throttle economic vitality. For the sake of restricting economic exchanges, there were important state monopolies (in salt, iron, liquor and other essential commodities) and the state-run workshops. The state even controlled the supply of skilled artisans by registering them with the government and forcing their sons to follow their fathers' occupation. Markets were regulated by the state, as were the activities of the guilds of the merchants and artisans. The fiscal measures of the state were usually designed in such a way that the role of the merchants was minimized.[34] In all, there was no limit to state economic intervention in the pursuit of its interests, which were equated with the public good. It was the state's own limited capability and the fragility of the basically subsistence economy that set the limits. Still, the existence of a sacrosanct private economic sphere beyond the encroachment of the state was not recognized.

The state-dominated social order was largely perpetuated, in an even more glaring form, in Nationalist and Socialist China. This can be explained by the predominant role of the state in the development of a backward society and the coercive, mobilizational and organizational power at the disposal of the modern state. In the case of Socialist China, state domination went to the extreme of state control over the means of production and the virtual disappearance of private property. State intervention in society also reached a new height with the "New Life Movement" of the Nationalist government and the effort to mold a "Socialist Man" in Socialist China.[35] In colonial Hong Kong, a basically state-dominated social order has existed for more than one and a half centuries, but a different conception and pattern of state-society relationship appeared, which underwent some noticeable changes only in the last two decades. As a matter of fact, these changes, inaugurated by the exigencies of a modernizing society and of late by the confusions springing from the 1997 issue, have, however, left the basic nature of the social-political order of Hong Kong unscathed.[36] Thus, the state-dominated social order of Hong Kong, very different from the examples above, logically furnishes a setting for the development of a type of Chinese mentality in many ways very different from that of the Chinese on the Mainland.

## The Nature of Governance in Hong Kong

The colonial government of Hong Kong differs from the governments in traditional, Nationalist and Socialist China in several very significant and conspicuous ways, which explains its vitally different relationship with the Chinese people. While these distinctive features of the Hong Kong government have evolved gradually to adapt to the changing environment, it is certain that, at least up to 1986 (the year of the later of the two surveys on which our study is based), the nature of governance in Hong Kong has remained largely intact since its installation in 1843, when the first part of the colony was ceded to Britain by the moribund Qing government.[37] The scheduled restoration of sovereignty to China in 1997 threatens to undermine the fundamental character of Hong Kong as it has evolved over the years.

The most intriguing issue in any discourse on the nature of governance in Hong Kong should undeniably be the legitimacy of its authority. The fact is that Britain has been able to maintain continuous and stable rule over Hong Kong for about 150 years (except for the brief period of Japanese occupation during the Second World War) without suffering from large-scale dislocations nor from nationalistic onslaughts and this should provide *prima facie* evidence that the colonial government has managed to enjoy a certain level of legitimacy among the Hong Kong people, if by legitimacy we mean the degree to which the ruled feel obligated to obey the orders from the rulers. In both traditional and modern China, the legitimacy of any government is without exception based on ideological justification that forces upon the government the responsibilities to be a model of morality and to educate the people in moral deeds. Whether in the forms of the Mandate of Heaven, the Three People's Principles or Marxism-Leninism-Mao Zedong Thought, all Chinese governments are obsessed with legitimation by ideological dogmas which delineate their role in the cosmic order, the social order, the world order or in the inexorable process of historical development.

The establishment of colonial rule in Hong Kong was based, until several decades ago, on military force. In the long span of colonial rule, subtle versions of the doctrines of the economic prowess and cultural superiority of the white people, and the civilizing mission of the colonizer, had occasionally emerged to justify colonial dominance. Still, there has not been an elaborate, systematic theory, explicitly articulated, to buttress the legitimacy of authority in Hong Kong.

To disentangle the enigma of colonial legitimacy and its surprising immunization from nationalistic challenge, even in the period immediately after World War II when nationalism sparked off worldwide anti-colonial movements, several considerations are important. The most significant explanation must be that colonial rule has created vested interests in society which identify themselves with continued colonial presence. The reluctance of the local Chinese elites to support the claim of the Nationalist government to sovereignty over Hong Kong in the aftermath of the war, and the aversion of most of the Hong Kong Chinese to the Chinese takeover in 1997 (while recognizing the *de jure* legitimacy of Chinese sovereignty over the place) express vividly the preference of the Hong Kong Chinese for continued colonial rule as opposed to rule by the government of their motherland. In fact, their attachment to the colonial regime can partly be explained by the lack of an alternative to independence. This independence would be militarily and practically unfeasible and culturally (given the unitary political tradition) unbearable. To the majority of Hong Kong Chinese, the colonial government is the only option until a more acceptable government is in place in an economically less backward China.

But it would be a mistake to consider that the legitimacy of the colonial government is based primarily on "negative" grounds (its coercive capacity and it being the lesser of two evils). There is a certain *a priori* character to colonial authority. In the first place, it is very natural for the Chinese subjects to transfer their traditional conception of authority as a "given", a fixture in the cosmic order, to their colonial master. In fact, they might not be sensitive to "legitimacy" as a crucial concern in their relationship to their government. Something pertinent to the issue of legitimacy might cross their mind when they experience cultural or social discrimination, but usually without significant lasting effect. With the gradual decline in ethnic prejudices and blatant forms of discrimination and the rise to economic prominence of the Hong Kong Chinese, their reception of colonial authority has progressively improved. Another factor which contributes to the sense of the "givenness" of colonial authority relates to the sequence of formation of Hong Kong as a British colony. Hong Kong was a barren island on the eve of its acquisition by Britain. Only after the installation of the colonial government and the build-up of an administrative and physical infrastructure did the Chinese come in large numbers. Hence, unlike other British colonies in other parts of the world, the colonial government of Hong Kong existed prior to the inflow of colonial subjects. The colonial subjects, therefore, are a self-select group who voluntarily subscribe to colonial rule. Before the Second World War, most Chinese just came and went, without any plan to settle down in Hong Kong permanently. They generally did not question the status of the colonial government as "their government," as such the "givenness" or *a priori* nature of colonial authority was tacitly taken for granted. It was only after the maturation of the post-war generations that the legitimacy of the Hong Kong government gradually became an issue among a section of the populace, but still it has not become a salient political issue.

On the whole, it can be said that, while the colonial authority in Hong Kong is not blessed by the more secure ideological legitimation possessed by traditional and modern Chinese governments, it still enjoys a decent level of legitimacy which bolsters its rule. The degree of legitimacy might have increased with time through the sheer process of habituation and the fact that the colonial government can claim credit for the miraculous post-war economic prosperity of Hong Kong. The rational and efficient administration of the Hong Kong government and the generally incorrupt civil service also contribute to the acceptability of the government by the people.

In addition to the fact that the colonial government is less "natural" or "given" than traditional or modern Chinese governments and less legitimized on ideological grounds, other facets of colonial governance also detract from the legitimacy of its authority, and hence are conducive to ambivalent, suspicious and cynical attitudes toward it, though not to the point where colonial rule is in jeopardy.

Unlike traditional or modern China, where ultimate political power is theoretically obtainable by any Chinese, by means fair or foul, in Hong Kong ultimate political power is beyond the grasp of the Hong Kong Chinese. Even in the civil service, which prides itself in recruitment based on merit, Hong Kong Chinese, until recently, were excluded from the top positions. Thus, opportunities for upward political mobility, so extolled in China, are restricted in Hong Kong. Because of this, the demarcation between the rulers and the ruled is absolute with the rulers forming an exclusive caste of their own. This is a politically alienating condition, which can only be partly ameliorated by enlightened and benign rule. The fact that the rulers are a separate socio-cultural group, which distances itself from the overwhelming majority of the ruled by linguistic barriers, aggravates the sense of alienation and powerlessness among the ruled.

The distance between the colonial government and the people is increased by the very character of the Hong Kong government, which is a "pure," secluded and faceless bureaucracy. One of us has coined the term "minimaly-integrated social-political system" to portray the social order of Hong Kong,[38] underscoring the gap between the polity and society. Despite efforts from the government and from different groups in society, such a gap has never been effectively filled by intermediary mechanisms.[39] The rise of protest activities and other unconventional tactics of political influence indicates the communication problem between the two parties and that the predominant power lies in the hands of the government.[40] This intermediary gap can be placed in perspective by comparing Hong Kong with traditional and modern China. In the latter, there is an interflow of those with political influence between state and society. In traditional China, for instance, the gentry (degree-holders) and officials played different but complementary roles in society. What is more important is that they belonged to the same cultural and status group. Furthermore, there was a continual interchange of personnel between these two groups, thus bridging the gap between state and society as well as between the rulers and the ruled. The same intermediary role is played by party members in modern China. In Hong Kong, it is a rare community leader who is also an ex-bureaucrat, especially an ex-ranking-bureaucrat. For the expatriate bureaucrats, the role of community leader eludes them, or they do not have the appetite for it. The very character of state-society linkage in Hong Kong is not conducive to a higher level of state-society integration. An autonomous and "pure" bureaucratic government, unchecked by any substantial social forces, is bound to be an isolated or secluded entity.

The faceless character of the colonial bureaucracy reinforces its secluded position. In Hong Kong, the tendencies for the Chinese people to personalize political authority, and to identify with, and to feel secure in, fatherly or charismatic political figures find no responsive chord in the faceless bureaucrats. The centralized, rational and collectivist Hong Kong bureaucracy forbids its members from projecting their own personal images, nor does it tolerate the intrusion of explicit personal sentiments and considerations in its activities. The bureaucrats appear to the Hong Kong Chinese as cold, impersonal, unconcerned with human feelings, hidebound and aloof. Even though the bureaucracy as a whole adopts a paternalistic stance, the lack of paternalistic figures in its midst precludes affective identification with the government by the people and leaves feelings of cynicism and alienation unallayed. It is no wonder that when a rare figure, who could lay claim to some charismatic traits appeared, he could leave personal imprints on the mind of the people.[41]

The doctrines of social non-interventionism and *laissez faire* professed by the colonial government further minimize the integration of state and society. It is easy to understand why social non-interventionism is practised. The forcible taking of Hong Kong as a British colony did not involve any manifest cultural mission to assimilate the incoming Chinese people into Western culture, nor was this a feasible action. The British colonial tradition, moreover, tends to respect the cultural and social arrangements of the colonized and deny the possibility that alien peoples can be socialized into non-white British. The sheer number of the colonized in comparison to the handful of colonizers would make social intervention extremely difficult and costly. Besides, despite the fact that the Chinese society of Hong Kong is a society of immigrants and sojourners, the social fabric, knitted together by a web of primary (particularly the family) and quasi-primary groups, has been resilient and effective in stabilizing the Chinese society, thus obviating the need for governmental intervention. While basically the doctrine of social non-interventionism is to the liking of the Hong Kong Chinese with their tendency to keep the government at arm's length, social development in the last several decades had pushed the government to a more interventionist direction. Still, the role of the government in its more interventionist stance is to provide the necessary social facilities and services for an increasingly complex society and to supplement, to a certain extent, resource deficiencies in a society where the originally traditionalist support network is in decline. The interventionist goal of the government is conceived of only modestly. Instead of changing the organizational patterns in society, the intention of the government seems to be to preserve the old while augmenting it with the new. Though public actions may not necessarily lead to the attainment of this goal, the government, however, knows full well that any inadvertent actions on its part to disrupt the social fabric will severely redound upon the government and strain inordinately the state-society relationship.

The practice of social non-interventionism has two drawbacks for the relationship between the government and the Hong Kong Chinese. In ordinary circumstances the Chinese people would shirk the risk-prone entanglements with authorities, but in extraordinary situations, such as community problems, shortfalls in public services, public disorder, etc., the government is normally seen as the only party that can and *should* help, and it is not possible for the government to ignore these pleas without producing popular discontent. In the last few decades, with the rapid modernization of Hong Kong, the government found itself increasingly overloaded with demands for social services, public facilities and resolution of social problems. The decent performance of the government in satisfying these escalating aspirations, and the fact that it appears to be willing to be responsive, would definitely have had an impact on the political attitude of the Hong Kong Chinese.

The second drawback is in the manner that social non-intervention has been carried out by the government and this has had alienating effects. Specifically, the government, while leaving society basically alone, fails to discharge the moralizing and pedagogical functions, that are deemed by the people as a crucial responsibility of a government. In effect, the government "refuses" to serve as a model of moral virtues, and conversely it does not harbor much moral expectations for the people. By the same token, the people are discouraged from pressing moral demands on the government.

Therefore, the state-society relationship is not embedded in a moral network. Thus the lack of moral linkage between the rulers and the ruled cannot but impart a sense of cynicism to a society, even one still infused with traditional values.

If social non-interventionism is easily understandable, economic *laissez faire* certainly is not. It is almost a universal rule that late industrializers require greater state participation in economic development.[42] The state's role in amassing capital for producer goods such as iron or coal in Germany, Japan and Russia is well-known. Its role in fostering import-substitution industries as in Latin America has also been well documented. Even in export-oriented industrializers such as South Korea, Taiwan and Singapore, the state's role in developing entrepreneurship, raising capital, targeting export items and curbing labor demands is prominent. In contradistinction to others, the role of the Hong Kong government in the economy has so far been minimal. The government has confined its economic function to the provision of a viable political and physical infrastructure for the economy to prosper. Even so, some crucial public facilities (electricity, gas, telephone, etc.) are run by private monopolies granted by the government. In the past twenty years, the government had resisted almost all calls for a more interventionist economic role, even though it had, willy-nilly, gradually adopted a more active role in economic development.[43]

Before the Second World War, when Hong Kong was still basically an entrepôt dominated by trade and commerce, the *laissez faire* stand of the government was understandable. But, when Hong Kong made the transition to manufacturing in the midst of the Korean War, and when the international embargo on China severely undermined its entrepôt status, the role of the government in the economic process remained surprisingly small. Still, the process of transition was so successful that, by the end of the 1950s, domestically produced exports, particularly textiles and apparel, had surpassed re-exports, making Hong Kong the first of the "Four Little Tigers" to enter the export game. That the government was relieved from the arduous task of guiding industrialization in Hong Kong can be explained by several factors, which together might argue for the fortuitousness of Hong Kong's economic fortune.

In the first place, the timely inflow of capital and labor from China on the eve of export-oriented industrialization in Hong Kong freed the state from the role in capital formation, entrepreneurship or labor supply.

> That surge in manufacturing can be traced to refugees from the mainland. Revolution brought Hong Kong a huge supply of politically unorganized labor and a significant segment of the Shanghai capitalist class that had been developing since the beginning of the century. Equally important for the inflow of capital, however, was the technical know-how, skills and even machinery that refugees brought with them. Hong Kong's industrialization is virtually synonymous with the development of the textile and apparel industries, which were almost entirely in local hands. Immigrants set up the first spinning mill in 1947, the first combined spinning and weaving mill in 1948, in conjunction with British capital.[44]

From the outset, the private sector's dominance of the economy was established. In a certain sense, Hong Kong was more fortunate than South Korea and Taiwan in that it did not have to go through the initial stage of import-substitution to lay the groundwork for later export-oriented industrialization. Instead, the period of import-substitution industrialization for Hong Kong took place in China (especially Shanghai) in a disguised form.

Secondly, some development functions in Hong Kong have been assumed by banks, trading companies, and larger manufacturers, thus further relieving the state from the need to intervene.

> Private banks played a leading role in reconstruction. Most merchants had lost inventory during the Japanese occupation, and firms had no credit standing. The Hong Kong and Shanghai Banking Company took a long-term view of the economy, playing the role of central bank and extending large sums of money to public utilities and key industrial firms, often without collateral. The trading companies were also important to development: when entrepôt trade flagged, they took the initiative in developing alternative trade in local manufactures, particularly with the United States. This trade included not only arms-length purchases but also the provision of specifications, the guaranteeing of loans, and the supply of credit and raw materials. Subcontracting and the putting out system provided a start for many local firms, creating a virtuous cycle in the growth of large and small manufacturing firms not seen in Singapore. Small manufacturing enterprises continue to contribute significantly to total manufacturing output.[45]

Thirdly, as a result of the abundant supply of local capital, Hong Kong was spared the desperate need to court foreign investments and loans. This minimal dependence on foreign capital has two significant consequences: the formation of a powerful local bourgeoisie and the limited power of foreign capital to direct the economic and political strategies of the Hong Kong government (which might lead to a more interventionist stance). A caveat, however, is in order here. In Hong Kong, the distinction between local and foreign capital is not sharp. There is a long history of British and overseas Chinese enterprises, both commercial and manufacturing, headquartered in Hong Kong. But these enterprises have, over time, developed a local identity, and it is not unreasonable to conclude that *laissez faire* has allowed "national" firms to dominate Hong Kong's economic landscape.

Lastly, the role of the state in enforcing labor acquiescence in Hong Kong through repression, control, corporatization and coercion is less than in Taiwan, and much less than in South Korea, Singapore and Latin America. In fact, the labor regime in Hong Kong is quite liberal, and in the last two decades the government had taken steps to improve labor conditions and strengthen the role of labor in their relationship with employers. Nevertheless, Hong Kong to this day lacks minimum wage legislation, centralized wage machinery, compulsory collective bargaining, and other conventional elements of industrial relations.[46] In effect, labor peace in Hong Kong is enforced in a decentralized manner by the economic elites. Hong Kong workers generally face repressive labor controls at the hands of employers and powerful foremen at the enterprise level, despite new labor laws that seek to reduce abuses of power. To some extent, the government encouragement of trade unions in the mid-1970s countered this sort of blatant anti-unionism. The dominance of pro-China unions in the manufacturing sector, ironically, is instrumental in maintaining labor quiescence because of China's interests in an economically prosperous Hong Kong. The dominance of light export industries in the manufacturing sector that employs a large number of young female workers and the ease of horizontal labor mobility also militate against powerful trade-unionism. But the most relevant factor in the limited role of the state in labor control seems to be the structural characteristics of the economy, which do not feature large-scale state or private enterprises or heavy industries with a geographical concentration of industrial workers.

> Economic structural factors . . . help explain the greater effectiveness of enterprise-level controls in Hong Kong and

> Taiwan, and the relatively greater role of state-level controls in Singapore and South Korea. Latin American industrialization was associated with a marked concentration of the industrial work force in large, urban-based manufacturing plants. In East Asia such a characterization applied to South Korea and Singapore but not to Hong Kong or Taiwan.[47]

Hong Kong government data show a decline in the percentage of workers employed in factories of at least two hundred persons. From a high of 50 percent in 1966, it dropped to 29 percent in 1980 and 26 percent in 1985.[48] The prominence of small-scale production in Hong Kong has resulted in a relatively greater organizational dispersion of the growing industrial proletariat, thus taking the thrust out of any militant labor movements.

The government practices of *laissez faire* and social non-interventionism are arguably not solely the result of its doctrinal beliefs and the limited need for governmental involvement. Political considerations are also involved. The limited intrusion of the government in social-economic affairs has objective depoliticizing consequences which, while compartmentalizing state and society, do seclude the colonial rulers from their subjects and hence secure colonial rule.

Together, *laissez faire* and social non-interventionism lay the basis for a sharp demarcation between the "public" and the "private," and tacitly indicate a limited conception of politics and the capability of political power. Even though this separation of the "public" and the "private" is a *de facto* rather than a *de jure* one in Hong Kong's state-dominated colonial order, the mere fact that this distinction has been made and popularly recognized for such a long time gives it some sort of "social contract" status agreed upon between the government and society. Social consent is given to the government as a *quid pro quo* for its recognition of the legitimacy of private interests, acceptance of the autonomous status of the private sphere and abstinence from interference in private affairs except in extraordinary circumstances and with general approval. Needless to say, there is no institutional guarantee for the "public-private" distinction, it has to be contingent upon the self-imposed restraint of the government. So far, the government has meticulously observed this separation of spheres. This conception of the "public" and the "private" in Hong Kong contrasts pointedly with that in China where the concepts of political power and of the illegitimacy of private interest prevail and the "private" is not protected against arbitrary onslaughts from the "public."

Another difference between Hong Kong and China has to do with the former's limited government and its less than secure legitimacy as the colonial ruler. The limited functions assumed by the Hong Kong government and the manifold activities of the private sector that have society-wide reverberations make it quite difficult to equate the "public" or public interest with the government; the claim of the government to represent public interest will be discounted by society. As a result, the very nature of the state-dominated social order in Hong Kong provides fertile soil for a continuous tussle between state and society as to where public interests lie and the extent to which the government represents public interests.

Paradoxically, colonial rule itself, by virtue of its success, spawns the conditions which raise doubts about its *raison d'être*. More specifically, colonial rule inadvertently becomes the vehicle for the transmission of ideas and practices which eventually make it untenable, and colonial rule is also the crucible for the emergence of forces bearing a negative image of colonialism.

One of the most important features of British colonial rule is the rule of law, which, to a considerable extent, protects the security of person and property of the colonized and secure for them some important civil rights, which were only obtained by the people in the governing country after centuries of bloody struggles. While the colonial rulers retain the prerogative to make oppressive laws relatively unchecked by their subjects, they are, to a certain extent, restrained by the democratic tradition and public sentiment in their home country. In Britain, especially, the independence of the judiciary, the belief in the supreme rule of law (even the sovereign is not above the law) and the degree of effectiveness of the law in restraining abuse of political power ensure that colonial rule in Hong Kong is benign and enlightened.

The common law tradition of the British, compared to the continental law tradition in Europe, enables their legal system to more fully counterbalance political power. The respect for social custom and convention, the tradition of *stare decisis* (the "sacred principle" of English law by which precedents are authoritative and binding, and must be followed), the prominence of judge-made law and due process all provide the basis for legal autonomy. Furthermore, "the common law was supposed to contain within itself broad basic principles regarding the procedure and limitation of governmental organs which no one of them could undertake to change."[49] The rule of law and the independence of the judiciary are further bolstered by the very constitution of the legal community. Unlike Continental Europe, in England there does not exist any distinct judicial profession. Judges are usually appointed among the practicing lawyers and they are included in the lawyer's guild. Thus, judges and lawyers share the same socialization experiences, interests and legal outlook. In Continental Europe, on the contrary, the judges are in fact considered a species of government officials and cannot escape identifying with or being sympathetic to state interests. Organized into a distinct group, quite separate from the practicing lawyers, or "members of the bar," the judges are members of a hierarchically organized bureaucracy. Men enter into this bureaucracy after appropriate training and remain in it for the rest of their lives. A prime motive for the individual judge in following the precedents in the interpretation of the law is the ministry's (viz., the state's) influence upon promotions. The dangerous potentialities of the dependence of the judiciary upon the state were revealed in the extent to which judges in Germany and Italy betrayed their judicial trust under Fascist influence.[50]

The development of an all-inclusive professional guild in England is of the greatest consequence for the independence of the judiciary. It is only against this background of a consolidated legal profession, priding itself upon its mastery of the "artificial reason" of the law, that the emergence of judicial "independence" can be evaluated. The fraternal community of bench and bar and the primary reliance on collegiate control on judicial behavior forbid the encroachment of the state. The security of tenure of the judges embedded in the principle of *quamdiu se bene gesserint* (during good behavior) further precludes state interference as the standard of conduct implied by that principle is set by the collegial and fraternal organization of bench and bar. The compelling force of professional ethics has been given governmental recognition.[51]

While the whole English legal tradition is not replicated in Hong Kong, there are enough of the elements of independence of the judiciary, the fraternal organization of bench and bar and fair application of the law to set it miles apart from traditional and modern China. In Hong Kong,

> [T]hough the judges are formally appointed by the Governor, he is bound by law before doing so to take the advice of the Judicial Services Commission—an independent statutory body presided over by the Chief Justice and upon which, as

> well as the Attorney General, serve a High Court Judge, a barrister and a solicitor in private practice, and a prominent layman . . . The judges, both of the Supreme Court and also of the District Court, have security of tenure in office until they reach retirement age; they are irremovable unless and until the Judicial Committee of Her Majesty's Privy Council in London, after due process of law, advises the Queen that the particular Judge "ought to be removed from office for inability arising from infirmity of body or mind, or for misbehavior."[52]

The judges of the Supreme Court, secure and independent in office, ensure the supremacy of the law above all other powers in the state. It is they who rule upon the prerogative writs (e.g., *habeas corpus*, *certiorari* and *mandamus*), which any individual in Hong Kong may issue, to test the legality of any of the government's actions which affect that individual. Moreover, neither the government nor even the Governor himself has any control over criminal proceedings. The Attorney General, subject to direction from no one, has sole responsibility for them. But his power is only to charge, or to stop the proceedings by entering a *nolle prosequi*. He cannot convict. It is the independent judiciary, in appropriate cases with the assistance of a jury of one's fellow citizens, which has the task of deciding a man's guilt or innocence, and thereafter of imposing the proper penalty on those found guilty.[53]

It must be admitted, however, that because utilization of legal means to resolve conflict has its costs, access to it is inequitably distributed among the people of Hong Kong. The claim of the legal system to be the stalwart of justice and the fact that the rule of law in Hong Kong is to a large extent a reality, therefore have to be balanced by the fact that the legal system has yet to prove that it does not mete out differential treatment to different sectors of society. The *de facto* discrimination against the have-nots and in favor of the haves would most likely evoke feelings of cynicism even with the general endorsement of legal justice in Hong Kong.

Colonial rule, despite its authoritarian character, ironically also has its quasi-democratic features, and it is therefore no wonder that the "democratic" elements in the past anti-colonial movements owed their birth to colonialism as the "school for democracy." Hong Kong presents no exception to this, it might even be said that the way Hong Kong has been governed makes it, in some senses, a more effective "school of democracy."

The system of consultation, centering upon the councils and committees at all governmental levels, gives the people an opportunity to participate in the management of their own affairs. "In such councils it was possible to secure some experience of the public business and the ways in which it might be approached, of the give and take of politics, and of parliamentary procedure. The more extensive the range of powers and functions of these councils, the more effective the experience was likely to be."[54]

In spite of the fact that these advisory organs are dominated by the executive by virtue of his power to make appointments to them and his prerogative to ignore their advice, the system of consultation still is a halfway house which gives some taste of democratic procedures and stimulates demands for more. Steps to strengthen the consultative system by introducing elective elements in them and by expanding their influence have been taken since the late 1960s and particularly during and after the Sino-British negotiation over the future of Hong Kong. Though there are obvious limits on institutional changes in Hong Kong,[55] the quasi-democratic consultative governance of Hong Kong should not fail to impart its effect on the political values of the Hong Kong Chinese.

Education in the political process is not confined merely to participation in the quasi-democratic institutions introduced by the colonial government. It also flows from the rational and legalistic bureaucratic administration. Except on the top levels, the meritocratic principle has been abided by in the recruitment of civil servants. As the repository of power and status, the civil service has been, and still is, a greatly coveted channel of upward social mobility for the ambitious Hong Kong Chinese. In comparison with the traditional Chinese or even the modern Chinese bureaucracy, that in Hong Kong is much less afflicted by nepotism or personalism and suffers less from the paralyzing effect of intra-bureaucratic rivalries or factional strife. Despite their arrogance and self-righteousness, Hong Kong's civil servants are much less corrupt and venal. Even though bureaucratic hegemony is the norm in Hong Kong, there still remain some means for the common people to seek redress against officials through internal bureaucratic procedures, litigation, various public bodies, or the mass media. The pertinence of a rationalized administrative system patterned after Western models to democratic training was aptly appreciated by Emerson:

> By itself the creation of an honest, impartial, and efficient administration is, of course, not necessarily a stepping stone to

> democracy since such an administration may quite as well serve an autocratic regime, but without it the emergent democracies cannot hope to survive. Its democratic bearing becomes more evident when other features of its development are taken into account. The recruitment of the civil service on the basis of merit rather than of traditional status, the separation of the public purse and business from the person of the ruler and his immediate entourage, and the assumption that all the people are entitled to equal treatment and under the rule of law work in their different fashions to establish conditions essential for democracy. As the "nativization" [in Hong Kong, "localization"] of civil service progresses, more and more of the local populace are drawn into association with the government and secure training in the conduct of a modern state, no longer wholly vested in a remote and alien bureaucracy well above their heads. On this score, again, the British and American practice have been superior to those of the French who have notoriously staffed the middle and even some of the lower ranks of the colonial service with Frenchmen rather than with people of the country; while the Dutch in the Indies fell somewhere midway between the two approaches.[56]

The pertinence of the civil service has been further enhanced by the recent acceleration of localization in Hong Kong.

The "soft" authoritarian rule of the colonial government also contributes to quasi-democracy. Secure in the belief that it is the only political option for the people of Hong Kong, it feels no imperative to create a political infrastructure to buttress its rule. Thus, unlike other "hard" authoritarian systems, in Hong Kong there are no government parties, government-sponsored corporatist structures or supportive, state-initiated mass organizations. In the same vein, the government has no need to resort to suppression to sustain colonial rule. Consequently, while there is a dearth of *positive* channels of political participation, the people of Hong Kong are still able to enjoy a tremendous amount of *negative* political freedom (freedom from government oppression). A case in point is the relatively free press in Hong Kong, which stands in stark contrast to the absence of an all-powerful propaganda apparatus in the hands of the government. In fact, Hong Kong's compact society possesses a highly developed mass media structure which spans a wide spectrum of political colorations. Even though the government retains suppressive power (enshrined in the harsh press laws still existent in Hong Kong), it is rarely used except in crisis situations. As such, freedom of speech and expression is largely taken for granted and is difficult to rescind. Compared to traditional and modern China, where thought control is vigorous and considered a legitimate function of governance, the negative political freedom enjoyed by the Hong Kong Chinese should have an impact on their ethos.

All in all, the nature of governance in Hong Kong comprises a set of inconsistent elements, viz., authoritarianism, ambiguous legitimacy of authority, limited government, benign and enlightened rule, separate but blurred public and private spheres, rule of law and quasi-democratic appurtenances. Some of these features are compatible with traditional or modern Chinese governance, while others are additives to Chinese political culture. Together they furnish a peculiar but congenial ambiance for the fostering of a very particular ethos among the Hong Kong Chinese.

## The Nature of Chinese Society in Hong Kong

Not only does the nature of governance in Hong Kong differ from traditional and modern China, but the Chinese society in Hong Kong can also be distinguished the Chinese society as it is commonly understood. In order to provide the backdrop for making sense of the ethos of the Hong Kong Chinese, it is necessary to highlight these differences but we must not forget that Hong Kong and China still share many of the same cultural characteristics. As Hong Kong society has undergone, and is still undergoing, rapid social change, any portrayal of it has to take into account its dynamic dimension.

Unlike traditional and even contemporary China, Hong Kong is an industrializing, modernizing and predominantly urban society exposed to Western acculturation and immersed in cosmopolitanism. All these grand-scale forces should exert enormous influence on the mentality of the Hong Kong people, even though it would be almost impossible to disentangle specific cause-effect relations.[57] Though at different speeds, the life-style, patterns of consumption, cultural tastes and career aspirations are approaching the modern, Western standard. Aside from these materialistic changes, it is also easy to detect subtle changes in normative expectations, though no systematic understanding of them is available.

The main distinction between Hong Kong and other Chinese societies is the lack of a settled population until after the Second World War. In the past, there were incessant inflows and outflows of people who were forever in search of economic opportunities and escape from political turmoil or suppression. As a society of immigrants and their offspring, the Chinese society of Hong Kong cannot avoid manifesting some degree of artificiality. The fact that Hong Kong inhabitants came to the place voluntarily underlines the "self-select" character of the Hong Kong population. In other words, the sociocultural profile of the Hong Kong Chinese must be vastly different from that of China.[58] The immigrants to Hong Kong were more urbane and modernized than their counterparts in China, and, in a sense, they were more ready or willing to "uproot" themselves from their Chinese soil. In short, they might be more adventurous, "individualistic," self-reliant and less encumbered by traditional inhibitions.

A society of immigrants also features truncated patterns of social organization as it is impossible to transplant whole social or community formations to a new environment. Even the family and kinship structures have to be modified to adapt to the exigencies of survival. At the same time, the role and functions of other primary and quasi-primary groups have to be enhanced, and their organizational forms altered to meet the new demands on them. The proliferation of these traditional groups in the history of Hong Kong testifies to the adaptability of tradition to an alien and modernizing environment. The adaptability of the Hong Kong Chinese and their society should result in simultaneous adherence to tradition and willingness to change, but in both there is a conspicuous element of self-selection exercisable by the individual(s) concerned. As such, a sense of individual efficacy *vis-à-vis* one's environment might be the result.

The tenacity of tradition in the Chinese society of Hong Kong has been drastically weakened by the absence of the agrarian-landlord and gentry-scholar-official classes in the colony. The nonexistence of these classes means that there have been no powerful custodians to uphold and enforce Confucian morality and virtues, nor are there any cultural hegemony to influence the substance of education. The disappearance of Confucianism from the content of Hong Kong's civil service examinations even deprives the residual Confucian presence of instrumental value, and relegates it to cultural backwaters. Confucian influence lingers on, but this is contingent more on the natural influence of social customs and family socialization than on any institutional underpinnings. Confucianism still has to face the unrelenting incursions of modernization and Westernization. Moreover, it has to contend with the anti-traditional thrust of the Chinese socialists, who have not failed to impinge on Hong Kong.

As a result, the Chinese elites in Hong Kong are made up of an assortment of people whose claim to elite status is doubtful or downright presumptuous. The early Chinese settlers who came to Hong Kong could even be dismissed as the "scum" of Chinese society, and the Hong Kong government initially was unable to "improve" the composition of the Chinese immigrants.

> Hong Kong government authorities were much concerned in the first ten years of the colony's existence about the type of Chinese who came to the island. Conditions were not conducive to attracting wealthy Chinese of respectable background, who could strengthen Hong Kong's economy by promoting local and Southeast Asia trade in China products. There had been some optimists who believed that the Chinese would welcome the opportunity to live and trade under an "enlightened, benevolent government," but they had underestimated traditional Chinese xenophobia and inbred loyalty to China as the motherland.[59]

Gradually an embryonic Chinese elite appeared and was made up of contractors, merchants (including opium monopolists[60]), compradores, government servants and those employed by the religious missions. Later on a more established Chinese elite appeared, but they took on a totally different character from traditional Chinese elites. According to Smith,

> [T]he Chinese elite of nineteenth-century Hong Kong consisted of interpenetrating advisory, financial, and professional groups. Members of this elite played an important role in bridging the social and cultural gaps between the Chinese and the British in the colonial society. In some cases, they played a further important role in the modernization processes of China. Yet they were almost all of humble origin. . . .
>
> Ho Ping-ti, in his study of social mobility in China, argues that the most important rung in the ladder to elite status was success in the Chinese civil service examinations. [In contrast,] the first rung in nineteenth-century Hong Kong was education at an English-language school, and further, that people typically progressed after their education, from

> government servant (usually as interpreter) to compradore, capitalist, and finally appointment to the Legislative Council.[61]

Since the Second World War, with the rise of Hong Kong as an industrializing society, the role of wealth in elite status has been greatly enhanced, though not necessarily displacing education, government service and proficiency in English. From the preceding description we can note several salient features of the Chinese elites in Hong Kong:

(1) Most of them came from humble origins, a mark of the openness of Hong Kong society. Ethnicity is only a partial deterrent to upward social mobility.

(2) The elite class is an open and non-exclusive group. The elites cannot control the entry of new elements into their ranks, nor can they forestall any downward exit of their members. Thus the Chinese elites are forever in flux. There is no closed upper caste to severely restrict mobility opportunities in society.

(3) Elite status is not based on cultural accomplishments (for example, distinction in Confucian learning), moral excellence or political achievements, but, most importantly, on economic success. In traditional and Socialist China, politics is the determinant of elite status, which in turn brings economic fortune. It is the other way round in Hong Kong: it is usually wealth which leads to political recognition (but not necessarily to political power) in the form of appointment to advisory bodies and the award of honors.

(4) The values embodied in the Hong Kong Chinese elites, because of the origins and character of these elites, differ from those of their counterparts in China. Their moral status is shaky, and they have no sense of cultural or moral mission. The dominance of this amoral elite, together with the shunning of the moralizing role by the colonial government, means that there is no powerful group or institution to safeguard tradition and Confucian virtues, thus unleashing the floodgate for modernizing intrusion. The crass materialism inherent in the economically-based Chinese elites and the growing opportunities for economic mobility ineluctably leave their imprints on Hong Kong ethos, and they are not counterbalanced by the "spiritual" and anti-merchant dogmas so pervasive in traditional and modern China. As a result, materialism and utilitarianism run rampant. The spread of Christianity by the missionary schools that many of the elites attend might temper the rampant materialism among the populace, but their modest influence proves too weak to make a noticeable dent in the

Chinese psyche, particularly when it runs against the spirit of a booming economy.

(5) The nature of the Hong Kong economy further enhances the economic clout of the local bourgeoisie. The establishment of Hong Kong's light industrial base prior to the significant entry of foreign capital has left economic power in the hands of the indigenous capitalists. This explains their social stature and political influence. The over-dependence on foreign direct investment in the initial stage of state-directed industrialization in Singapore, on the contrary, accounts for the weakness of the indigenous bourgeoisie who can only cut a niche in the less strategic sectors of the economy there. The dependence of the economy of Hong Kong on foreign trade and the openness of overseas markets add to the social stature of the indigenous bourgeoisie. Dependence on foreign trade helps to create an image among the people that the wealth of Hong Kong is obtained from abroad, under the enterprising leadership of the local capitalists who pry open foreign markets and create employment at home. These economic leaders, instead of being the scions of entrenched interests, have managed to rise from humble origins. This heroic image of the economically successful not only mitigates potential sentiments of class antagonism, it might even foster popular opposition to any blatant and clumsy governmental attempts to contain free-wheeling private economic enterprise. Of even more importance might be the consequent breakdown of the traditional "zero-sum" conception of economic goods. The displacement of this economically enervating dogma by a conception of unlimited availability of economic goods should not fail to have "revolutionary" impact on the ethos of the Hong Kong Chinese.

On the other hand, the very nature of economic development in Hong Kong produces other potentially antagonistic effect on the outlook of the Hong Kong Chinese. Reliance on foreign markets and growing dependence on foreign direct investment as a means of technology transfer induce a sense of economic inefficacy among the people, who have no means to control their economic future. The recent rising current of international protectionism exacerbates this feeling of helplessness, which casts a shadow on the economic pride so potent in the ethos of the people. Furthermore, the economic growth of Hong Kong has been bought with the costs of inequitable distribution of income and wealth among the people. As a measure of income inequality, the Gini coefficients in Hong Kong for the years 1966, 1971, 1976 and 1981 are 0.487, 0.411, 0.435 and 0.447

respectively. Though one can of course take comfort in the fact that compared to most other developing countries (including the more developed Latin American countries), Hong Kong has so far managed to combine economic growth with equitable distribution of income;[62] still, income inequality in Hong Kong is staggering and had widened in the early 1980s. The government, through the provision of social services, subsidized housing and so on, has already played a part in reducing the level of income inequality, but these measures are far from sufficient to make a great impact. The government does not have the capability to make a frontal attack on this problem. There is a gradual restructuring of the Hong Kong economy resulting from a number of causes: foreign protectionism; competition from the new NICs (newly-industrializing countries); the sudden availability of cheap labor in China; the need to strive for high-technology export-products; the need to court foreign capital; the less optimistic future prospect of the world economy as well as the economy of Hong Kong; and the exodus of local capital due to the 1997 malaise. All of these things point to a less sanguine view of income distribution in the future.

The feeling of economic dependence is coupled with that of political dependence. With no possibility of independence, Hong Kong Chinese are dependent on the alien colonial rule of the British, and in the future will come under Chinese rule. The impossibility of the conversion of economic power into ultimate political power in the past, now, and in the future, is likely to produce uncomfortable feelings of political frustration. But, at the same time, it will fuel an even more exaggerated emphasis on economic achievement and on a conspicuous display of wealth and consumption patterns, inadvertently fomenting nascent "class" feelings.

The time factor is of enormous importance in understanding the changing ethos of the Hong Kong Chinese. Hong Kong's industrialization really took off in the 1950s, but its major effect on the standard of living on the people came probably as late as the 1970s. If we take the view that value changes lag behind structural and economic changes,[63] then it should be reasonable to expect the co-existence of old and new values in Hong Kong. Symptomatic of this should be some sort of schism in the outlook of the younger and older generations. The time available for structural change to erode old values should not be sufficient to impart a homogeneous ethos among the Hong Kong Chinese. Normative conflicts and behavioral inconsistencies within and between individuals should be commonplace phenomena in Hong Kong; these conflicts and inconsistencies should be considered as logical outcomes in a fast-changing society.

Secular changes in Hong Kong society and the recent appearance of the momentous 1997 issue, whose long-term effect on Hong Kong ethos have yet to be fully comprehended, have also to be taken into account in interpreting the findings in regard to the Hong Kong ethos. Hong Kong's population has become younger and more educated. The percentage of people in the age group of 15-34 was 28.3 percent in 1961, but it increased to 29.7 percent in 1971, soared to 40.7 percent in 1981, then dropped a little bit to 39.4 percent in 1985. The percentages of the population with less than primary education in selected years from 1961-81 were: 42 percent in 1961, 39.3 percent in 1966, 31.9 percent in 1971, 25.6 percent in 1976 and 22.1 percent in 1981. Contrariwise, those with secondary education or above were 16.3 percent in 1961, 19.3 percent in 1966, 23.6 percent in 1971, 31.4 percent in 1976 and 41.2 percent in 1981.

The role of the government in society has also expanded, though its impact is more on the absolute amount of resources devoted to social services and infrastructural facilities than on the size of the public sector, which remains largely stable. Public expenditure as a percentage of Gross Domestic Product (GDP), for instance, was 14.6 in 1979-80, 17.8 in 1981-82, 19.1 in 1982-83 and 16 in 1984-85. Another measurement produces similar results: government consumption as a percentage of GDP (at constant 1980 market prices) was 7.1 in 1974, 6.6 in 1979 and 6.8 in 1984. On the other hand, the rate of increase in public employees is quite fast. The authorized establishment of public service contained 114,692 persons in 1976-77, but the figures jumped to 151,809 in 1981-82 and 181,719 in 1985-86.

Growing involvement of government in social and (to a much lesser extent) in economic affairs has overloaded the existent limited channels of political participation. The increasing resort to unconventional influence tactics and extra-institutional modes of demand-making (e.g., demonstration, protests, parades, etc.) has irreversibly changed the political landscape of Hong Kong in the last twenty years.[64] The tolerant attitude toward non-violent protest actions and their modest effectiveness in eliciting a response from the government have given unconventional influence tactics a semi-institutionalized status in the political culture of Hong Kong.[65] The proliferation of various types of "pressure groups" from the grassroots, instigated by a section of the growing middle stratum of Hong Kong, coupled with the expanded influence of the vested economic interests, are symptomatic of a higher level of political activism, though Hong Kong's basic political character remains unchanged.

This political activism receives a significant boost from the 1997 shock, though it is far from clear whether a long-term trend of increasing political activism will take hold or whether the sudden rise of politicization in the last half-decade represented only a temporary interlude in a depoliticizing trend. Still, its effect on our findings in the 1985 and 1986 surveys should be discernible.

The scheduled return of Hong Kong to China in 1997, in spite of the latter's promise (enshrined in the Sino-British Agreement signed in 1984) to allow Hong Kong to maintain the capitalist system and its original lifestyle for fifty years after the departure of the British, has plunged Hong Kong into a quagmire of uncertainty. The social, economic, political and cultural distinctiveness of Hong Kong, which sets it apart from China and used to be taken for granted, suddenly appears to have only a short lease of life. This sudden awareness might engender a reinforced feeling of attachment to the things as they presently are, a reluctance to accept changes in the *status quo* and a sharpened sense of a Hong Kong identity.

On the whole, the Chinese society of Hong Kong differs from traditional and modern Chinese society in many essential ways: its high degree of modernization, industrialization and urbanization; its dominance by market forces; the erosion of tradition; the adapted changes in the family and other primary and quasi-primary structures; the lack of a moralizing elite and the dominance of an economic elite; the fluidity of society and the extent of social mobility; the self-select character of the immigrant-settlers; the high standard of living; the exposure to foreign influence; the rapidity of social change and its political and economic dependence. Its "borrowed time, borrowed place" character,[66] grossly magnified by the 1997 malaise, can in fact stand alone to differentiate Hong Kong sharply from China. The high degree of societal autonomy from the state and the more or less spontaneous development of society are also an experience which modern China has yet to undergo.

In the subsequent description and analysis of the ethos of the Hong Kong Chinese, we shall make reference to the distinctive features of the polity and society of Hong Kong and draw on them to interpret the data. To anticipate the conclusion of this study, it can be said that the particular ethos of the Hong Kong Chinese is firmly grounded on the peculiar social-political order of Hong Kong.

# 2

# Individual, Social and Economic Values

A conception of man and an orientation toward human nature provide the benchmarks for making sense of human cultures. Attitudes toward the individual are, in general, the cornerstone of a system of social and political values. We, therefore, start with an analysis of the conception of the individual in the ethos of the Hong Kong Chinese. This will then become the basis for an exegesis of their social, economic, legal and political values.

## Conception of the Individual

Conspicuously absent from the Chinese conception of man is the idea of individualism in the Western sense, nor is there any positive valuation of the virtues of individuality. Among the components of the concept of individualism, several are of paramount importance: the ultimate principle of the supreme and intrinsic value, or dignity of the individual human being; the notion of autonomy or self-direction; the notion of privacy; the ideal of self-development; the conception of an abstract individual with given interests, wants, purposes, needs, etc.; the ideas of human liberty and rationality.[1] In short, the individual is highly valued and takes precedence over society or any other collectivities. Implicit in the Western concept of individualism are a positive view of human nature, a low degree of fatalism and theories of individual rights and equality.

The concept of individuality is derived from the need for personal development or self-actualization inherent in the doctrine of individualism. Its central point is the need for the expression of each person's uniqueness. "Individuality is concerned with the interior qualities of the person, with expressivity, and subjective conscience, and the development of sensibility, consciousness, personality and will."[2] The attainment of self-development inevitably runs counter to social constraints, and it is the removal of those social constraints, which are detrimental to self-actualization, that is emphasized in the doctrine of individuality, as witnessed, for example, in the Romantic movement of the late eighteenth and early nineteenth centuries.

The ascendancy of individualism in the last several centuries in the West was related to the particularity of its historical development. Up to the present moment, there is no place in the world where a full-blown doctrine of individualism has been successfully transplanted, and this includes such places as Spain, Portugal and Greece that might be loosely said to belong to the West. The enormous difficulties encountered in the transfer of concepts cross-culturally can readily be seen in Hong Kong, where the persistence of Chinese culture is strong.

The origin of individualism in the West can be traced to antiquity and goes back to the religious foundation of Western society.

> [A]n emphasis on the subjective individual emerged in Western cultures because of the accidental presence of Christian beliefs about the soul. As a result of the destruction of the original Jewish-Christian church under Roman Imperial conditions, the Christian community emerged as a de-tribalized group of individuals bound together by faith and members of a community called the church. Because Christianity was originally a Jewish movement, which emerged and developed inside a Greek culture, there was less space for the influence of particularistic tribal allegiances. Christianity began to develop as a complex community with diverse ethnic origins. These circumstances favoured the development of an emphasis on the individual soul. The Christian emphasis on personal belief and loyalty to a universalistic god was further developed inside a Roman context, where Roman legal notions of the *personal* began to merge with Christian emphases on the soul. In other words, there was a fortuitous combination of a particular aspect of Roman legal theory and Christian theology to produce the notion of a subjective personality with rights and obligations. . . . [W]ith the institutional development of the Christian church as a universalistic institution in

> feudal Europe, the confessional came to be used as an instrument for the control of heresy and political protest. The notion of conscience began to be used for largely political reasons, that is, to achieve control over the Christian hinterland, particularly in remote and mountainous regions. However, the confession in the society of the court also contributed to the flowering of a court culture, which to some extent was quite individualistic or at least favoured the individual development of personality. . . . [T]his had a particularly important consequence for the emergence of women as private and unique individuals. Thus Christianity provided many of the ingredients that were necessary for the development of conscience and personality, and these ingredients were combined with a variety of other cultural circumstances in Europe.[3]

Subsequent events in the historical development of the West—the Reformation, the rise of Protestantism, the discovery of the individual in medieval and early modern Europe (the Enlightenment), the rise of the cities, the Commercial and Industrial Revolutions and the Age of Revolution (sparked off by the French Revolution)—propelled the doctrine of individualism to the forefront of ideological discourse.

Traditional China presents a vastly different path of historical development. Though long-term changes can be identified, the social order of traditional China was, however, quite stable and the changes it had undergone were basically cyclical. Most importantly, absent in Confucianism and in many of the other schools of philosophy was the idea of a transcendent God: there was no God in relation to which the individual had a special role, no notion of individual equality before God, and no concept of individual salvation in another world. The pre-occupation of Confucianism with secular human affairs, the "societalization" of the cosmic order and the sacredness of group life were not congenial grounds for the assertion of the individual. The equation of self-development with realization of oneself in society and the observation of social status-role demands further submerged the individual beneath society and social groups.

But that does not mean that traditional Chinese thinking did not recognize the individual. In fact, traditional Chinese philosophies did have definite ideas about individual equality, rights, duties, and freedom. However, the particular way in which these values were articulated makes them compatible with steep status inequalities and the subordination of the individual to society and state. These values still form an integral part of the concept of man in the ethos of the Hong Kong Chinese, despite the infusion of modernizing influences.

## Orientation toward human nature

The conception of human nature in most agrarian societies is conditioned by the economies of scarcity and the corresponding image of "limited good" or constant-pie orientation.[4] Because people are seen as embroiled in a relentless game in which survival is at stake, it is difficult to nurture a favorable view of human nature. As a result, misanthropic sentiments are pervasive in traditional societies. In traditional China, the absence of interpersonal trust has been extensively documented in both scholarly works and in casual commentaries.[5] Aside from the zero-sum view of worldly goods, the inordinate stress on the family plus limited opportunities to deal with strangers and poor communications and transport facilities all contributed their part to interpersonal mistrust.[6]

Some traditional Chinese views (particularly Confucianism and Mohism), however, took a more sanguine view of human nature. The propagation of Confucianism as the state religion had complicated the popular view of human nature, though not transforming it. All men were deemed to have the potential to become good by cultivating their evaluating mind. In the case of Mencius, human nature was even declared to be good. By focusing on the human condition at birth, the Confucians were able to arrive at a theory of a natural (or biological) equality of men.

> . . . [A]ccording to the Confucians, the content of human nature is threefold: first, a number of constant activities that man shares with other animals (eating, drinking, sleeping, sex); second, certain social activities unique to man (the statement of what these are varies from thinker to thinker); and third, an evaluating mind that can assess the natural nobility or baseness, rightness or wrongness, propriety or impropriety of an object, act, position, or event. Man can use his evaluating mind to guide his innate social tendencies along the proper lines. These three components are shared by all human beings and make them biologically [naturally] equal.[7]

The fact that all men was naturally equal, however, did not mean that all men were *actually* equal, for environmental factors came into play to cause differences in moral excellence among men. The availability of appropriate training techniques and qualified teachers was also of crucial importance. "Two environmental factors were particularly stressed: economic well-being and education. Following Mencius' observation that men whose livelihood is insecure are not likely to perceive and perform the 'right' actions, Confucian works occasionally suggest that the government intervene in the economic life of the country, purportedly to guarantee the people the economic security necessary to reliable moral discrimination.[8]

The Confucian conviction of the malleability of human nature and the importance of the social environment blends uncomfortably with the people's cynicism and suspicion of human nature. The influence of modernization, on the other hand, has been suggested as a salutary one:

> *Calculability* or trust: By our definition the modern man should have more confidence that his world is calculable, and that people and institutions around him can be relied upon to meet their obligations. We assumed that the modern man would be more prepared to trust a stranger than would the traditional man. He would not agree that everything is determined either by fate or by the whims and the inborn character of men.[9]

The modernized Hong Kong Chinese's view of human nature is complex. It falls short of the expectation of modernization theorists and reflects the imprint of tradition. In our 1985 survey, 57.8 percent of the respondents agreed and 4.2 percent strongly agreed that human nature was evil, therefore there must be war and conflict in the world. Ironically, 74.1 percent agreed and 4.7 percent agreed very much that human nature was good and if it turned bad, it was the work of the environment. The respondents seemed to emphasize the molding power of environmental factors while remaining uncertain about the valuation of human nature. The belief in the malleability of human nature can be further corroborated by the fact that 75.1 percent of the respondents agreed with the statement that except for diehard criminals, all criminals could be rehabilitated provided that people in society made the effort.

Uncertainty about the valuation of human nature plus the belief that people could be transformed appeared to produce a modest level of interpersonal trust. 42 percent of the respondents disagreed or strongly disagreed with the statement that most people could not be trusted. This compared favorably with similar findings by Almond and Verba. In their cross-national study of the United States, United Kingdom, West Germany, Italy and Mexico, the percentages of respondents who agreed that "most people can be trusted" were 55, 49, 19, 7 and 30 respectively.[10] In terms of "abstract" interpersonal trust, the Hong Kong Chinese appear to be fairly modernized.

But "abstract" social trust has to be qualified by actual experience in concrete situations. 57.1 percent of respondents agreed and 2.6 percent strongly agreed that "in these days one really doesn't know whom to rely on or trust." Only 30.1 percent disagreed or strongly disagreed. Therefore, in order for "abstract" social trust to be translated into "real" social trust, actual cooperative experience in an institutional framework which fosters interpersonal rapport is needed. The moderate level of actual social trust in turn is implicit in the attitude of the Hong Kong Chinese toward individual equality and individual rights.

## Individual equality and individual rights

Embedded in the concept of the individual equality of Confucianism is an idea of individual freedom. However, instead of the Western individualistic view of freedom, which stipulates that individuals should be as free from interference in their activities as it is possible to be, freedom in the Confucian sense is conditional. Confucians, in their penchant for moralizing, only allowed the freedom to do good, which was defined in the Confucian way.

> The freedom advocated in Confucian ethics is the freedom to do good or the freedom to choose what is good. It is ethical freedom of choice. But such freedom of choice has its own ground and its own limits. It is a limited freedom. There is no such thing as an unlimited freedom.[11]

In the mind of Confucians, the limitation of freedom in such a manner would not impose an undue burden on the individual, as there was an inherent tendency in the evaluating mind of the individual to seek out the Confucian good. Therefore, the limitation on one's freedom only facilitated the realization of one's natural inclination. The *a priori* specification of the content of the evaluations to be arrived at by the human mind made it possible for natural equality and actual social inequality to co-exist. As Munro points out:

> From a philosophical standpoint, the Confucians would have been on firmer ground if they had based their doctrine of

> natural equality simply on the thesis that all men evaluate and choose; indeed this position is still found in contemporary Western philosophy. But in the Confucian doctrine there was an antecedently determined *content* to the evaluations made by the mind: that is, it was assumed that certain specific things would be judged superior and inferior, proper and improper, right and wrong. It followed that nature demanded a hierarchy of social positions, and the Confucians continued to advocate some kind of social aristocracy, no matter how imbued they became with egalitarian sentiments.[12]

This particular Confucian view of individual freedom, however, finds only faint echoes in the mind of the Hong Kong Chinese. Their preponderant obsession with personal freedom is a well-known fact, though this personal freedom has more to do with basic civil rights and socio-economic freedom; the freedom of political participation has so far received only lukewarm support.[13] Unlike the Confucians, the Hong Kong Chinese appear to reject any *a priori* specification of the content of freedom, nor do they confine freedom to only the ethical or moral realms. Neither would they support the Confucian view that the government has the right and responsibility to restrict freedom for the common good.

Several relevant findings will make these points clear. 68.1 percent of the respondents claimed that the goal of law was to protect the citizen's right to choose any moral criteria, in contrast with the 17.2 percent who saw the goal of law to compel the citizen to abide by society's criteria of right and wrong. Even though "social stability" ranked very high in the mind of the Hong Kong Chinese and they were worried about rampant social problems, still less than half (39.1 percent) of respondents agreed or strongly agreed that social problems sprang from too much individual freedom. Among the many freedoms conceivable, freedom of speech is of overriding importance to the Hong Kong Chinese, and this is reflected in the finding that an overwhelming 96 percent of respondents agreed or strongly agreed that "everyone should have freedom of speech." The furor in 1987 ignited by the Public Order (Amendment) Ordinance, which was construed by the mass media as meaning the government was attempting, to curb freedom of speech attested to this preoccupation with freedom of expression.

Because of the almost sacrosanct status given to freedom, any attempt by the government to restrict it will not be tolerated. Only 34.8 percent of respondents concurred that sometimes the government must force the people to do something against their wishes for the sake of the common interest. Most of them (52.9 percent), however, rejected this as the prerogative of the government. It is also interesting to note here that respondents were more likely to support this prerogative of the government if they believed that man's nature would make war unavoidable,* if they considered that most people were not trustworthy, and if they did not think that human nature was good.

The Hong Kong Chinese view of individual freedom differs sharply from the Confucian standpoint, and even the attitude prevalent in modern China, thus testifying to modernizing influence and the lack of elite and institutional support for tradition in Hong Kong. Nevertheless, this refutation of tradition does not necessarily drive the Hong Kong Chinese to embrace wholesale the Western view of freedom. Implicit in the Western view of freedom is a general acknowledgement of the binding power of some universal principles that provide the guidelines for the exercise of freedom. These universal principles undergird the Western legal system. The Hong Kong Chinese, interestingly, fail to evince acceptance of binding universal principles. Of course that does not mean that they have an unrestricted view of individual freedom, for social norms and mores have their part to play in restraining individual freedom and make social order possible. What is relevant here, however, is not that freedom is untrammelled to the Hong Kong Chinese, but that it is guided by a morality which is situational in character. This gives both a measure of flexibility and a degree of fluidity or openness in the social relationships among the Hong Kong Chinese. The operation of situational morality, derived from the traditional Chinese ethos, has been considerably mitigated by modernizing influences and the institutionalization of law and other formal practices, but the relative or situational conception of morality still lingers on in the ethos of the Hong Kong Chinese.

In traditional China, situational morality owed its existence to the view of the individual as a concrete being enmeshed in a stratified social order where everybody had a definite set of obligations and privileges according to his status-role and degree of closeness to a particular set of concrete persons.

* Throughout the book, a relationship is said to exist between two variables or phenomena when the chi-square value is significant at the 0.05 level.

> In the Confucian tradition, morality was particularistic. One's moral obligations to others were defined by their positions within one's network of personal affiliations. In Confucian moral discourse, the configuration of Chinese society was, as the great Chinese anthropologist Fei Xiaotong [Fei Hsiao-tung] expressed it, "like the rings of successive ripples that are propelled outward on the surface when you throw a stone into water. Each individual is the center of the rings emanating from his social influence. Wherever the ripples reach, affiliations occur. The rings used by each person at any given time or place are not necessarily the same. . . ."
>
> In such particularistic configuration, the nature of one's moral obligations to another depended on the precise nature of one's relationship to the other: for instance, a son's obligations to his father were different from a father's obligations to his son. And the intensity of one's obligations depended on the closeness of the relations. As Fei described it, the further the ripples of one's social relations were propelled, the fainter they became. Thus, one's obligations to immediate family members were more intense than obligations to distant kin.[14]

Yet the network of personal relations that defined the sphere of one's closest loyalties is highly elastic, thus situational or particularistic morality would call for differential treatment of others according to particularistic norms. "In contrast to Confucian morality, Western moral discourse is universalistic. One's moral obligations toward another are defined by general norms equally applicable to all persons of a particular category. . . . In such a universalistic group configuration, the nature of one's moral obligations to another is determined by what specific common groups one belongs to and by what norms govern the conduct of everyone in such groups."[15] Moreover, there is, in Western moral discourse, also the idea that there are universal norms applicable to all irrespective of conditions. Such an idea was more or less anathema to traditional Chinese and its underdevelopment severely affected the functioning of the law and the bureaucracy.

To measure the influence of situational morality in the ethos of the Hong Kong Chinese, we asked our respondents to choose among three moral "options": first, sticking to their own moral principles in disregard of results, second, modifying these moral principles if adherence to them would bring adverse consequences, third, acting in disregard of any moral principles if adherence to them would bring adverse consequences, or acting in disregard of any moral principles in order to achieve personal goals. The findings testify to the persistence of situational moral discourse. The first option was taken by 21.9 percent of respondents and the third one by a minuscule 3.4 percent, while the second option was chosen by 63.9 percent of them. Hence, flexibility in adapting moral principles to changing situations instead of strictly abiding by them is still the norm in Hong Kong.

Obsession with individual freedom on the part of the Hong Kong Chinese naturally leads them to be concerned with their individual rights. In traditional China, there was no concept of the natural or inborn right of man. In place of the idea of natural right was the belief that individual rights were derived from society and hence were subordinate to societal interests.

> Rights are entrusted by society to the individual; society is the source of rights. The individual apart from society has no rights to speak of. Since society bestows rights, at times of necessity it can also remove rights; at least it can limit their scope.[16]

Such a conception of the social origin of individual rights was and still is starkly expressed in the concept of political right in China. Political rights are granted, and thus can be withheld, by the state for instrumental collective purposes:

> As constitutions defined them and laws and political practice spelled them out, political rights in China were consistently regarded as a grant given by the state to the citizens, to enable them to contribute their energies to the needs of the nation.[17]

The purpose of political rights has never been to protect the individual against the government. The use of rights for self-seeking purposes cannot be part of their legitimate purpose. If rights are granted, the individual is expected to use them cautiously and with restraint. By the same token, the concept of social right is equally restrictive:

> The people's only claim in the Mencian [*minben* 民本] conception of government was for welfare, and even this was not a right they could demand but a responsibility the ruler was urged to shoulder for both moral and prudential reasons.[18]

Underemphasis on rights in China has a correlation in an overemphasis on duties, which signifies the dominance of society over the individual.

> [I]t was not the rights of the individual that were considered most important. Of most importance were the duties or

> obligations of the individual. According to Confucian ethics, in order to be a man or to be a sage, it is necessary, first, to perform one's duties, not to claim one's rights. It is a fulfillment of duties that can make a man into a man or into a sage.
>
> The duties of the individual are the moral principles according to which one should act with regard to oneself and to others.[19]

When individual duties, predominantly social in nature, are underscored, the detrimental effect of the absence of a concept of natural individual freedom are further magnified.

Thinking in the same terms as traditional Chinese, Hong Kong Chinese also harbor a theory of the social origin of individual rights. 65.6 percent of respondents agreed and 3.7 percent agreed very much with this statement: "The rights possessed by a person in society are not in-born. It is because of his good performance that society gives him the rights as rewards." Only a tiny minority (20.5 percent) disagreed or strongly disagreed with it.

Such a conception of individual rights explains why Hong Kong Chinese are not hesitant in denying these rights to people who pose as a menace to social order. Only 32.8 percent of respondents agreed to give the right to vote to those who voted *blindly*. 68.6 percent agreed that someone who didn't even know what he was talking about should not be allowed to speak in public. 70.3 percent would take away the right of expression from a newspaper which distorted the facts. 62.7 percent thought that the government should prohibit assemblies of people who advocated something which the people were against (such as the legalization of homosexuality). When social order is at stake, even the procedural rights of the defendant in a criminal trial might be sacrificed. For example, only 30.2 percent of respondents were definitely against the use of illegally obtained evidence to convict a suspect.

To be sure, it is difficult even for people reared in Western civilization to practice tolerance and to fully respect the rights of others. In the United States, "[o]nly a minority of the mass public fully appreciate why freedom of speech and press should be granted to dissenters and to others who challenge conventional opinion."[20] The data in the United States also showed that "a large majority of the population would deny to unpopular groups the use of the community's facilities to express unpopular opinions suggest that most Americans have only a crude sense of the meaning of a 'right' as that concept has evolved in the American experience."[21] In reality, the idea of individual rights is difficult to learn, and more difficult to practice even in a country such as the United States which prides itself on its libertarian tradition.

> [D]espite their ubiquity and their apparently singular hold on the American public mind, libertarian norms are difficult to learn. Though easily voiced in the abstract, they raise, in principle and practice, complex issues that make extreme demands on our understanding and patience. Some rights . . . clash with each other. Others violate our ideological outlook or sense of moral decency . . . Still others deeply offend religious sensibilities . . . while others are affronts to patriotism . . . Freedom of speech or press may also be used in ways that outrage our sense of social justice. . . .[22]

The difficulty is further compounded in a culture which celebrates equality of opportunity and competition among individuals.

> In a culture which strongly emphasizes achievement and reward, the notion that one enjoys an ineradicable and inviolable claim which one has done nothing to earn is difficult to grasp. It is far easier to grasp the idea that a right is a *privilege*, a reward for proper conduct or conformity to community standards—and it is precisely in these terms that the concept of a right is often understood (or, more accurately perhaps, misunderstood). By this reasoning, those who behave disreputably or who endanger the society by their conduct or who fail to play the game by the rules should be denied the benefits enjoyed by more deserving citizens.[23]

Hong Kong shares with the United States the same relentless competition among individuals, but lacks the soothing influence of the American libertarian tradition. The relatively low respect for the rights of others is, therefore, not difficult to understand. Consequently, despite the modest level of abstract social trust displayed by the Hong Kong Chinese, they have yet to substantiate it with a decent demonstration of tolerance.

**Personal efficacy and fatalism**

Fatalistic ethos and low personal efficacy are dominant traits in the scarcity economies of traditional societies.[24] Most of traditional Chinese eked out only a bare existence.[25] The magnification of individual achievement in Confucian ideology, the ostensibly equal opportunities offered by the state for upward social mobility through state service, and the openness of the Chinese economy, to a certain extent, ameliorated fatalistic feelings. The open and dynamic socio-economic order of Hong Kong dangles before the eyes of Chinese unlimited opportunities for individual success unprecedented in the extended history of China.

Hong Kong Chinese have a limited use of fate as an explanatory factor for success or failure.[26] Individualistic variables (education, hard work, foresight, etc.) have more often been cited instead of fate.

In our 1985 survey, the findings pointed to a loosening grip of fatalism in the ethos of the Hong Kong Chinese. 52.3 percent of respondents disagreed or strongly disagreed with the following statement: "Nowadays the people of Hong Kong can only adopt the attitude of 'let tomorrow look after itself.' " 44.9 percent disagreed or strongly disagreed (as compared with 42.4 percent who agreed or strongly agreed) with the statement "To design long-term plans for oneself will make one unhappy because most of the times these plans will not materialize." Even more evidently, 80.2 percent of them disagreed or strongly disagreed with the statement "Whether one will be successful or not is determined by fate, it is useless to make the effort." Obviously it is this rejection of fate as the determinant of one's future that propels Hong Kong Chinese to strive hard for success.

The weak belief in fate, however, is not automatically translated into a high level of personal efficacy, which is the belief in one's ability to change one's environment. Despite the economic success of Hong Kong, the double sense of economic and political dependence, which has recently been aggravated by international protectionism and the 1997 malaise, might have diminished the sense of efficacy which the Hong Kong Chinese *should* evince. Thus, we should not be astonished to find that 54.3 percent of respondents agreed or strongly agreed that "in face of future uncertainties, we can only adjust as best we can," and only 38.3 percent had a different view. The combination of the belief in individual effort with a fairly low sense of personal efficacy *vis-à-vis* one's environment is a reflection of the peculiar social context of Hong Kong.

## Personal goals

One of us had in the past pinpointed the centrality of material values in the ethos of the Hong Kong Chinese.[27] The expression Lau had used to depict the Hong Kong Chinese ethos, "utilitarian familism," underscored their longing for material possessions and the use of materialistic criteria for normative judgments.[28] Later on Lau, in view of the weakening of the family institution in Hong Kong, coined another term "egotistical individualism" as a portrayal of the core values of the Hong Kong Chinese,[29] but materialism still looms large there. The abundant opportunities available for the acquisition of material goods, and the relatively short time in which Hong Kong has left material scarcity behind, stimulate rampant material desires.

Gradually, however, the emphasis on material values has declined, though they still occupy a central position in the ethos of the Hong Kong Chinese. In the 1985 survey, 14.7 percent of respondents strongly agreed and 70.3 percent agreed that the most important personal goal was to make as much money as possible without breaking the law. Only 11.8 percent failed to agree. Other findings, however, revealed a slight erosion of material values. The 1986 survey showed that while 40.5 percent picked "income" as the major consideration in job selection still more than half of them would look for other attractions. Similarly, in spite of the fact that 81.4 percent of respondents rated money as important or very important in a happy life, only 8.5 percent of them named it as the most important element. To the respondents, health was the most essential element in a happy life, as it was chosen by 55.1 percent of them. Furthermore, the importance of income was less to respondents who were younger and more educated. Though rigorous longitudinal data are unavailable for comparative purpose, our impression is that the dominance of materialism has slightly abated among the Hong Kong Chinese.

## Individual-society relationship

Under utilitarian familism or egotistical individualism, individual and family interests are without exception ranked above societal or collective interests. In fact, society is seen as an arena where individual interests are pursued, and social interests are important to the extent that this arena has to be preserved for the sake of individual interests. In other words, aside from serving individual interests, social interests have no other legitimate claim for recognition.

But utilitarian familism and egotistical individualism in their ideal-typical forms are not the ethos of the Hong Kong Chinese *in toto*. Other normative influences, particularly those originating in traditional China, are also at work. Social interdependence in the complex industrial society of Hong Kong would naturally breed an awareness of the larger society and its interests. The fact that Hong Kong has gained a settled population should also contribute to a more popular concern for Hong Kong society. What is more pertinent here is that Confucianism assigned a secondary place to individual or sectional interests, and sought to suppress their assertion. Private interests failed to receive legitimate recognition in traditional China, nor were there institutional channels available for the proper reconciliation of conflicting private interests. When society was ranked all-important and when social harmony was determined as the primordial social interest, authoritarian control of private individuals was the inescapable outcome. This traditional view stands in sharp contrast to utilitarian familism and egotistical individualism. To the Hong Kong Chinese, this ideological dissonance cannot be easily resolved.

Consequently, there is a basic contradiction in the ethos of the Hong Kong Chinese. It has been established that utilitarian familism is a dominant theme there, so is the growing salience of egotistical or acquisitive individualism. But the hold of tradition still persists. *Hence, whether the modern theme or the traditional theme occupies the central position will be contingent upon the situation at hand. The ready availability of the traditional outlook, however, means that private interests in Hong Kong can be curbed without too much difficulty if collective interests in a particular situation can be demonstrated to be of supreme importance.* Moreover, shifting back and forth between the traditional and modern outlooks is eased by the "situational morality" of the Hong Kong Chinese, which does not impose hard and fast rule on moral choice.

The traditional theme of the primacy of social interests in the ethos of the Hong Kong Chinese is manifest in two of our findings. In the 1985 survey, our respondents were presented with the following statement: "Someone says that there is in society something called 'public interest,' which is more important than any private interest. For the sake of the public interest, private interests can be curbed or even impaired. But there are also people who say that there isn't the so-called 'public interest,' therefore private interests are most important. No one can impair private interests on the pretext of public interest." The respondents were asked to choose between the two points of view. The result was illustrative. As many as 62.6 percent of them recognized the presence of the public interest, whereas only 21.1 percent repudiated the idea of public interest. Thus, public interest still looms large in the mind of the Hong Kong Chinese.

Another finding relates to the guardianship of public interest. In the 1985 survey, a general statement was posed: "The people of Hong Kong are selfish, and forces in civil society cannot be relied upon to maintain social stability. Only a government with authority can be depended on to restrain these selfish people and to avoid conflict and confusion." More than half of them (57.9 percent) agreed or strongly agreed with this statement, while only 25.3 percent disagreed with it. In interpreting this piece of evidence, it must be borne in mind that it only establishes in a general sense the need for authority on the part of the Hong Kong Chinese. But this authority is not necessarily the same as the incumbent colonial government, even though the two somehow overlap. To anticipate later discussions, in some senses the Hong Kong government fails to be the private-interest curbing authority the Hong Kong Chinese have in mind, because it sometimes is seen as one among the many self-regarding private interests.

## Social Values

The general recognition of public interest and the need for authority to bolster social order by curbing private interests underscore the predominant value of social stability in the ethos of the Hong Kong Chinese. This strong need for social stability is apparently rooted in the lack of enough trust in other people and insufficient sense of personal efficacy. But it also is derived from the succession of social turmoil and disorders which plagued modern Chinese history, from which many of the elderly Hong Kong Chinese have fled. Even Confucianism as a doctrine was a form of reaction against the social breakdown in the Spring and Autumn and the Warring States Periods. Thus, when Western thinkers tried to design political systems as vessels to contain irrepressible conflict, Confucians (and legalists as well) aimed at designing systems where no such conflict would appear. From a psychoanalytic point of view, this yearning for social stability and aversion of conflict might originate from the very Chinese personality, a product of the particular Chinese child-rearing techniques.[30]

### Social stability and social conflict

In the mind of the Hong Kong Chinese, the normal state of a society is stability. In our 1985 survey, 65.1 percent of the respondents agreed, and 4.3 percent agreed very much that a normal society ought not to have much important conflict, while only 20.1 percent disagreed. In the same vein, but referring specifically to Hong Kong, 47.2 percent agreed and 5 percent strongly agreed with the statement that the foundation of Hong Kong's prosperity and stability was fragile and could easily be undermined by some undesirable elements in society. Such a conception of social order naturally leads the Hong Kong Chinese to dislike social actions which smack of "radicalism" and thus threaten social peace. Thus, 53 percent of respondents disagreed or strongly disagreed with the following statement: "There is an increasing number of Hong Kong people who dare to confront the government. This is a healthy phenomenon."

As we mentioned earlier on, Hong Kong Chinese consider the government as the authority responsible for upholding public interest and maintaining social order, but, the extent to which the incumbent government is the embodiment of this authority is murky. On the one hand, the decline in the authority of the Hong Kong government since the inception of the Sino-British negotiation over the future of Hong Kong was lamented by 57.1 percent of the respondents. But since only just over half of them agreed with the relevant statement ("The erosion of the authority of the Hong Kong government is a bad thing, because it will lead to conflict and confusion in society."), the role of the Hong Kong government in social stability is recognized, but not overwhelmingly, by the Hong Kong Chinese. On the other hand, slightly less than half of the respondents (46.3 percent) agreed or strongly agreed with a seemingly contradictory statement: "The erosion of the authority of the Hong Kong government is a good thing, because it will then pay more attention to public opinion in order to win the citizens' goodwill and support." (Incidentally, 32.2 percent disagreed or strongly disagreed.) The manner in which these two statements was phrased (the inclusion of explanatory phrases in them) might seriously influence the answers given by the respondents, but still the ambiguous role of the Hong Kong government as the bulwark of social stability in Hong Kong is underlined by the findings.

### Social egalitarianism

Intrinsic to Confucianism was a strand of natural individual equality, which could, to a certain extent, be realized in society if the distribution of wealth was not too unequal. As a matter of fact, traditional rulers were enjoined by Confucians to decrease economic inequality in society. The charity works of the traditional state and its control of the merchants were means to prevent economic polarization and hence to safeguard the foundation of the ruling dynasty.[31]

On the face of it, the dominance of the market and the *laissez faire* policy of the government should generate a high level of tolerance for income inequality in Hong Kong. The government has played a prominent role, through social services and public housing, in reducing staggering economic inequalities, though it has refrained from direct intervention in income distribution in Hong Kong.

Under these circumstances, therefore, it is interesting to find that the idea of social egalitarianism is still a significant element in the ethos of the Hong Kong Chinese. In the 1985 survey, 55.3 percent of respondents agreed or strongly agreed that a good society was one where there was not much difference in incomes (39.9 disagreed or strongly disagreed). Specifically referring to Hong Kong, 63.6 percent thought that the gap between the rich and the poor should not be that large. 19.6 percent considered the existing gap to be about right, while only a minuscule 1.7 percent thought the gap too small. Surprisingly, however, this conception of the good society and the perception of economic inequality in Hong Kong had not led our respondents into believing that their society was not a fair one. 49.8 percent of them considered Hong Kong society as fair or very fair, while only 38.2 percent thought otherwise. This more or less equal split in opinion among the Hong Kong Chinese seems to show some sort of uneasy balance between traditional egalitarian ethos and the spirit of a market economy. Yet, the impact of these contradictory views about economic equality on policy demands seems to be minimal, since, as will be seen later, the egalitarian ethos is not translated into distributive and redistributive demands by the Hong Kong Chinese.

In regard to this aspect of economic egalitarianism as an ideal, it is interesting to compare the Hong Kong Chinese perspective with that of the Americans, as both of them boast of their *free* economic systems. The difference between the two lies in the Americans' failure to set up economic egalitarianism *even as an ideal.* "Attitudes toward the distribution of income make clear that Americans do not support radical egalitarianism. On the contrary, a substantial income gap is considered fair by all the leadership groups."[32] American "[p]eople generally use a principle of differentiation, and thus differentiating norms, in the economic domain—the arena of the workplace, marketplace, and social structure."[33] As such, ideal and reality are more congruent in the United States than in Hong Kong.

## Traditional virtues

To the Confucians, the basic social virtue was filial piety that was the keystone of the whole social order. The crucial importance attributed to filial piety lay in the belief that embedded in filial piety was the right attitude to authority and this made a stable hierarchical Confucian order possible.[34] The emphasis on filial piety underscored the centrality of the family and kinship network in Confucian thought. Human sentiments and benevolence were deemed to originate from the closeness of family members and radiate outward to all other social spheres.

> [Confucian scholars] agreed unanimously that the realization of benevolence must begin with the love of children toward their parents. This means that, in the complicated relations among men, filial piety forms the primary and most fundamental unit of mutual connection between two or more persons, in which the practice of benevolence must first be fulfilled. By inference, all other relations among human beings should emanate from this basic virtue as their source; otherwise, they may not stay on the right course of benevolence for the attainment of peace and prosperity.[35]

The lingering hold of filial piety in the mind of the Hong Kong Chinese can be seen in the fact that 23.5 percent of respondents in the 1985 survey strongly agreed and 64.1 percent agreed with the statement that the first thing to do in order to build a good society was to have everyone practising filial piety. In the 1986 survey, it was found that 71.6 percent of respondents agreed that an unfilial person must be a no-good rascal. A substantial minority in the 1986 survey (36.6 percent) even went as far as to say that there weren't evil parents in the world. The support for filial piety as a social virtue even leads the Hong Kong Chinese to support its legalization as a punishable "crime." 77.1 percent of respondents in the 1985 survey agreed or strongly agreed that the government should enact laws to punish those children who failed to take care of their elderly parents. Likewise, 85.9 percent of respondents in the 1986 survey agreed or strongly agreed that the government should enact laws to force people to take care of their elderly parents. In the same survey, 54.6 percent of respondents agreed or strongly agreed that parents should live together with their married children and 85 percent were willing financially to support their parents. It is also noteworthy that the assumption of their duties and responsibilities toward their parents was far from reluctant, since that had not engendered grievances among the respondents. In the 1986 survey, for example, 53.8 percent of respondents were satisfied and 7.6 percent very satisfied with their relationship with parents, while 77.5 percent of the parents were satisfied or very satisfied with their children.

With respect to kinship relations, the time lag between normative orientation and reality is unmistakable. In the 1986 survey, it was found that more than half (55.8 percent) respondents maintained infrequent visits with their relatives; only a tiny 14.3 percent did so. But, in general, the value of kinsmen was stressed. 75.2 percent of respondents in the 1985 survey agreed with the following statement: "In order for people to live more happily, Hongkongese should strengthen their ties with family members and relatives so that they can better provide mutual help." At the same time, the respondents were willing to assume their responsibilities toward their relatives. 74.6 percent of respondents in the 1986 survey admitted that they had the responsibility to help relatives in financial trouble, and 77.4 percent claimed that they would assume the responsibility heartily. In assuming this responsibility toward relatives, it is noteworthy that no idea of *quid pro quo* was involved. In general, the Hong Kong Chinese took for granted the willingness of relatives to render help to themselves. For example, in a survey of four localities conducted by us in the summer of 1982, the percentages of respondents in Kwun Tong, Tuen Mun, Tai Hang Tung and Sai Ying Pun who denied that the relatives' willingness to help was decreasing were 69.2, 76.4, 100 and 86.7 respectively. They were, however, a little bit less certain about the ability of their relatives to help, as shown in the fact that the percentages of respondents who denied that the relatives' ability to help was decreasing were 65.3, 48.1, 83.3 and 68.8 respectively. This expectation that help from relatives would be forthcoming when it was needed, however, failed to be converted into moral demands on their relatives. 66.6 percent of respondents in the 1985 survey did not think that their relatives had the responsibility to help them when they were in financial difficulties. The percentage found in the 1986 survey was similar (66.8 percent). Even so, 49.4 percent in the 1986 survey thought that in fact if their relatives helped them, they would do so heartily.

Despite the assumption of the readiness and willingness of the relatives to help, Hong Kong Chinese still feel a sense of unease in having to receive help from their relatives. "That support is perceived to be available from the extended family does not imply that individuals are eager to accept such support. Such support may imply dependence and, perhaps, reciprocal obligations . . ."[36] 75.9 percent of the respondents in the 1985 survey admitted that they would have an uncomfortable feeling of indebtedness when they accepted help from their relatives.

Ironically, those who feel discomfort in receiving help from relatives, though obviously straying away from "traditional" are far from being the "modern" man as commonly understood. It is more likely that they are the "marginal people" who are unable to attach themselves to "tradition," but at the same time fail to find their anchorings in "modernity." This observation can be corroborated by several findings. They agreed more with the statement that one should let tomorrow took care of itself. They tended to have a dim view of others' trustworthiness. They were more pessimistic about the future conditions of the Hong Kong people. Relatively more of them denied the utility of long-term planning. They had a stronger tendency to adjust passively to changes in the environment.

Nevertheless, when the Hong Kong Chinese are in trouble, and help from both government and relatives is available, they are more willing to accept help from the latter. 70.9 percent of respondents in the 1985 survey opted for their families when in economic straits, only 6.3 percent of them selected the government. Contrariwise, 35.1 percent would rely on themselves, 31.5 percent would go to their relatives for help, and 22.6 percent to their friends. These findings clearly highlight the resilience of the family institution as well as the moderate politicization of private needs in Hong Kong. A comparison of Hong Kong with other societies should bear this point out. In a comparative study of India, Japan, Nigeria and the United States, it was found that in three of the societies concerned, people opted for support from government when support from both government and family was perceived as available. The percentages preferring government *vis-à-vis* family were 62-38 in India, 45-55 in Japan, 57-43 in Nigeria, and 52-48 in the United States.

> The data suggest a good deal of ambivalence about the sources of support in time of need. One might have expected a clear preference for family aid (given that both were perceived to be available) in societies such as India, Nigeria and Japan where family ties remain tighter than in the U.S. And in the U.S. as well a desire to remain independent of the government might have led to the same result. But in Nigeria, India

> and the U.S. majorities prefer aid from the government when both are available. Family aid, this suggests, has its drawbacks as well. It can entail obligations and it can drain limited family resources.[37]

This preference for resources from one's primary network to government contributes to maintaining some distance between government and society and reduces the extent of politicization in Hong Kong.

### Satisfaction with society and perception of its future

Overall, Hong Kong Chinese are satisfied with Hong Kong society and their life in it. In the 1985 survey, 74.4 percent of respondents were satisfied or very satisfied with the existent Hong Kong society. 75.3 percent were satisfied or very satisfied with their livelihood. The latter percentage decreased slightly in the 1986 survey, but still 63.6 percent were satisfied or very satisfied. Moreover, they expected their livelihood to improve in the future, while they looked back with satisfaction at improvement in their livelihood in the past. Thus, the 1985 survey showed that 49.2 percent of respondents considered that their livelihood was better than five years ago, while only 21.1 percent thought it was worse. 30.5 percent were optimistic about their livelihood five years later, and only 11 percent thought that it would deteriorate. Thus, Hong Kong Chinese derive satisfaction from their society and their station in it.

Despite their general satisfaction with Hong Kong society, the Hong Kong Chinese have a rather negative image of their society, even though it does not severely detract from their satisfaction with it. A relevant finding is that in the 1985 survey 41.5 percent of respondents opined that Hong Kong society was full of problems and evils, while 39.9 percent considered it stable and orderly. In the same survey, it was found that 36.9 percent of respondents agreed or strongly agreed with the statement that the situation of the Hong Kong people had deteriorated, and 43.8 percent disagreed or strongly disagreed. But more intense pessimism took hold in the 1986 survey. 50.3 percent thought that it was likely or very likely that after the return of Hong Kong to China the standard of living would stagnate or even deteriorate. After 1997, 60.3 percent expected a reduction in personal freedom, 56.9 percent anticipated a reduction of civil rights, and 52.3 percent expected degeneration of the judicial system. Only 35.7 percent thought that the *status quo* could remain unchanged for fifty years, and a mere 17.3 percent were optimistic that Hong Kong people could enjoy a happy and blissful life after 1997.

This rather gloomy view of the future of Hong Kong society, however, is coupled with a relatively high sense of collective or social efficacy. For example, 61.7 percent of respondents in the 1985 survey thought that Hong Kong people had the ability to govern well. But only 22.3 percent of respondents expected the Chinese government to freely allow the Hong Kong people to govern themselves. By the same token, 62.3 percent of respondents agreed or strongly agreed with the following statement: "The economic and political conditions of Hong Kong are extremely vulnerable to external influences, therefore the Hong Kong people cannot control their fate." This frustrated sense of social efficacy must feed into the limited sense of personal efficacy mentioned before and produce a short-term time perspective among the Hong Kong Chinese. This, in fact, seems to be true as only 45.3 percent of respondents in the 1986 survey considered that they had the capability to plan and prepare themselves for the future.

## Economic Values

The brilliant performance of the capitalist economy of Hong Kong and its relative autonomy from the political sector have created an aura of sacredness around it. The lingering presence of the traditional value of economic egalitarianism and the staggering income inequality produced by capitalist development might impede full-scale and unconditional acceptance of capitalist values, but, so far, Hong Kong has only witnessed feeble demands for economic redistribution. Ambiguous feelings toward the wealthy can be detected, but they still are the model for popular admiration and emulation. In short, the capitalist system of Hong Kong is founded upon solid normative orientations.

### Attitude toward the capitalist economy

There is pervasive normative support for the capitalist economy of Hong Kong, and it is no wonder that the preservation of capitalism in Hong Kong after 1997 constitutes a crucial part of the Sino-British Agreement. Studies done in the past had already found that Hong Kong was seen as a land of opportunity by Hong Kong Chinese.[38] In our 1985 survey, an overwhelming 87.6 percent of respondents agreed or strongly agreed that Hong Kong was a place full of developmental opportunities. Hence, it is individual efforts that count in one's success or failure.

The preference for equality of opportunity and individual competition is also evident in the fact that in the 1986 survey, 73.3 percent of respondents preferred a society afflicted by inequalities but with freedom and development opportunities to one that had equalities but was devoid of freedom and development opportunities. The value placed on economic competition is also reflected in the fact that 71.8 percent of respondents in the 1985 survey agreed or strongly agreed with the statement that those who succeeded under conditions of intense competition, such as Li Ka-shing and Y. K. Pao, ought to be the model for the youngsters to admire and learn from.

The support for a free economy is also seen in the fact that in the 1985 survey 54.5 percent of respondents disagreed or strongly disagreed with the statement that those who advocated a "free economy" were in fact people who intended to rapaciously exploit workers.

## Economic inequalities

When economic success is explained in individualistic terms, the staggering income inequalities in Hong Kong can be tolerated, particularly when the "trickle down" effect resulting from past economic growth has, in effect, raised the standard of living of the people.

84.2 percent of respondents in the 1986 survey agreed that in Hong Kong, provided a person had the ability and worked hard, he should have the opportunity to improve his social and economic status. Because of this belief and the fact that many wealthy people do rise from the ranks of the humble, 48.1 percent of respondents in the 1986 survey thought that most rich people obtained their wealth by individual means. Only 27.5 percent explained the success of the rich as resulting from economic exploitation or illicit channels. In the same vein, the 1985 survey showed that 55.4 percent of respondents did not agree with the statement that the money of the rich was acquired through exploiting the toiling masses.

Nevertheless, there are still elements of ambivalence in the normative orientation of the Hong Kong Chinese. For example, while economic success is largely explained in individualistic terms, poverty is deemed to relate somewhat more to social factors. In the 1986 survey, 34.7 percent of respondents explained poverty by means of social causes while a smaller proportion of them (31.4 percent) alluded to individualistic factors. Another pertinent point is that substantial numbers of Hong Kong Chinese believed that many wealthy people owe their success to illicit activities. 41.1 percent of respondents in the 1985 survey agreed or strongly agreed that many rich people used improper means to get money, while 35.8 percent disagreed.

In view of the fact that the Hong Kong Chinese are aware of the huge number of the impoverished in their society (61 percent of respondents in the 1986 survey said that there were many or a lot of poor people in Hong Kong), it is astonishing to find that most Hong Kong Chinese would not accept ways to reduce economic inequalities involving expropriation of the rich. For example, 55.8 percent of respondents in the 1985 survey disagreed or strongly disagreed with the suggestion that the government should compel the rich to do charity work. The fact that the extent of disagreement was not overwhelming might reflect the ambivalent attitude of the respondents toward the rich.

## Perception of class and class action

The belief in equality of opportunity, the expectation that one's efforts will pay off, general acceptance of the legitimacy of income distribution through the market and actual experience of improvement in one's standard of living, all work to dampen perception of classes and class conflict. Previous studies had shown that the Hong Kong Chinese did not have a dichotomized image of social class. Instead, a finely graded stratification structure, based on the criterion of wealth, was generally held.

> First, there is no general consensus as to the class structure, only a conceptually fragmented picture of social class. Second, underlying more than half of the classification schemes employed by the people are the dimensions of wealth and income, though other criteria such as political or administrative power, educational achievements and "morality" are occasionally inserted to complicate the general scene. Third, many of the "conceptual schemes" are non-exhaustive, which is to say that they do not cover the whole populace. They hence tend to represent what the people regard as the most important ingredient of success or failure in Hong Kong. Fourth, closely related to the previous point is that in some classification schemes, individual status or class

> categories are based on different criteria, thus resulting in a juxtaposition of several class categories which are strictly speaking non-comparable. Finally, the fragmented conception of class structure tends to impede the formation, at least in an ideological sense, of two polarized and antagonistic classes, or the possibility of class conflict. In short, social classes as structural forces in shaping interpersonal relationships and political actions are relatively insignificant in Hong Kong. [39]

The feeble sense of class division and class conflict might have produced an image of class structure which encapsulates a majority of people in a single "class," since people fail to see much difference in their life-situations. In the 1986 survey, 73.3 percent of respondents asserted that their livelihood was as good as that of the average Hongkongese. 7.8 percent thought that they had a worse livelihood, whereas 17.4 percent considered that their living standard was above average. Because of this tendency to "homogenize" classes, it is not surprising to find that in the same survey most respondents classified themselves as "middle class" people. More precisely, 31.9 percent declared themselves to belong to the lower-middle class, 36.7 percent to the middle-middle class and 2.4 percent to the upper-middle class. Only 2.4 percent claimed to belong to the upper class, while 26.3 percent relegated themselves to the lower class. When this distribution of responses is compared to the assignment of one's parents to different "class" categories, a subjective sense of upward mobility appears, which might further mollify any feelings of class antagonism. In the same survey, 44.2 percent of respondents classified their parents as belonging to the lower class, 25.6 percent the lower-middle class, 20.2 percent the middle-middle class, 3.3 percent the upper-middle class and 1.3 percent the upper class. Therefore, the expectation of equality of opportunities and the perception of Hong Kong as a land of abundant opportunities seem to have been vindicated in the mind of the Hong Kong Chinese.

Needless to say, many Hong Kong Chinese might harbor feelings that they have not been able to obtain the socio-economic status they *ought* to obtain or deserve. In the 1986 survey, 71.4 percent of respondents were not satisfied with their educational achievements. However, their actual achievements did not differ too much from the achievements they aspired to. Similarly, 56.2 percent of respondents in the same survey considered their actual monthly income as "fair." Even those who were bothered by their "unfair" monthly income had an idea of "fair" income which was close to the amount they actually earned. 29 percent of them considered as "fair" a monthly income which was 20 percent or less higher than the actual one, 27.5 percent rated as "fair" an income between 20 to 40 percent higher. Only 24.6 percent wanted an increase of more than 60 percent in their monthly income. Consequently, dissatisfaction with what one actually gets is mild among Hong Kong Chinese.

The faint perception of class division or class conflict has resulted in limited collective actions of a "class" character. This explains the prevalent labor quiescence in Hong Kong, as well as the insignificant incidence of strikes and lockouts. Still, on the ideological level, there is widespread sympathy for trade unionism in Hong Kong, even though less than 20 percent of industrial workers have joined trade unions, a figure less than that obtained in the mid-1950s (35 percent). In the 1986 survey, only 15 percent of respondents had joined trade unions. Among those who hadn't joined, close to 75 percent expressed no intention to do so.

Sympathetic support for collective action among workers had already been found in previous studies. In a study of young Hong Kong workers, it was found that at least at the attitudinal level the respondents concerned were sympathetic to the interests of their fellow workers, as they claimed that they would be willing to participate in class actions to further their common interests.[40] In our 1985 survey, for example, 61.2 percent agreed or strongly agreed that Hong Kong's trade unions should be more powerful and more influential. Nevertheless, this sympathy on the normative level is not translated into action. Thus, only 26.3 percent of respondents in the 1986 survey expressed willingness to participate in industrial actions proposed by fellow workers. Accordingly, the privatized nature of the Hong Kong workers identified in past research seems to persist to this day.[41]

## Conclusion

The individual, social and economic values of the Hong Kong Chinese represent a mixture of old and new orientations; these orientations maintain an uneasy co-existence.

The freedom enjoyed by the individual in an open socio-economic system provides the condition for individual success and individual expression. Personal freedom is the predominant value in the Hong Kong Chinese people's view of the individual. Nevertheless, the value of the individual emphasized by the Hong Kong Chinese seems to be an instrumental one, and a person is valued primarily by his achievements rather than by any Western conception of the intrinsic value of the individual. The Confucian idea of the natural equality of men still lingers on, but it seems not to have much effect on interpersonal relationships. While the Hong Kong Chinese have progressed quite a bit in their decent level of abstract social trust, still, in their action tendencies, mistrust of others is the dominant theme. Hong Kong Chinese have no qualms in restricting the enjoyment of civil rights by others if those rights would engender social disorder. The uncomfortable feeling of political and economic dependence also erodes the sense of self-control which would normally be pervasive in the mind of the successful economic people.

The emphasis placed on social order and social harmony and the loathing of social conflict still persist strongly in the ethos of the Hong Kong Chinese. Many of the traditional virtues centering upon the family are still strong, thus simultaneously producing depoliticizing effects and buttressing the competitive capitalist system and its concomitant economic values. Thus, the autonomy of the capitalist economic system is given some normative support, which immunizes it from arbitrary intrusion from both society and polity. For example, social egalitarianism is prevented from conversion into class antagonism, and unease about income inequality is not translated into demand for redistributive political actions.

Overall, the ethos of the Hong Kong Chinese establishes a clear demarcation between the public and private spheres and the relative autonomy of the social, economic and political sectors. These new conceptions of the nature of the social order represent a substantial transmutation of the traditional ethos and hence are the central elements of their identity. However, as these conceptions are not based on secure institutional guarantees, but instead are the result of past practices and the tolerance of the colonial government, they are always subject to modification by environmental changes. The relatively low sense of individual and social efficacy of the Hong Kong Chinese thus produces a feeling of helplessness among a people with a strong belief in individual efforts.

# 3

# Political Values

Structurally speaking, the monocratic and bureaucratic colonial regime in Hong Kong bears a striking resemblance to the imperial bureaucratic regime of traditional China and the "democratic centralism" of Socialist China, though in the latter case the hegemony of the Chinese Communist Party complicates the picture. The authoritarian colonial system provides a fertile ground for the transplantation and perpetuation of the parochial-subject,[1] hierarchical and apathetic political culture of the traditional Chinese. The preservation of traditional Chinese political culture might be even more complete, and individual elements of it even further accentuated, because of the closed nature of alien colonial rule. Nevertheless, colonial rule's very nature is one made up of a benign character, a self-imposed limitation of government functions, legalistic orientation and a consultative mode of rule. This has not only considerably counteracted some of the negative impact of alien rule on the traditional political culture of the Hong Kong Chinese, but has also spawned a more sophisticated and differentiated political culture among them. The resulting political values are an admixture of old and new elements, which, however, do not constitute a harmonious whole. Admittedly the value "system" of the mass public in general is fraught with internal contradictions that can only be partially resolved through a myriad of psychological processes,[2] but still, it may be reasonable to argue that the evolution of the political values of the Hong Kong Chinese has not taken a smooth or gradual trajectory. In fact, it seems that the evolutionary process has speeded up since the late 1960s, with the increasing involvement of the government in the social and, to a lesser extent, the economic spheres, and accelerated even more since the early 1980s with the onset of the Sino-British negotiation over the future of Hong Kong. The progressive political assertions of the activist segment of the populace, and the accommodating stance taken by the government toward it, also produce educative effects on the political beliefs of the man on the street.

On the whole, despite all these developments, the tenacious staying power of tradition and the absence of fundamental structural changes in the political system of Hong Kong combine to enable the old elements to dominate the political values of the Hong Kong Chinese. Nevertheless, the new elements do have momentous importance and their continual reinforcement should portend significant changes in mass political values. In the meantime, their presence has created serious strains in the existent political ethos, notably in the conception of government and its role in society, which represents a conspicuous departure from the traditional Chinese political culture as commonly understood.

## Attitude toward Politics

In traditional China, the monopolization of power by government, the exaggeration of, and obsession with, social harmony, the non-recognition of the legitimacy of private interests and social conflicts, and the normally unhappy government-people encounters, all of these things had engendered a deep-rooted anti-political attitude among the people. The term "politics" carried a legion of negative meanings such as the pursuit of private interests to the detriment of public good, chicanery, violence, personal feuds, immorality, government harassment, corruption, personal status ambitions and so on, which together constitute a form of indictment of the arbitrariness and rapaciousness of political power in a state-dominated social order.

The political experience of the Hong Kong Chinese has mitigated the seriousness of anti-political feelings. Table 3.1 lists the distribution of responses to a series of probing questions in the 1985 survey, which were designed to throw light on the various facets of anti-political attitudes. The findings here present a complex attitudinal orientation which is ambivalent in substance.

It appears that unconditional abhorrence and a fear of politics has

TABLE 3.1
Attitudes toward Politics
(in percent)

| Statement | Agree very much | Agree | Disagree | Disagree very much | Don't know/ No answer |
|---|---|---|---|---|---|
| 1. Democratic politics will facilitate the appearance of dangerous careerists. | 1.2 | 40.3 | 32.6 | 1.2 | 24.6 |
| 2. The purpose of political participation is to improve the livelihood of myself and my family. It is not for the sake of realizing political ideals. | 1.0 | 51.6 | 27.1 | 1.0 | 19.2 |
| 3. Even if many people vote blindly, their right to vote should not be denied. | 0.9 | 43.4 | 44.2 | 2.6 | 8.9 |
| 4. "Politics" means the oppression of a group of people by another group for the sake of the latter's self-interests. | 1.4 | 31.4 | 43.3 | 2.9 | 21.0 |
| 5. Politics is dirty. | 3.0 | 26.1 | 45.5 | 3.0 | 22.4 |
| 6. Politics is dangerous. | 3.1 | 41.9 | 32.1 | 1.7 | 21.3 |
| 7. Political leaders are unworthy of trust. | 2.6 | 27.0 | 42.5 | 1.3 | 26.6 |

abated among the Hong Kong Chinese. Anti-political sentiments, however, linger on as a plurality of respondents (45 percent) agreed or strongly agreed that politics was dangerous and a similar proportion (41.5 percent) agreed or strongly agreed that "democratic politics will facilitate the appearance of dangerous careerists." Nevertheless, there seems to be improvements in other areas such as trust of political leaders, right to vote, perception of politics as dirty and the non-oppressive aspects of politics. Unlike the moralistic conception of politics in traditional political doctrines, the attitude toward politics of the Hong Kong Chinese is primarily instrumental, as the majority of respondents related political participation to the enhancement of private interests. Despite facts to the contrary, political power was conceived both as the means to promote public ends (hence it should be controlled only by the government) and as the means to status itself (in this sense power was something to be enjoyed rather than deployed to achieve measurable results[3]). From the developmental perspective, the transition from a moralistic to an instrumental approach to politics represents a significant step in the transformation of a political culture. In order for this transition to occur, the relevance of government and politics to the people must be greatly increased. In Japan, for example, the sudden expansion of channels of political influence after the post-War reforms has brought the government closer to the people, leading to a sudden awareness by the people of the utility of government to them and promoting an instrumental attitude toward politics. In the study of Japanese political culture by Richardson, it was found that the "Japanese take a strong interest in what politics can do for them, their community or their occupation. . . . The fact that more voters are knowledgeable on issues directly affecting their interests, at the same time lacking opinions on more general belief questions, is a corollary of this more general tendency toward pragmatism."[4] In general,

> [M]arked increases in instrumentalist expectations seem to be characteristic of the transition from more authoritarian and parochial to more popular and cosmopolitan political styles. This is the broad implication both of American nineteenth century experience and, more recently, of political life in some post-colonial nations of Africa and Asia.[5]

In Hong Kong, the increasing perceptions of government as the benefactor and the primary solver of social and even private problems are critical in the formation of an instrumental orientation toward politics on the part of the Hong Kong Chinese.[6] A growing sense of dependence on the government for a variety of things related to daily living makes it well-nigh impossible for people to avoid politics. As this increased "approach" stance toward politics by the Hong Kong Chinese has been reciprocated by the accommodationist position of the government in the past two decades, a more favorable attitude toward politics might thus result.

## Conception of Political System

It is quite unlikely that the common person has any idea about the abstract concept of a "political system." Be that as it may, we still tried to fathom, in a rough manner, what a "political system" meant to the Hong Kong Chinese in our 1986 survey through a battery of test items. The findings are shown in Table 3.2.

Several observations can be drawn from the table. In the first place, there was an overwhelming endorsement of the existent political system, whatever it meant to the respondents. This finding, however, is not surprising at all, as it falls in line with other findings. In our study of four localities in Hong Kong in the summer of 1982, a similar question was asked.

> On the whole, the "benign" authoritarian, and bureaucratic political system in Hong Kong appears to be supported by the respondents: 53, 55.9, 48.6, and 57.5 percent respectively of the residents of Kwun Tong, Tuen Mun, Tai Hang Tung, and Sai Ying Pun agreed with the statement that under existing circumstances the political system of Hong Kong, while far from perfect, was the best that they could get. Only a tiny proportion (12.4, 14.2, 18.3, and 13.7 percent respectively in the four localities) disagreed with such an evaluation. This favourable attitude towards the political system apparently is based upon the performance of the government.[7]

Secondly, because of the general support for the existing political system, any attempts to drastically alter it would be opposed. Thus, 79.3 percent of respondents agreed and 7.2 percent strongly agreed that any political reform should be gradual. The passive response of the Hong Kong Chinese to the call for "democratization" in Hong Kong by the democratic activists recently indicated their basically conservative orientation.

Thirdly, there also appears to be a reformist or idealistic strand in the political ethos of the Hong Kong Chinese. Almost half of the respondents (49 percent) agreed or strongly agreed that political leaders elected by the people would perform a better job than the present Hong Kong government, while only 24.5 percent disagreed or strongly disagreed. In another occasion, it was found that 55.7 percent of them thought that, in general, the people and social leaders in Hong Kong knew better than the government what was good and what was bad for Hong Kong. Moreover, as evidenced in Table 3.2, they were

TABLE 3.2
Conception of the Political System
(in percent)

| Statement | Agree very much | Agree | Disagree | Disagree very much | Don't know/ No answer |
|---|---|---|---|---|---|
| 1. I think the existing political system is good enough. If there is any problem, it is mainly because of the faults of some government officials. | 1.3 | 51.0 | 31.4 | 0.7 | 15.6 |
| 2. The chance of success for democratic reform in Hong Kong will be good. | 2.3 | 52.4 | 15.5 | 0.5 | 29.2 |
| 3. The emergence of political parties will make the political system of Hong Kong better. | 0.5 | 34.3 | 27.5 | 0.8 | 36.9 |
| 4. Political leaders elected by the people will perform better than the incumbent Hong Kong government. | 3.4 | 45.6 | 24.0 | 0.5 | 26.5 |
| 5. Any political reform should be gradual, it must not be hasty. | 7.2 | 79.3 | 1.0 | 0 | 7.2 |
| 6. It will be better for Hong Kong to be governed by a few capable men than to talk about political reform. | 4.7 | 54.2 | 24.4 | 1.0 | 15.6 |
| 7. Whichever kind of government is immaterial, provided a minimum standard of living can be safeguarded for myself. | 4.2 | 56.6 | 31.2 | 2.6 | 5.5 |
| 8. Although the political system of Hong Kong is not perfect, it is the best we can have under existing circumstances. | 2.6 | 71.7 | 16.6 | 0 | 9.1 |

optimistic about the chance of the success of democratic reform in Hong Kong, for 54.7 percent rated the chance as very good.

On the face of it, it is difficult to square this favorable reception of elections and optimism about democratic reform with the lukewarm response to the democratic appeals on the part of the Hong Kong Chinese. On closer scrutiny, however, the riddle is not difficult to explain, and the solution lies in the particular conception of democracy in the mind of the Hong Kong Chinese. When they were asked about what was a democratic government, the answers chosen by the respondents are revealing. A plurality of them (43.9 percent) would classify a government as democratic if it was willing to consult public opinion, without requiring that public opinion must be followed. 23.2 percent, the second largest proportion, considered democratic government as a government elected by the people. 15.8 percent thought that a government that could lead the people is democratic, while 0.7 percent would deem a government democratic if it gave to the people whatever they wanted. In Western democratic theory, election is the *sine qua non* of democratic government, but it doesn't appear to be the crucial element in the mind of the Hong Kong Chinese. Since the Hong Kong government prides itself on its activeness in consulting public opinion, and since this self-proclaimed virtue of the Hong Kong government is, to a certain extent, even shared by the people, democratic reform, if it is defined as refinements in consultative government, would not constitute drastic institutional changes in the mind of the respondents; they would embrace it and were optimistic about its success. The validity of this argument can be borne out by the findings in Table 3.3.

In Table 3.3, it appears that those who were more optimistic about the probability of success of democratic reform were more likely to define democratic government as consultative government.

The profound importance of consultative government in the ethos of the Hong Kong Chinese can be examined from another angle. Our respondents were asked about the most important factor in social stability. 14.5 percent of them picked traditional virtues (*li yi lien chi* 禮義廉恥 [rules of propriety, righteousness, modesty and sense of shame]),[8] 37.5 percent chose law, 29.6 percent a sound political system and 7.3 percent strong leaders. The fact that institutional factors such as law and political system were preferred more should testify to the modernity of the political values of the Hong Kong Chinese. Nonetheless, as shown in Table 3.4, the preference for law and for political institutions as the factors for social stability is fully compatible with the preference for consultative government as democratic government. Surprisingly, it was those who rated strong leaders as most crucial to social stability that were more inclined to define democratic government as elective government. It might be that those who favored election saw it as the vehicle to deliver to them strong leaders, whom they saw lacking in the faceless bureaucracy currently presiding over Hong Kong.

TABLE 3.3
Probability of Success of Democratic Reform by
Selected Conceptions of Democratic Government
(in percent)

| High probability | Consultative government | Government that can lead | Elective government | Sub-total (N) |
|---|---|---|---|---|
| Strongly agree | 61.1 | 5.6 | 27.8 | 94.5 (17) |
| Agree | 50.9 | 17.3 | 29.1 | 97.3 (365) |
| Disagree | 51.8 | 24.6 | 19.3 | 95.7 (109) |
| Strongly disagree | 25.0 | 25.0 | 25.0 | 75.0 (3) |

TABLE 3.4
Most Important Factor for Stability by
Conception of Democratic Government
(in percent)

| | Consultative government | Government that can lead | Elective government | Total (N) |
|---|---|---|---|---|
| Traditional virtues | 52.2 | 12.0 | 28.3 | 92.5 (85) |
| Law | 53.8 | 18.9 | 25.4 | 98.1 (259) |
| Political institutions | 57.1 | 18.6 | 21.4 | 97.1 (204) |
| Strong leaders | 26.5 | 26.5 | 44.9 | 97.9 (48) |

$\chi^2 = 33.06$, d.f. = 20, $p < 0.05$

In fact, the preference for consultative government seems to camouflage a fear of politics. Hence, it can be hypothesized that those who are less fearful of politics would place more emphasis on election as the criterion of democratic government. The data show that this seems to be in fact the case. In Table 3.5, respondents who agreed that politics was a repression of one group of people by another were more prone to define democratic government as consultative government, and vice versa for those who disagreed. This might provide a further clue explaining the riddle of the seemingly co-existence of political idealism and behavioral conservatism among the Hong Kong Chinese.

TABLE 3.5
Politics as Political Repression by
Selected Definitions of Democratic Government
(in percent)

| | Democratic government as | | | |
|---|---|---|---|---|
| Politics as political repression | Consultative government | Government that can lead | Elective government | Sub-total (N) |
| Strongly Disagree | 36.4 | 13.6 | 45.5 | 95.5 (21) |
| Disagree | 48.0 | 21.1 | 28.6 | 97.7 (287) |
| Agree | 53.3 | 16.7 | 26.0 | 96.0 (218) |
| Strongly Agree | 54.5 | 36.4 | 0 | 90.9 (10) |

Going back to Table 3.2, the growing emphasis placed on law and institutions has, however, not displaced the importance attached to good leaders, who were appreciated as the kingpin of any political system in traditional political thought. In Confucian teachings, "[f]or its governing, the state could not rely solely on a complete and perfect set of institutions."[9] Moreover, "the administration of government lies in getting proper men. Such men are to be got by means of the ruler's own character. That character is to be cultivated by his treading in the ways of duty."[10] However, "Confucius' stress on the 'superior man' was not intended to substitute a government by men for government by laws, but rather to implant the concept of government by men within a system of government by law."[11] Traditional China was often described as government by man instead of government by law and castigated as such, even though it had developed one of the more advanced and rational-legal bureaucratic institutions among traditional societies. These institutions are the same as those that provided the stimulus to institutional changes in the modern West.[12] In view of the centuries-old valuation of good leaders in China and the tendency of Chinese to personify government and to identify government with prominent political figures, the emphasis on good leaders by the Hong Kong Chinese appears natural, and this emphasis might even be further accentuated by the lack of identifiable leaders in Hong Kong in the first place.[13]

While it is incontrovertible that the importance of institutions and law is widely recognized by the Hong Kong Chinese, it is not possible to conclude then that the importance of rule by the traditional superior man has thus been irreversibly displaced. At most we can conclude that the question of whether rule by institutions or rule by man is more important to the Hong Kong Chinese is still a moot point. They obviously see the centrality of a good political system, but they are also fully aware that good institutions, in order to function well, have to be manned by good officials and leaders. Thus, more than half of our respondents (52.3 percent) agreed or strongly agreed with the following statement: "I think the existing political system is good enough. If there is any problem, it is mainly because of the fault of some government officials." On another occasion, they seemed to place more emphasis on rule by man than rule by institutions, as 58.9 percent of them agreed or strongly agreed that "it will be better for Hong Kong to be governed by a few capable men than to talk about political reform." In short, while the Hong Kong Chinese have not yet "progressed" to the stage where the concept of rule by man is relegated to oblivion, they have, however, embraced institutions as an integral part of the political system to an extent unknown in traditional and modern China.

The "progress" made by the Hong Kong Chinese in their political values can be measured by their attitude toward political parties. Since the appearance of political parties in the last decade or so of Manchu rule in China, the term "political party" has become a *bête noire* to the ordinary Chinese. This abhorrence of political parties might even be exacerbated among the Hong Kong Chinese, since many of the more elderly of them fled to Hong Kong for political reasons. The term "political party" conjures up images of confrontation, factions, totalitarianism, corruption, political plots, ideological indoctrination, closed political arenas and adversarial politics. The attitude toward political parties thus provides an acid test of the level of "modernity" of the political values of the Hong Kong Chinese. In our 1985 survey, 34.8 percent of respondents agreed or agreed strongly that "the emergence of political parties will make the political system of Hong Kong better." Even though we lack previously collected data to serve as a reference point for comparative purposes, we feel that it might not be unjustified to conclude that the Hong Kong Chinese have formed a fairly favorable attitude toward political parties as an integral part of a political system. Nevertheless, since 36.9 percent of them either answered "don't know" or gave no answers at all, we must say that the topic of political parties is still a very controversial subject to the Hong Kong Chinese and they have difficulty in arriving at an established opinion on it. In this connection it is noteworthy that a higher percentage (57.6) of those who disagreed that political parties would improve Hong Kong's political system also defined democratic government as consultative government as opposed to those who agreed (43.9 percent). Conversely, a higher proportion of those who agreed that political parties would make Hong Kong's political system better (35.1 percent) defined democratic government as government elected by the people (see Table 3.6). In other words, those who were more favorably disposed toward consultative government were less receptive of political parties, while the reverse was true of those who preferred elective government.

TABLE 3.6
Attitude toward Political Party by
Selected Conceptions of Democratic Government
(in percent)

| Parties will improve Hong Kong political system | Consultative government | Government that can lead | Elective government | Sub-total (N) |
|---|---|---|---|---|
| Strongly agree | 75.0 | 0 | 0 | 75.0 (3) |
| Agree | 43.9 | 17.6 | 35.1 | 96.6 (231) |
| Disagree | 57.6 | 21.2 | 17.2 | 96.0 (195) |
| Strongly disagree | 33.3 | 33.3 | 33.3 | 99.9 (6) |

Finally, the instrumental orientation toward politics we have mentioned in the previous section also colors people's conception of a political system. Thus, 56.6 percent of the respondents agreed and 4.2 percent agreed very much (see Table 3.2) with this statement: "Whichever kind of government is immaterial, provided a minimum standard of living can be safeguarded for myself." This finding qualifies the idealistic strands in the conception of a political system detected before. Accordingly, in the ethos of the Hong Kong Chinese, "modern" democratic tenets have made their presence felt, but they seem to occupy a subsidiary position and fail to be synthesized with the traditional elements. Even so, their impact on other facets of the political ethos is palpable.

To set the stage for later discussions, comparative evidence from the relatively new democracy of Japan can be noted. In Japan, the newness of democracy had resulted in a sudden upgrading of the standards for political evaluation with political reality lagging far behind. The new evaluative standards furnished by the superficially understood and tenuously held democratic dogmas thus exacerbated the level of political cynicism in the political culture because old political practices were suddenly viewed from a modern perspective:

> Just as Americans who believe in liberty as a general principle would deny freedom to various political minorities, many Japanese seem to accept the ideals of democracy to some degree while rejecting the possibility that real life conforms to these ideals. Indeed, *it is not at all unlikely that acceptance of democratic norms may actually contribute to cynicism and thus ambivalence in some cases.*[14] (italics ours)

Even though Hong Kong does not have the comparable democratic experience of Japan since the Meiji Restoration and, particularly the post-War period, colonialism as a "school of democracy" has, nevertheless, enabled many democratic precepts to creep in and establish themselves as the standards for evaluating the government and other political processes.

## Attitude toward Government

The complex attitudinal syndrome toward government of the Hong Kong Chinese is the result of a *mélange* of conditioning factors—traditional political values, "imported" Western political ideas, actual political experience, the behavior of the Hong Kong and Chinese governments, the influence of political leaders and activists and the less-than-given nature of the authority of the colonial regime. Consequently, the attitudinal syndrome is suffused with ambivalences and ambiguities, which not only fail to provide clear guides to political action, but also exert a dampening effect on political involvement. The overall impact of the largely "unexpected" 1997 issue on the attitude toward government is hard to ascertain at this stage, for its effects are diverse and multi-faceted. The 1997 malaise simultaneously gives an impetus to political participation, raises political fears, and causes political withdrawal. Furthermore, in the meantime, it is not possible to predict whether the present confused state in popular attitudes toward government represents a transitional state moving in a definite direction or a continuing condition, because the future political development of Hong Kong is still a fluid matter.

Table 3.7 presents the findings on various attitudes toward government by the respondents in the 1985 survey. The general picture arising from the seemingly contradictory findings is a favorable, yet cynical, orientation toward government in general, and the Hong Kong government in particular.

What is most remarkable in Table 3.7 is the finding that a plurality of the respondents were able to recognize an autonomous political institution embodied in the Hong Kong government that functioned in accordance with a distinctive set of principles. Thus, 47.1 percent of them disagreed or strongly disagreed with this statement: "Managing government is akin to business management, as the most important thing is profit-making." Given the traditional conception of government as the guardian of public goods and as a moralizer along with the disdain for crass money-making behavior, this ability to distinguish the intrinsic differences between the political and economic institutions is understandable. It also shows that despite the pervasive penetration of economic reasoning in materialistic Hong Kong, the political sector and the government are still able to maintain a distinctive identity. This might be attributed to the fact that the colonial government, by virtue of its secluded nature, has, so far, been able to maintain its institutional distinctiveness by minimizing its entanglements with society and the economy. Another piece of evidence also provides indirect testimony to the autonomy of the political sector. 53.2 percent of respondents disagreed or strongly disagreed with the statement that only those who had prestigious occupations and had done well in them could make good (political) leaders. Hence, even though the Hong Kong Chinese admire achievers in the social and economic spheres, they do not necessarily consider the achievers as "natural" political leaders. Seemingly, they are capable of distinguishing between political skills and non-political skills.

The ability to identify a separate and autonomous political sector apparently is related to the acceptance of the idea of public interest. We have already reported that 62.6 percent of the respondents in the 1985 survey admitted the existence of a so-called public interest in society. Accordingly, the autonomy of the government or the political sector will be granted and recognized by the people if it is seen to be pursuing public interest, in whatever ways they define public interests. On the other hand, if the government is not seen as the guardian of public interests, a strong element of political cynicism toward it is unavoidable, even though a distinctive identity and institutional autonomy are still granted to it. On this point two pieces of evidence are revealing. 65.3 percent of respondents agreed and 5.9 percent strongly agreed with this statement: "Most of the time the Hong Kong government avows that it is the protector of public interests. In reality, it always promotes its own interests." In the same vein, a substantial proportion of respondents (44.4 percent) agreed or strongly agreed with the statement that the Hong Kong government mainly takes care of the interests of the wealthy (rather than public interests). Thus, the Hong Kong government was either seen as but one of a multitude of self-regarding private interests, or as the bulwark of the dominant private interest in Hong Kong. Because the Hong Kong government is seen as having forsaken the right to represent public interests, the people are reluctant to offer automatic compliance to its wishes, even though, for a variety of other reasons, resistance to government actions and law violations are comparatively rare in Hong Kong. Nonetheless, the cynical and suspicious sentiments are palpable. Hence, 55.7 percent of respondents in the 1985 survey declared that the people and social leaders knew better than the government what was good or bad for Hong Kong, while only 21.5 percent demurred. 52.9 percent of them rejected the prerogative of the government to compel people to do things against their wishes on the grounds of "public interest." Thus, while the ruling coalition in Hong Kong, dominated by the bureaucracy and supported by business elites, has provided the political infrastructure undergirding the post-War economic miracle, it has not been able to assign a high level of "givenness" or "naturalness" to the authority of the alien colonial government.

The less-than-given nature of the legitimacy of the colonial regime, however, has not thrown its rule into jeopardy. It is especially because of the performance of the bureaucracy, and also because of sheer habituation and the lack of viable political alternatives that the Hong Kong government has secured a legitimate basis for continued

TABLE 3.7
Attitudes toward Government
(in percent)

| Statement | Agree very much | Agree | Disagree | Disagree very much | Don't know/ No answer |
|---|---|---|---|---|---|
| 1. Managing government is akin to business management as the most important thing is profit-making. | 1.8 | 37.7 | 42.5 | 4.6 | 13.4 |
| 2. Government should treat the people like a father treats his children. | 8.2 | 72.9 | 13.0 | 0.8 | 5.1 |
| 3. A good government should concentrate on improving the livelihood of the people. It should not pay too much attention to long-term political ideals or isms. | 5.9 | 65.3 | 16.9 | 0.4 | 11.5 |
| 4. Most of the time the Hong Kong government avows that it is the protector of public interests. In reality, it always promotes its own interests. | 5.7 | 55.3 | 23.5 | 0.5 | 15.0 |
| 5. There is an intimate relationship between the activities of the government and my daily living. | 4.0 | 74.3 | 11.9 | 0.7 | 9.1 |
| 6. Hong Kong government is a good government. | 1.0 | 60.2 | 21.1 | 0.5 | 17.1 |
| 7. Hong Kong government takes care mainly of the interests of the wealthy. | 4.8 | 39.6 | 42.5 | 1.2 | 11.9 |

and unchallenged rule. The general acceptance of the Hong Kong government can be seen in Table 3.8, which illustrates the different levels of trust in the Hong Kong, British and Chinese governments in the 1985 survey.

Similar findings were obtained in the 1986 survey, where 76.4 percent of respondents trusted or very much trusted the Hong Kong government, 56.6 the British government, and only 31.8 the Chinese government. The crucial importance of government performance in political trust can be corroborated by several findings. In our study of four localities in 1982, "the percentages of respondents who said that the government's performance was good or average were 15.2 and 59.1 in Kwun Tong, 18.4 and 52.1 in Tuen Mun, 22 and 50.5 in Tai Hang Tung, and 15.5 and 54.4 in Sai Ying Pun."[15] In Table 3.7, 61.2 percent of respondents agreed or strongly agreed that the Hong Kong government was a good government. Likewise, in the 1986 survey, 43.6 percent of respondents rated the performance of the government as good or very good, while 46.6 percent considered it as about average. Only a minuscule 9.5 percent thought that the government had done a poor or very poor job. Thus, despite the less-than-given character of colonial authority and the suspicious and cynical feelings of the public, the linkage of the government with the economic success of Hong Kong and its efficient administration have nevertheless much improved the status of the government in the eyes of the people.

The intimate relationship between government and people began two decades ago with the growing dependence of the changing Chinese society on the government and the government's increasing involvement in social-economic affairs. The new slogan of the government, "positive non-interventionism," by adding the qualifier "positive," demonstrates that the government is prepared to intervene

TABLE 3.8
Trust in Governments

| | Distrust very much | Distrust | Trust | Trust very much | Don't know/ No answer |
|---|---|---|---|---|---|
| 1. Hong Kong government | 3.9 | 12.9 | 68.2 | 3.9 | 14.0 |
| 2. British government | 3.5 | 30.9 | 37.8 | 1.7 | 26.1 |
| 3. Chinese government | 8.1 | 34.8 | 29.7 | 1.8 | 25.6 |

in society if the situation calls for it. This increasingly close relationship between the people and the government is also perceived by the Hong Kong Chinese, as 78.3 percent agreed or strongly agreed with the statement that "there is an intimate relationship between the activities of the government and my daily living." Needless to say, there is a "vicious circle" here once the government has started to intervene in society by providing various goods and services, it will stimulate rising expectations and also rising frustrations among the people. In fact, this argument can be generalized. "When the government produces services, people come to expect more. They also rely more on the government when there is nowhere else to turn—in particular when the family is too poor to help. The strain on resources when the state is committed to social services for a non-affluent population is evident. The result may be unsatisfactory services—something that . . . only heightens awareness of government potential."[16]

The important place of the government in society, as perceived by the Hong Kong Chinese, can also be seen in an earlier study of ours.

> The increasing awareness of the relevance of the government to one's livelihood naturally fosters a sense of dependence on the government for the satisfaction of one's needs. If the emphasis on self-help and the avoidance of governmental contacts were the norms in the past, the findings of this survey seem to show that these norms are fading fast. Two types of problems were distinguished in this survey, community problems and personal or family problems, and the respondents were asked to identify the person or organization most responsible for their solution. In the replies, the prominence of the government as the primary problem-solver is astounding.
>
> [A table] shows, in no uncertain terms, that the government is the most frequently quoted agency responsible for solving community problems. [Another table] adds a further consideration. Not only is the government held to be responsible for the solution of community problems, but it is thought to be the most effective means of getting things done.
>
> Parallel with the dependence on the government as a problem-solver there is inevitably a sense of diffidence on the part of the people: they feel unable to solve local problems through their own initiative and efforts. And this is, in fact, the case here. What is even more surprising is that this sense of dependence on the government is extended to the realm of

> personal and family problems. The Chinese people have often been applauded for the resilience and resourcefulness of their family and kinship network, and it is precisely these qualities of the Chinese family that enable it to distance itself from the potentially threatening political authorities. But . . . a significant proportion of the respondents held the government responsible for the solution of their personal and family problems, and the number of people replying that they themselves or their family were responsible was, in contrast, far from impressive. This finding is even more puzzling since the most important family problem named by respondents was a financial one, which on the face of it should have only an indirect relationship with the government. But that is not the end of the story. Compared with those who held the government responsible for the solution of personal and family problems, an even larger proportion claimed that only the government was capable of solving them. The percentages of those who strongly emphasized this capacity of the government and those who were less enthusiastic were 37.9 and 12.7 in Kwun Tong, 33.3 and 12.8 in Tuen Mun, 43.1 and 7.3 in Tai Hang Tung, and 30.1 and 8 in Sai Ying Pun.
>
> In all, what transpires from the above findings is that the people of Hong Kong are fast adopting an active and even interventionist conception of government, and it is unavoidable that they should like to see the government measure up to their expectations. Such an expectation would severely tax the capabilities of a government which is used to basing its political legitimacy on its performance and would call for drastic revision of its cherished doctrine of limited government.[17]

This increasingly close relationship between government and people must be seen in an instrumental and pragmatic light. The government is perceived primarily as service deliverer and benefactor with unlimited resources. At the very least, there is no manifest evidence to show that individuals and groups in Hong Kong, in their attempts to obtain benefits from the government, see themselves embroiled in any sort of zero-sum game. The general impression seems to be that a bunch of noncompetitive individuals and groups are jointly making claims on the unlimited resources controlled by an alien entity, viz., the colonial government. As a result, vertical relationships between individuals or groups with the government are emphasized to the neglect of horizontal relationships among them. This condition of unaggregated demands enables the government, provided the total amount of demands does not become impossible, to deal with them separately without jeopardizing colonial rule. But, at the same time, the paucity of aggregating mechanisms also deprives the government of the leverage to contain, control or manipulate demands from society, thus leaving the government vulnerable to incessant attacks by the aggrieved. Yet, large-scale political actions against the government are difficult to organize. They are even more difficult to sustain.

The instrumental and pragmatic conception of the government-people nexus can be seen from the fact that 65.3 percent of respondents agreed and 5.7 percent strongly agreed with the following statement: "A good government should concentrate on improving the livelihood of the people. It should not pay too much attention to long-term political ideals or isms." Furthermore, this instrumentalism and pragmatism is reminiscent of traditional Chinese expectations of the government, that also carried a heavy paternalistic dimension. In fact, 72.9 percent of respondents agreed and 8.2 percent agreed very much with the statement that the government should treat the people like a father treats his child. Only a tiny 13.8 percent of them refuted the statement. Support for paternalism also implies that the claims of the people against the government are not entitlements belonging to the people, which the government has the duty to respect, but instead are pleas or petitions for governmental beneficence.

In the last section, we have shown that the Hong Kong Chinese are capable of differentiating between the political and economic spheres and that they are basically reluctant to condone direct government interference in the economy, particularly in the area of income redistribution. However, given the growing dependence of society on the government, the readiness of the Hong Kong Chinese to seek government action in solving public and private problems and given the importance attached to governmental paternalism, we are led to think that the general conception of government has to be an interventionist, activist or expansive one. This orientation reflects the idea of the omnipotence of the state among traditional and modern Chinese. From previously reported findings, one might say that the perceived functions and powers of government might, to an unknown extent, be circumscribed by the demand for autonomy of the economy and the need to safeguard cherished personal freedoms. To what extent the economy or personal freedoms are seen as completely outside of political intervention is difficult to determine. From the fact that the Hong Kong Chinese are not reluctant to deny rights to others if they are seen as posing a threat to social order, we might conclude that even personal freedoms are not immune from political onslaughts in situations popularly defined as "threatening." In the case of the economy, the staggering economic inequalities, the strong negative elements in the evaluation of the wealthy and the perceived future economic difficulties in Hong Kong would dampen the subjective resistance of the Hong Kong Chinese to governmental interference in the economy. We might even venture to say that the limited economic functions of the Hong Kong government are self-imposed by the very economic doctrine of the government itself, which so far has been able to ward off demands on it to play a more interventionist role in the economy. A government without such restrictive economic doctrines or one without the necessary political autonomy might have to succumb to popular pressures to intervene.

What is more significant, however, is that governmental intervention in social affairs is not only condoned by the Hong Kong Chinese, but is actually demanded. Since social intervention on the part of the government perforce requires economic intervention in order to procure the necessary resources or provide the necessary conditions, to what extent social interventionism and economic *laissez faire* can co-exist is still a question which has not yet been addressed the minds of the Hong Kong Chinese.

## Functions of the Government

The role of the government in law and order and in establishing and maintaining the physical infrastructure for economic and social development is widely internalized by the Hong Kong Chinese. These functions are what enter into the definitions of economic *laissez faire* and social non-interventionism that have been practised by the colonial government for such a long period. Whether the Hong Kong Chinese, given their traditional heritage of an expansive and interventionist government, have really endorsed such limitations on the functions of the government is still not clearly known. Hence, extent to which the present limited government is supported by the values of the Hong Kong Chinese is still controversial. In the past two decades, the Hong Kong Chinese clamored for increased government facilities and services. They, however, still seemed to dislike the entry of the government into the social and economic realms.

In order to tap into the Hong Kong Chinese conception of the social, economic and cultural functions of the government, a series of probing questions were asked of our respondents in the 1985 survey. The results are tabulated in Table 3.9.

TABLE 3.9
Perception of the Functions of Government
(in percent)

| Statement | Agree very much | Agree | Disagree | Disagree very much | Don't know/ No answer |
|---|---|---|---|---|---|
| 1. Government should enact a law to penalize those children who fail to take care of their elderly parents. | 9.0 | 66.1 | 18.5 | 0.9 | 5.5 |
| 2. Officials should set examples and teach the people correct morals and behavior. | 9.4 | 83.6 | 3.1 | 0.3 | 3.7 |
| 3. Government should use legal means to deter divorce. | 0.7 | 22.3 | 62.8 | 4.6 | 9.6 |
| 4. The profusion of social problems is the fault of the government. | 0.8 | 28.6 | 56.3 | 1.0 | 13.3 |
| 5. Government is primarily responsible for resolving social problems. | 9.0 | 80.2 | 6.0 | 0 | 4.8 |
| 6. Government should force the rich to become more charitable. | 3.1 | 35.3 | 53.2 | 2.6 | 5.7 |
| 7. Government should find a job for everyone, so that no one will be unemployed. | 9.0 | 67.3 | 18.6 | 1.0 | 4.0 |
| 8. Government should provide a place to live for all the people of Hong Kong. | 17.9 | 75.1 | 4.8 | 0.5 | 1.7 |

Some surprising findings have been obtained, the most important of which is the acceptance of an influential role for the government in the moral sphere, though our respondents were careful to distinguish between public and private moralities. In this connection, the conclusion that can be drawn is that the moralizing function of the government is still quite prominent in the ethos of the Hong Kong Chinese.

An overwhelming majority of the respondents, 93 percent, agreed or strongly agreed that officials should set examples and teach the people correct morals and behavior. The shirking of such functions by the colonial government would obviously disappoint the people. In regard to the established, non-controversial moral norms, there was a call for the government to enforce them. For instance, filial piety has long been the central "public" morality of China, hence 75.1 percent of respondents agreed or strongly agreed that the government should enact a law to penalize those children who failed to take care of their elderly parents. But there is a limit to the moralizing role of the government. For the private or relatively controversial moral norms of recent origin, the responsibility of the government to enforce them is only dimly recognized. The issue of divorce provides a test case. Divorce poses a threat to the cherished family ideal, hence it was frowned upon and severely discouraged in traditional China. Modernization nevertheless has gradually changed popular attitude toward divorce in Hong Kong, but it is still a controversial topic which divides the populace. In the 1986 survey, 37.6 percent of respondents refused to accept divorce while 41.4 percent did so. But it appears that divorce is also largely seen as a private affair which is beyond the reach of society, not to mention the government. Therefore, the government is not given the "right" to interfere with divorce between people. Thus, 67.4 percent of respondents in the 1985 survey disagreed or strongly disagreed that the government should use legal means to deter divorce. In conclusion, like the traditional and modern Chinese, the moralizing role of the government is generally accepted by the Hong Kong Chinese; however, such a role is restricted to the established public moral realm. This realm seems to be a shrinking one with the rise of individualism as an increasing number of previously public moral norms will be transformed into private moral norms, though undoubtedly some moral norms (e.g., smoking in public places) hitherto considered as private will be progressively transformed into public moral norms.

While the interventionist role of the government in the moral sphere is generally condoned, intervention in the economic sphere fails to receive strong support. Despite the strand of egalitarianism in traditional Chinese economic thought, and traditional norms that obligated the wealthy to be philanthropic as a means of reducing economic inequalities, the Hong Kong Chinese are nevertheless reluctant to resort to administrative means to redistribute income. Thus, less than half (38.4 percent) of the respondents agreed or strongly agreed with the statement that the government should force the rich to become more charitable. This finding resonates with the general picture of the economy as autonomous from politics in the mind of the Hong Kong Chinese.

Support for non-interventionism in the economic sphere, however, stands in stark contrast to calls for interventionism in social problems and public services. As mentioned earlier on, if the Hong Kong Chinese are given a choice between help from government and help from family, the latter will be chosen. However, the complexity of modern Hong Kong society has already reached a point where the government has to assume responsibility for a lot of public concerns, and the people basically have to depend on it for many aspects of their well-being. The involvement of the government in many public and social services since the late 1960s has already rendered anachronistic its vaunted doctrine of social non-interventionism; this leaves a gap between ideology and reality that continues to infuse elements of inconsistency and hesitancy into the government's social and welfare policies as they waver between the poles of social self-dependence and governmental engagement.

The Hong Kong Chinese, despite their inevitable dependence on the public sector for their well-being, are nevertheless still capable of making a distinction between society and polity. Social problems and shortfalls in public services are explained largely in terms of endogenous societal factors. The responsibility for them is not shifted to the political sector as a ploy to demand public action. In Table 3.9, 57.4 percent of respondents disagreed or strongly disagreed with the argument that the profusion of social problems was due to the fault of the government. This line of reasoning echoes that of the traditional Chinese, and it reflects, just as in traditional China, the distinct demarcation between civil society and government in Hong Kong.[18] Unlike traditional China, the distinctness of the demarcation in Hong Kong should be even greater because of the self-imposed limits on the functions of political power by the colonial government.

Absolving the government of responsibility for social problems however, does not relieve it of the obligation to solve them. Hence, fully 89.2 percent of respondents attributed to the government the primary responsibility for solving social problems. Implicit in this finding is an obvious lack of confidence in self-help or in social efficacy on the part of the Hong Kong Chinese. As the appearance of social problems are related to deficiencies in public and social services, it logically follows that the government should also make provisions for them. Not surprisingly, 78.3 percent of respondents agreed or strongly agreed that the government should find a job for everyone so that no one would be left unemployed. In a similar vein, 93 percent felt that the government should provide a place to live for all the people.

Simultaneous support for social and moral interventionism and support for economic non-interventionism on the part of the Hong Kong Chinese is intrinsically contradictory, and the contradiction will be sharpened when a choice has to be made between the two. This contradiction will be intensified under certain conditions: decreasing availability of resources with a slowdown in economic growth; a faster increase in demand for social and public services than the speed of economic growth; more emphasis on social well-being or economic equity than on economic growth; a more "integralist" view of the government as part of the social order rather than an outside benefactor with a bottomless reservoir of resources. It is the last situation, when social actors are perceived of as competing among themselves for a limited pool of resources rather than fighting separately against a resourceful government, when people will be forced to choose explicitly between priorities. But, up to now, all these conditions have not matured to the point of compelling people to choose between social and moral interventionism and economic non-interventionism, or to raise in their mind the need for political equality (equitable distribution of political power) to mitigate economic inequalities and make available more social and public services. In short, there is, as yet, no conclusive evidence to decide whether economic non-interventionism or social/moral interventionism is more important in the ethos of the Hong Kong Chinese. There is, however, a hint that when a critical choice has to be made between the two, economic non-interventionism might be relegated to lesser importance. In the 1986 survey, the respondents were asked to choose between two arguments about social welfare. The first stated that existing social welfare was inadequate for it did not make it possible for the suffering people and families to improve their living conditions. The other argument countered the first by saying that a too large or too comprehensive social welfare system would lead many self-reliant people into indolence and dependence on welfare. 52.3 percent of respondents agreed with the first argument while only 29.7 percent endorsed the second one. This finding definitely cannot furnish evidence that economic non-interventionism will be in jeopardy when the hard choice between social well-being and economic freedom has to be made; however, it seems to indicate that the support for the free capitalist economy might not be an absolute or unconditional support. *The traditional Chinese tendency to put social (and political) interests over and above economic interests seems to have a residual influence even in a free-for-all capitalist system.*

## Political Involvement

In keeping with the modest level of individual and social efficacy of the Hong Kong Chinese, a relatively low sense of political efficacy is also found. This low sense of political efficacy might, to a certain extent, be strengthened by the 1997 malaise and the entry of China as a political center of gravity in Hong Kong. A low sense of political efficacy inevitably impedes active political involvement and infuses a certain element of unconventionality in political actions. However, there is also a redeeming feature in the area of political involvement in Hong Kong. That is, Hong Kong Chinese evince a decent level of administrative efficacy, which apparently is derived from the more accommodationist stance of government officials. This sense of administrative efficacy might have somewhat alleviated the frustrations fostered by feelings of political inefficacy.[19]

Even though there is a general perception of the intimate relationship between the activities of the government and personal and social well-being, political interest remains low in Hong Kong. In a survey commissioned by the *South China Morning Post* in 1986, political matters ranked very low in the priority list of tasks for the government, way below issues such as housing, law and order, transport, education, and social welfare. Only 1 percent of respondents listed the structure of Hong Kong government as the most important task for the government.[20] The lack of political interest among Hong Kong Chinese, however, does not bother them at all. In the 1985 survey, 72 percent of respondents took the view that since the people were very busy, their failure to concern themselves with public affairs was excusable. This low interest in politics directly affects people's level of activity in political discussions. As shown in Table 3.10, our respondents maintained rather infrequent discussions of public affairs with others except probably with "those superior in knowledge."

TABLE 3.10
Frequency of Discussion of Public Affairs
(in percent)

| Discussion with: | Very frequently | Frequently | Seldom | Very seldom | Don't know/ No answer |
|---|---|---|---|---|---|
| 1. Family members | 2.1 | 20.5 | 39.2 | 32.6 | 5.6 |
| 2. Relatives | 0.8 | 7.3 | 37.4 | 48.4 | 6.1 |
| 3. Friends | 2.7 | 38.5 | 28.6 | 25.7 | 4.6 |
| 4. Those superior in knowledge | 1.7 | 31.8 | 27.8 | 31.9 | 6.8 |
| 5. Community leaders | 0.4 | 4.4 | 19.7 | 63.8 | 11.4 |

Underlining low political interest is a pervasive sense of political powerlessness, which has been documented extensively in the literature.[21] In our 1982 study of four localities, it was found that the "paralyzing sense of political powerlessness has not been much allayed. People still feel that they do not really count in the decision-making structure of their society. The government continues to be a monolithic enigma. In Kwun Tong, Tuen Mun, Tai Hang Tung, and Sai Ying Pun, 53.6, 62.2, 56, and 40 percent respectively of the respondents felt that the government's work was too complicated for them to understand. In general, less than 20 percent of them thought otherwise. Faced with a government whose rationale and operation they have difficulty in identifying with, the people's sense of political efficacy is bound to suffer. Most of the respondents (73.3 percent in Kwun Tong, 75 percent in Tuen Mun, 78 percent in Tai Hang Tung, and 77.9 percent in Sai Ying Pun) thus believed that they could have little influence on the government's local policies."[22]

Several years later, the feeling of political powerlessness not only persisted, in fact, it became more severe. In our 1985 survey, 66 percent of respondents agreed and 9 percent agreed strongly that politics and government were complicated and difficult to understand. An alarmingly large percentage of them (84.7 percent) thought that they had little or very little influence on the policy of the government. In the 1986 survey, an even larger proportion of respondents (87.9

percent) denied that they had any power to change the actions of the government.

Continual fear of authority might partly account for the high sense of powerlessness among the Hong Kong Chinese, this is in spite of the increasingly tolerant attitude of the government toward its critics and opponents and in spite of the general perception that the authority of the government has eroded since the onset of the Sino-British negotiations. (In fact, 44.6 percent of respondents agreed or strongly agreed with the statement that "since the Sino-British negotiations over Hong Kong's future, the authority of the Hong Kong government had suffered," in contrast with the 36.5 percent who disagreed or strongly disagreed.) Thus, still 43.6 percent of respondents agreed or strongly agreed that "we should never antagonize those with authority, for fear that they might take revenge on us." Only a slightly larger percentage (48.5) of respondents disagreed or strongly disagreed. Nevertheless, the erosion of the authority of the Hong Kong government has not created the image of a power vacuum at the top. What they do see is a reinforced authority complex at the pinnacle of the political hierarchy made up of the Hong Kong government, the Chinese government and the British government that has reversed its past practices by increasingly participating in the governance of Hong Kong. Accordingly, 52.2 percent of respondents agreed or strongly agreed with this statement: "Since the signing of the Sino-British Agreement, the Hong Kong government has received assistance in many ways from the Chinese government. Therefore, the authority of the Hong Kong government has been restored to the previous level." Furthermore, 54.3 percent of them agreed or strongly agreed with another similar statement: "As an ordinary citizen, I find it even more difficult than it was in the past to influence the decision of the Hong Kong government at a time when Hong Kong is governed by the Chinese, British and Hong Kong governments." The replacement of authority, as it was constituted by the former Hong Kong government system, by an expanded authority complex comprising three governments has obviously exacerbated the sense of powerlessness among the Hong Kong Chinese. Needless to say, if the three governments act in tandem and present a monolithic image to the people, the effect on political powerlessness would be even more potent. If they bicker among themselves or engage in serious conflicts, we still do not think that the sense of powerlessness would be attenuated. In all likelihood, the result would be the specter of an authority crisis and its corollary, grave political fear.

Lack of political interest and feelings of political powerlessness however, do not stunt all forms of political involvement. In point of fact, given the increasing role of the government in social-economic affairs, it is impossible for Hong Kong Chinese to abstain completely from political participation. It would then be interesting to know what forms of participation people will take when participation is considered unavoidable, necessary or even desirable.

In the first place, Hong Kong Chinese, in general, accept an obligation or duty to be concerned with public affairs. In our 1985 survey, 80.2 percent of respondents agreed that every citizen had the responsibility to put forth his opinions about public affairs in order to help the government make better policies. Only 10.2 percent took the contrary view, and reasoned that by not expressing openly one's opinions future troubles could be averted.

Nevertheless, normative support for public political expression has not been translated into action. For example, the Hong Kong Chinese rarely make personal contacts with government officials. In our 1982 study of the inhabitants in four localities we found that,

> [t]he people are found to take the initiative in approaching the government only extremely rarely, though the experience of the contacts actually made is felt to be generally rewarding. In the same vein, despite their positive image of government officials the people seldom initiate contacts and discuss community problems with them. Only a minuscule 1.5, 4.2, 0.9, and 2.7 percent respectively of the respondents in Kwun Tong, Tuen Mun, Tai Hang Tung, and Sai Ying Pun had done so in the three months preceding the day of the interview.[23]

Personal contacts with government officials belong to a particular mode of political participation that is distinct from other more group-related modes and can take place even in situations of low political or democratic awareness. The generic mode of "particularized contacts" "involves the citizen as individual (or perhaps with a few family members) contacting a government official about a particularized problem—that is, one limited to himself or his family. Such activity combines high information but usually little pressure. It entails little conflict among social groups and little cooperation with others. But it does require a great deal of initiative."[24] Moreover,

> [t]his mode of activity has some interesting characteristics that differentiate it from other activities. People can take part in this way without the broad participant orientations that are

associated with other activity. Political interest, political information, and other "civic" orientations correlated positively with other political activities; they do not correlate with particularized contacting. The result is that in each nation, particularized contacting is unrelated to other political activities; i.e., the likelihood that an individual will engage in particularized contacting is unrelated to the likelihood that he will engage in other activities. It is a distinct mode of activity, in that it may be engaged in by those with no broad political concerns at all.[25]

Some factors are of foremost importance in inducing particularized contacts by fostering "parochial awareness." "The likelihood that an individual will mention the government as a potential source of aid in relation to a personal or social problem and actually expect such aid is affected both by the past experience an individual has had with government programs as well as by the extent to which alternative sources of aid (particularly from the family) are available."[26] More precisely,

> [p]arochial awareness is most frequent among those who have experienced government services but are dissatisfied with them; who, in addition, report that help from the extended family is unavailable; and who, in any case, would prefer not to take such aid. Citizens appear to learn that the government might be capable of supplying help for their particular problems if they have received some services. The fact that the services were not satisfactory only increases that awareness. Belief that one can count on the government (parochial expectation) is, however, found among the satisfied recipients of services.
>
> At the same time, the belief that one cannot rely on the extended family increases the likelihood that one will think of the government in time of need. But this does not make one optimistic about receiving such support. The relationship between the unavailability of family support and parochial expectations is not as clearcut as that between the former and parochial awareness. If the family can't help, one thinks of the government—but one is by no means certain one can rely on it.[27]

On the face of it, in view of the dependence of the Hong Kong Chinese on the government for the solution of their personal, family, and community problems, the inexorable involvement of the government in social welfare and public services, and the general satisfaction with government performance, we should expect to see a large amount of particularized contacts among the Hong Kong Chinese. However, as we have seen, such is not the case. In fact, compared to the countries studied in the Cross-National Program in Political and Social Change by Verba, Nie and Kim (Austria, India, Japan, the Netherlands, Nigeria, the United States, and Yugoslavia), the volume of particularized contacts in Hong Kong is very small, and smaller than all these countries.[28] This is puzzling for some other reasons. Firstly, most of our respondents in the 1985 survey (53.8 percent) thought that the government had the capability to help them solve their personal and family problems. If this was so, the government should be a natural target for particularized contacts. Secondly, a fairly substantial proportion of respondents, 39.1 percent, thought that the government would come to their aid when they and their families were troubled by problems. (A similar proportion, 39 percent took the contrary view.) Thus, the government was seen by many as an approachable or accessible source of help. Thirdly, our respondents expected fair and favorable treatment from officials if they contacted them, thus evincing a fairly high degree of administrative efficacy (or subject competence). Thus, 51.6 percent of respondents were certain that they would receive fair treatment (or the same treatment received by others) from government officials when they went to a government department for help. Only 24 percent did not think so. When they explained their position to the officials, 53.5 percent of respondents expected the officials to pay some attention to them, while 9 percent of them even thought that the officials would seriously consider their viewpoints. Only a small 17.7 percent expected to be given a cold shoulder by the officials.

Given all these factors favorable to particularized contacts, we should be justified in concluding that there is a great potential among the Hong Kong Chinese to make particularized contacts with government officials *when there is a strong need for them.* That this potential has only been minimally realized may well be explainable by several factors. First, the paralyzing sense of political powerlessness among the Hong Kong Chinese might deter them from really taking the initiative to contact officials. Secondly, the still booming economy might have solved many problems indirectly or by default. And finally, the still perceived availability of family resources and the lingering tendency to define and explain private problems in non-political terms make the government less relevant as an agency with the duty to help. Thus, even though Hong Kong Chinese think that the government has both the willingness and ability to help, they do not have enough motivation to demand it.

If particularized contacting, which requires little political awareness or group mobilization, is infrequent among the Hong Kong Chinese, it is therefore not surprising also to find a low incidence of "higher" modes of political participation. When the respondents were asked in the 1985 survey whether they thought that they could do something about a bill under consideration by government that in their opinion was unfair or harmful, 37.6 percent gave an affirmative answer while 48.9 percent reported a negative one; 38.7 percent of them mentioned that they would probably really do something to change the action of the government, in contrast with the 48.9 percent who would not or definitely would not do so. In the 1986 survey, when the respondents were queried as to whether they would do something about a bill proposed by the government which they deemed to be unfair or contain adverse effects for themselves, the plurality (46.6 percent) of them gave a negative reply. In fact, despite the modest proportion of people who claimed that they would take action to influence the government, the percentage of those who had actually done so represents only a minuscule portion of them.[29]

What is most interesting here, however, are the types of "effective" influence tactics as perceived by the Hong Kong Chinese. The basically closed political system in Hong Kong, dominated by what is thought to be a largely secretive and monolithic bureaucracy, and inadequate channels of political participation would naturally divert a portion of participation to unconventional channels. The emergence of unconventional politics is further abetted by the ambivalent attitude toward colonial authority, the enormous sense of powerlessness *vis-à-vis* political authorities, the more or less "institutionalization" of non-violent unconventional pressure group politics and the lack of politically aggregative mechanisms (such as political parties) in Hong Kong. The findings in our 1982 study of four localities can provide a pertinent starting point for a more in-depth discussion:

> While the inadequacy of the channels of political participation and the dearth of intermediate leaders in Hong Kong operate to sustain the feeling of impotence, the appearance of the pressure groups and the free, competitive mass media inject some new elements into the scene to

improve the situation somewhat. Broadly speaking, the pressure groups and the freewheeling mass media are intimately related, as it is the latter which enable the former to thrive and send their messages across to the people.

The impact of the joint functioning of the pressure groups and the mass media suggests alternative means of political influence to the people. The significance of the mass media in this respect can easily be measured using the figures in Table 1.6 [not reported here], which shows the preponderant role of the media in informing the public about local affairs and the means employed by others to cope with community problems.

The examples set by the activities of the pressure groups have the effect of enlarging the inventory of influence tactics in the minds of the Hong Kong Chinese. Although the unconventional methods so frequently adopted by the pressure groups still fail to win widespread acceptance, the people have somehow revised their political thinking and introduced new dimensions in their political outlook. . . . [S]ide by side with more conventional means of influence (such as having personal relationships with officials and filing complaints to the relevant government department), the people are not only quite aware of a variety of unconventional methods (petitioning the Governor, publicity campaigns, and electing representatives), but also seem to consider these as being among the more effective ways of getting the government to accede to their demands. Moreover, it can even be claimed that the people have become more favourably disposed towards political activism of various kinds. When asked about the possible reactions of others to their playing a more active role in tackling community issues, most of the respondents said that they did not expect to encounter hostilities of any kind.

What is most remarkable in this connection is that the tolerance on the part of the government is taken for granted.

To a lesser extent, the popular acceptance of unconventional methods of political influence has been extended to the more radical of them. Tactics which involve a quantum of confrontation or violence are increasingly rated as effective means to compel the government to give in. The respondents were asked their opinion on the use of such methods as demonstrations, protests, propaganda, or sit-ins to pressure

> the government; the responses given are instructive. The percentages endorsing such acts completely and partially were 15.5 and 19.7 in Kwun Tong, 16 and 13.5 in Tuen Mun, 16.5 and 12.8 in Tai Hang Tung, and 7.1 and 10.2 in Sai Ying Pun. It is still true that about half of the respondents (46.7, 54.2, 49.5, and 63.7 percent respectively in Kwun Tong, Tuen Mun, Tai Hang Tung, and Sai Ying Pun) were opposed to such disorderly behaviour. However, in view of the fact that the people never even contemplated this kind of radical tactics in the past, the appearance of a substantial minority in society to confer legitimacy on them is indisputably no small change.[30]

The importance of group-based and unconventional tactics of influence apparently has increased since the time the above study was done (1982). Table 3.11 lists the effective ways to influence government policy reported by the respondents in the 1985 survey. Together the three unconventional group-based tactics—mobilizing and organizing the people affected, exercising influence through political parties and other political organizations, and demonstrations and protests—were identified by 44.2 percent of the respondents. This shift of support for the new tools of political influence testifies to the increased political exposure and experience of the Hong Kong Chinese in the last few eventful years.

TABLE 3.11
Effective Ways to Influence Government Policy

| Ways suggested | Percent |
|---|---|
| Make use of relatives who are officials | 1.8 |
| Write letters to officials or meet them in person | 18.1 |
| Mobilize and organize the people affected | 25.7 |
| Exercise influence through political parties and other political organizations | 14.7 |
| Demonstrate and protest | 3.8 |
| Other methods | 1.8 |
| No way | 12.5 |
| Don't know/No answer | 21.5 |

Comparable findings were obtained in the 1986 survey. Aside from 46.6 percent of respondents who would do nothing when faced with an unfair and harmful bill proposed by the government, 3.9 percent would seek help from influential persons or organizations, 5 percent would register their opposition with the mass media, 7.8 percent would go to the District Boards (district advisory committees), 10.6 percent would approach officials, 1.3 percent would go to the Unofficial Members of the Executive and Legislative Councils, 11.3 percent would join petition campaigns and 3.9 percent would participate in protests, demonstrations and parades.

From Table 3.11 and the findings above, it can be seen that, while unconventional group-based tactics feature prominently in the minds of the Hong Kong Chinese as effective methods to change governmental actions, they are not normally resorted to in reality. However, the extent that these unconventional methods are being actually utilized by the people seems to have increased progressively over time.

Yet, notwithstanding the increasing acceptance of unconventional tactics by the Hong Kong Chinese, their attitude toward it is, at best, ambivalent. This attitude is conditioned both by the ambivalent attitude toward the colonial government and preoccupation with stability. As will be seen later, this ambivalence also characterizes popular attitudes toward pressure groups and their leaders.

On the one hand, 53 percent of respondents in the 1985 survey disagreed or strongly disagreed that it was a healthy phenomenon that an increasing number of people were courageous enough to confront the government in protests and demonstrations. This attests to a preference for order and respect for authority on the part of the Hong Kong Chinese. On the other hand, a plurality of them (46.5 percent) also agreed or strongly agreed that since the Hong Kong government was accustomed to bully the weak and fear the strong, therefore it was quite all right for some groups or individuals to take radical actions to force it to change its stand. Those who disagreed or strongly disagreed amounted to only 38.8 percent of the total. Such a finding reveals a sense of frustration on the part of the Hong Kong Chinese at the futility of conventional means of political influence.

Upon closer scrutiny, it is evident that the favorable reception of unconventional group-based influence tactics is conditioned by one's attitude toward politics. Those who take a less traditional view of politics are more likely to see these tactics favorably. This point receives some support in Tables 3.12 and 3.13.

Those respondents who were less inclined to see politics as either dirty or dangerous were more disposed to see political mobilization, protests and political parties (though, at this moment there is no political party in the strict sense in Hong Kong), as the effective means to influence government policy.

On balance, political involvement by the Hong Kong Chinese is still quite low, even though they are aware of, and have become accustomed to, some new influence tactics which contain an element of political confrontation. Hong Kong Chinese are still plagued by feelings of powerlessness, cynicism and alienation. Comparatively speak ing, these feelings do not necessarily lead to political passivity and inactivism. In India, for example, political involvement exists side by side with political alienation.

> India is a polity whose masses remain considerably "traditional" and highly aware of caste and its role in politics. Yet, many of these people are politically involved, often participating in acts beyond that of voting. The level of involvement is comparatively high and it is linked to attitudes which in the West would be considered contradictory or dysfunctional. Lower castes and illiterates with attitudes suggesting high criticism and rejection of the system, the regime, and its leadership, as well as high cynicism about the ordinary citizen's possible role in that context, and in addition, opposition to party conflict and the competitive style of political life—many of these people are the regular voters and the highly active.[31]

In Hong Kong, the lack of individual initiative or resources in political participation are not compensated for by the mobilizing efforts of political groups and leaders, which may explain the behavioral lethargy of the Hong Kong Chinese. Needless to say, as the Hong Kong government is an exclusionary bureaucratic regime rather than a populist or ideologically-inclined ruling force, mobilization from the top is precluded as a channel of political participation.

## Attitude toward Political Leaders

The unavailability of respected and trusted political leaders has been a perennial shortfall in the political system of Hong Kong. Bureaucratic hegemony and the non-existence of a meaningful electoral process almost completely preclude the emergence of popular, not to say

TABLE 3.12
Politics as Dirty by Selected Means to Influence Public Policy
(in percent)

| Politics as dirty | Personal relations with officials | Mobilizing people | Political parties | Protest actions | No way | Sub-total (N) |
|---|---|---|---|---|---|---|
| Strongly disagree | 30.4 | 39.1 | 4.3 } 22.8 | 4.3 } 2.8 | 13.0 | 91.3 (21) |
| Disagree | 21.5 | 36.2 | 24.2 | 2.7 | 10.6 | 95.3 (279) |
| Agree | 20.4 | 29.6 | 16.7 } 16.4 | 7.4 } 7.1 | 21.6 | 95.7 (155) |
| Strongly agree | 42.9 | 19.0 | 14.3 | 4.8 | 9.5 | 90.5 (19) |

TABLE 3.13
Politics as Dangerous by Selected Means to Influence Public Policy
(in percent)

| Politics as dangerous | Personal relations with officials | Mobilizing people | Political parties | Protest actions | No way | Sub-total (N) |
|---|---|---|---|---|---|---|
| Strongly disagree | 38.5 } 21.8 | 30.8 } 37.8 | 7.7 } 22.2 | 0 | 7.7 | 84.6 (11) |
| Disagree | 20.8 | 38.2 | 23.1 | 2.4 | 9.4 | 93.8 (199) |
| Agree | 22.9 } 24.6 | 30.3 } 29.7 | 19.6 } 19.1 | 6.6 | 17.3 | 96.7 (262) |
| Strongly agree | 45.5 | 22.7 | 13.6 | 4.5 | 9.1 | 95.5 (21) |

charismatic, leaders exercising diffuse and personal political authority. The impersonal and distant character of colonial bureaucratic authority at best enables it to be respected or feared, but it is not loved by the ruled, particularly when it is also alien and secluded. As such, the urge of the Hong Kong Chinese to personalize government and to identify with political leaders through an affective nexus is thwarted, producing alienation and powerlessness in its wake.

The dominance of the colonial bureaucracy not only obstructs the formation of an indigenous political leadership on the "national" level, but its unitary nature and its aversion to decentralization also impede the emergence of effective intermediate leaders. There are local leaders, of course, but they have not been given the necessary autonomy and power to act as effective intermediaries between the government and the people. They are, in large measure, made to function as para-administrative agents with a second-class status or as the channel for the downward transmission of governmental messages. Accordingly, local leadership is seen more as a status to be enjoyed than as a role to be played.

In the immediate post-war period, traditional leaders were able to find a small niche in the political system as a result of the limited penetrative capacity of the government, the shortage of public resources to deal with the multitude of social problems and the strength of tradition in Hong Kong. With rapid modernization, traditional leaders, who could still claim some measure of mass support, faded out and were replaced by modern Chinese elites, who on the strength of individual merit, obtained their leadership status through government co-option. As the Westernized Chinese elites, consisting mostly of professionals and businessmen, did not have organizational linkage with the people, the gap between government and the people widened.[32] Subsequent efforts by the government to create official and quasi-official mechanisms and the spontaneous formation of citizens' groups have only partially bridged the gap. As of 1986, the shortage of political leaders in Hong Kong remained serious.

Our 1982 study of four localities found that a preponderant proportion of the respondents were unable to name any local leaders. On the whole, the relationship between the leaders and the inhabitants was a distant one, as we see it described below.

> From the point of view of the residents, certain characteristics are important for good community leadership. . . . There were no great differences among the four localities. The will to

> enhance community well-being, the ability to enhance community well-being, and an acquaintance with community affairs were the traits that received the most emphasis. All of the characteristics have to do with the leaders' capacity to deliver services to the populace.
>
> Even though the requirements for good leadership are clear, to the residents, their leaders fall far short of expectations. . . . The slightly higher ratings given to the leaders of Tuen Mun and Tai Hang Tung are in recognition of their active leadership.
>
> The small differences in leadership evaluation did not, however, translate into actual contact with leaders. In Kwun Tong, Tuen Mun, Tai Hang Tung, and Sai Ying Pun, only 2%, 2%, 2%, and 1%, respectively, of the respondents had approached their local leaders in the 3 months before the interview. Of those who had not made any contact with local leaders, only a small proportion would like to have local leaders approach them directly (16% in Kwun Tong, 22% in Tuen Mun, 32% in Tai Hang Tung, and 26% in Sai Ying Pun). As before, Tuen Mun and Tai Hang Tung stood out among industrial and residential communities respectively.[33]

In our 1985 survey, a set of probing questions was designed to measure the people's attitude toward political leaders in general. The appearance of the 1997 negotiations and other related episodes had provided limited opportunities for indigenous leaders to assert themselves. Their efforts seemed to have moderately improved their collective image, as can be seen in Table 3.14.

The respondents in the survey affirmed the positive contributions of political leaders, while, at the same time, overrating their possible political contributions. Political activities were accorded a more respectable status that was a far cry from the basically anti-politics stance of the traditional Chinese. Political leaders were evaluated in a more favorable light, though that did not constitute popular trust in them. In fact, 47.8 percent of respondents said that there was no political leader in Hong Kong whom they felt they could trust. Only 24.5 percent had such a leader or leaders in mind. Furthermore, as we have already seen, the Hong Kong Chinese are able to distinguish between the requirements for political leadership and those for leadership in other non-political spheres.

In their search for political leaders, the Hong Kong Chinese obviously have in mind leaders whose first priority is the interests of

TABLE 3.14
Attitude toward Political Leaders
(in percent)

| Statement | Agree very much | Agree | Disagree | Disagree very much | Don't know/ No answer |
|---|---|---|---|---|---|
| 1. Most political leaders have engaged in illicit activities. | 1.4 | 27.1 | 40.9 | 1.3 | 29.2 |
| 2. Political activities are respectable and meaningful. | 0.8 | 44.9 | 29.7 | 0.5 | 24.1 |
| 3. If only we have political leaders who are upright and competent, most conflicts and problems in Hong Kong can be solved. | 3.3 | 60.2 | 22.0 | 0.8 | 13.7 |
| 4. Only those with prestigeous occupations and who excel in them can make good leaders. | 1.8 | 30.6 | 49.9 | 3.3 | 14.3 |

Hong Kong. This resonates with the increasingly salient Hong Kong identity and apprehensions about incorporating Hong Kong as a part of China. Thus, 55.1 percent of respondents claimed that they would render support to a political leader who was intent on mobilizing support from the people but failed to receive support from the Hong Kong and Chinese governments.

The formation of a favorable impression of political leaders is contingent upon particular perceptions of politics and government, and vice versa. The attenuated anti-politics stance of the Hong Kong Chinese seems to provide the context for a better reception of political leaders. Thus, as shown in Table 3.15, those who were less predisposed to see politics as dirty or dangerous were more able to recognize trustworthy social or political leaders in Hong Kong. It also follows that if trustworthy political leaders were recognized, the Hong Kong Chinese would be more disposed to use group-based tactics to influence the policy of the government, though not to the extent of embracing political parties or political protests, as seen in Table 3.16.

TABLE 3.15
Conceptions of Politics by Recognition of Trustworthy Leaders

| Conceptions of politics | Recognition of leaders* | $\chi^2$ | d.f. | p |
|---|---|---|---|---|
| 1. Politics is dirty | | | | |
| (a) Strongly disagree or disagree | 39.9 | 8.01 | 3 | 0.046 |
| (b) Strongly agree or agree | 27.1 | | | |
| 2. Politics is dangerous | | | | |
| (a) Strongly disagree or disagree | 42.6 | 9.85 | 3 | 0.020 |
| (b) Strongly agree or agree | 29.6 | | | |

* Percentages agreeing that there were trustworthy social or political leaders in Hong Kong.

In view of the importance of popular leaders in the political ethos of the Hong Kong Chinese, it might be logical to conclude that the rise of charismatic leaders could bring about some important changes in the political landscape of Hong Kong.

## Attitude toward Pressure Groups and Their Leaders

The term ''pressure group'' has a narrow and occasionally pejorative meaning in the political context of Hong Kong. It refers primarily to those citizens' groups that are community or neighborhood based, or they may be single-issue groups. Sometimes they are outside the institutional political arena and they tend to resort to unconventional, publicity-oriented tactics to pressure the government. The pressure groups reflect both the institutional gap between government and society and the imbalance in the distribution of political power in Hong Kong. They are particularly active in the areas of public policy and services, especially those with welfare or redistributive implications. As noted before, pressure tactics have fast become an institutionalized part of the Hong Kong political scene, but that, however, has not been true of pressure groups and their leaders, whose role in society is still ambiguous.

Both the 1985 and 1986 surveys showed that pressure groups and

TABLE 3.16
Political Leaders Not Trustworthy by Selected Means to Influence Public Policy
(in percent)

| Political leaders not trustworthy | Personal relations with officials | | Mobilizing people | Political parties | | Protest actions | No way | Sub-total (N) |
|---|---|---|---|---|---|---|---|---|
| Strongly disagree | 33.3 | 22.6 | 33.3 | 22.2 | 20.2 | 0 | 0 | 88.8 (8) |
| Disagree | 22.3 | | 39.2 | 20.1 | | 3.5 | 10.2 | 95.4 (270) |
| Agree | 24.0 | 23.8 | 26.3 | 21.0 | 20.5 | 3.6 | 20.4 | 95.2 (159) |
| Strongly agree | 22.2 | | 16.7 | 16.7 | | 0 | 27.8 | 83.3 (15) |

their leaders had yet to promote a favorable popular image of themselves. In the 1985 survey, 43.2 percent of respondents thought that pressure groups could not successfully achieve their goals, 21.3 percent considered that they could, while 35.6 percent didn't know or gave no answer. The effectiveness of pressure groups in improving the living conditions of the common people was also questioned. 44.1 percent of respondents rated their contribution to the improvement of living conditions as small or very small, 27.9 percent as large or very large, while 28 percent didn't know or gave no answer. Pressure groups were also perceived as a threat to society. 53.5 percent of respondents said that the activities of the pressure groups would endanger the prosperity and stability of Hong Kong. 18 percent did not think so, and 28.6 percent picked the non-committal replies of "don't know" or "no answer." The substantial proportion of non-committal responses to these questions indicates the novelty of pressure groups and pressure tactics in the Hong Kong political scene and their controversial nature. As such, a crystallized public opinion about them has not yet emerged. On the whole they still have a long way to go to establish themselves in the mind of the public.

Pressure group leaders, however, seem to fare somewhat better. Through skillful utilization of the mass media, a handful of pressure group leaders have been able to impress themselves on the public mind. The incessant resort to dramatic tactics has turned some of them into household words among the common people, though the images they have projected are not necessarily received positively. A telling find is that 58.5 percent of respondents reported no particularly trusted pressure group leaders, only 12.5 percent were able to do so, and 28.9 percent said they did not know or gave no answer. But the inability of conventional political leaders (particularly the established Westernized Chinese elites co-opted by the government) to serve as an effective intermediary between government and people, and the ambivalent attitude toward colonial authority inherent in the popular political ethos provide favorable conditions for some pressure group leaders to make themselves accepted as the "representatives" of some of the people. Their unconventional tactics, which contain an implicit anti-authority element, apparently also appeal to a public vexed by feelings of powerlessness, cynicism and alienation. If that is the case, then it is not surprising that 45.6 percent of respondents took the view that pressure group leaders could better reflect public opinion than the members of the Legislative and Executive Councils, only 23.7 percent took a different view; but, what is most interesting is that 30.6 percent of respondents were not able to come up with definite answers.

Similar results were obtained in the 1986 survey. Only 22.7 percent of respondents felt that the contributions of pressure groups to the improvement of the living conditions of the common people were large or very large. 32.8 percent thought that they were small or very small. 32.1 percent considered their performance in this aspect as only run-of-the-mill. But what is of importance here is that the respondents had a pretty positive impression of their motives in criticizing and making suggestions about public policies. 30.8 percent saw the pressure group's foremost motive as "serving society," 14.5 percent as "self-interest," whereas 40.8 percent interpreted their motives as a mixture of both. That this is a more positive view of the motives of pressure groups (and incidentally quasi-political groups as well) can be seen by the distribution of responses to the motives of the candidates for the District Board, Urban Council and Legislative Council elections: 24.9 percent "serving society," 19.5 percent "self-interest," and 38.6 percent a mixture of both.

As indicated earlier on, pressure groups and their leaders represent a new and still controversial phenomenon in Hong Kong. Intrinsic in the pressure group phenomenon are elements, some of which appeal to the political ethos of the Hong Kong Chinese, while others are repugnant to it. Pressure groups conflict with the anti-politics proclivity, the need for authority, the preoccupation with stability and the distrust of political leaders, all of which are facets of the political ethos of the Hong Kong Chinese; but, at the same time, they serve to assuage the hurt political feelings of a people who cannot find an alternative to potentially humiliating alien colonial rule. In fact, the sudden emergence of pressure politics in the last one and a half decades and its controversial nature serve as the means to clarify the basic political values of the Hong Kong Chinese: they were impelled to conduct a comprehensive search of their inventory of political values in order to make sense of and to ascertain the status of this "strange" phenomenon.

For those who take a negative view of politics, pressure groups are seen as a threat to prosperity and stability. As shown in Table 3.17, respondents in the 1985 survey who were more inclined to see politics as dirty or as dangerous and who had in mind no trustworthy leaders were more likely to see pressure groups as dangerous and reject them on that account.

In the same way, those who saw politics as dangerous were also

TABLE 3.17
Conceptions of Politics by Pressure Groups as a Danger to Prosperity and Stability

| Conceptions of politics | Pressure group a danger* | $\chi^2$ | d.f. | p |
|---|---|---|---|---|
| 1. Politics is dirty | | | | |
| (a) Strongly disagree or disagree | 21.4 | 13.16 | 3 | 0.004 |
| (b) Strongly agree or agree | 33.7 | | | |
| 2. Politics is dangerous | | | | |
| (a) Strongly disagree or disagree | 18.6 | 9.85 | 3 | 0.020 |
| (b) Strongly agree or agree | 29.7 | | | |
| 3. Political leaders are not trustworthy | | | | |
| (a) Strongly disagree or disagree | 20.6 | 12.48 | 3 | 0.006 |
| (b) Strongly agree or agree | 32.0 | | | |

* Percentages agreeing with the statement that the activities of the pressure groups would endanger the prosperity and stability of Hong Kong.

more likely to think that pressure groups were not successful in achieving their goals. Distrust of political leaders in general also has spillover effects on the perception of the trustworthiness of pressure groups in particular. Thus, those who considered political leaders untrustworthy were more inclined to think that pressure groups were unsuccessful in achieving their goals.

Those who take a negative or misanthropic view of human nature are also more disposed to denounce the pressure groups. Those who agreed or strongly agreed that the evil nature of human beings made war and conflicts inevitable were more likely to think that pressure groups would endanger prosperity and stability. In the same vein, those who deemed the majority of people untrustworthy were more likely to take the same view of pressure groups.

Similarly, those who have a more traditional orientation toward authority are less prepared to endorse a positive valuation of pressure groups. Thus, 57.4 percent of those who agreed or strongly agreed that one should not antagonize those in authority looked upon pressure groups as a menace to prosperity and stability, as compared with 41.2 percent of those who disagreed or strongly disagreed. Likewise, 82.9 percent of those who agreed or strongly agreed that powerful authority was needed to maintain law and order viewed pressure groups as a menace to prosperity and stability, in contrast with 64.9 percent of those who disagreed or strongly disagreed.

Those who detest social conflict and crave harmony are also less favorably disposed toward pressure groups. For example, those respondents who tended to agree that a normal society should have no serious conflicts were more likely to report that they found no trustworthy pressure group leaders. Closely related to this finding is another one on the acceptance of collective protests. 51.1 percent of those who agreed or strongly agreed that increasing protests against the government were a healthy phenomenon were able to find trustworthy pressure group leaders, as compared to 35.7 percent of those who disagreed or strongly disagreed.

Analogously, those Hong Kong Chinese who hold a favorable view of the existent social-political order are more likely to have a negative view of pressure groups. Thus, those who were satisfied with the existing Hong Kong society in the 1985 survey were more inclined to see pressure groups as a menace to prosperity and stability. Similarly, those who held the view that the existing political system was the best one available were less likely to say that pressure groups were successful in achieving their goals. Moreover, they were more likely to deem pressure groups a threat to prosperity and stability.

There are two findings on the factors affecting public reception of pressure groups that are more striking. One is that, despite the popularity gains of some pressure group leaders, they do not appear to be the kind of leaders whom the Hong Kong Chinese would like to embrace or identify with. It seems that pressure group leaders, if they are favorably received by a portion of the public, are received because the people are frustrated with the lack of "legitimate" political leaders in Hong Kong and the unresponsiveness of existing elites. Pressure group leaders appear to serve as the mechanism for the expression and release of frustrated feelings and ambivalent sentiments *vis-à-vis* the authorities. This point can, to a certain extent, be highlighted by the fact that those who considered that a few competent leaders were more important than political reforms in improving the administration of Hong Kong were more likely to say that pressure groups endangered prosperity and stability. Apparently, pressure group leaders were not viewed as the competent leaders the respondents would like to have in Hong Kong.

Another finding is that even those who hold a more liberal and open attitude toward political parties take a less favorable view of pressure groups, which implies that pressure groups should play no role in the political parties of Hong Kong, if any are formed. This view is in direct contradiction with the intention of many pressure groups to combine and form political parties with a reformist thrust. In our 1985 survey, 29.3 percent of respondents who agreed or strongly agreed that the appearance of political parties would make the political system of Hong Kong better said that pressure groups would endanger prosperity and stability, as compared to 18.4 percent of those who disagreed or strongly disagreed.

On the whole, it seems that pressure groups and their leaders, notwithstanding the generally unfavorable and ambivalent attitudes toward them, have a definite role to play in this particular juncture of political development in Hong Kong. But, it also appears that pressure tactics *per se* or as a single tactic are not sufficient to "legitimately" entrench pressure groups in the institutional structure. An entrenched status can most probably be obtained if the pressure groups can meet "mainstream" institutional politics at least halfway and make compromises with it. In the process, the radical thrust of pressure politics would inevitably have to be at least partially blunted.[34]

## Social and Political Spheres

As we have seen, Hong Kong Chinese are more prone to differentiate between the political and economic realms than between the social and political realms. The critical support for this observation is that Hong Kong Chinese are supportive of governmental intervention in social affairs whereas economic freedom and private interests are held to be supreme values in the economic sphere. The conceptual separation between the economy and the polity and the conceptual intermingling between society and the polity are reflected in the fact that statistical correlations between political variables and social variables are much stronger than correlations between political and economic variables.

Most importantly, there is not much statistical evidence about the relationship between evaluations of the economy and the government, but a favorable attitude toward the government is intimately related to favorable views of Hong Kong society. It is impossible to conclude definitely whether it is social satisfaction that is conducive to political satisfaction, or the other way round, but it appears plausible that a favorable attitude toward the government and the political system in general is contingent upon satisfaction with Hong Kong society.

The relationship between social and political satisfaction can be supported by several pieces of evidence:

(1) Those respondents who were satisfied with the existent Hong Kong society were more likely to expect fair treatment from officials when they were approached for help.

(2) Those who were satisfied with their livelihood also were more likely to expect fair treatment from officials.

(3) Those who had experienced improvement in their livelihood in the last five years likewise expected fair treatment from officials.

(4) A perception of Hong Kong society as stable and orderly is a powerful predictive variable for political satisfaction. The more a respondent was inclined to see Hong Kong as a stable and orderly society, the more likely he would (a) consider the political system of Hong Kong the best under existent circumstances, (b) repudiate the allegation that the Hong Kong government primarily catered to its own selfish interests, (c) rate Hong Kong government as a good government, (d) deny that the Hong Kong government mainly looked after the interests of the rich, (e) trust or very much trust the Hong Kong government, (f) trust or very much trust the British government, (g) trust or very much trust the Chinese government, (h) disagree or strongly disagree that the government was to be blamed for the proliferation of social problems.

The above finding also underline the instrumental conception of the government's social functions, the competent performance of which is critical to the acceptance of the existing political system. Compared to such idealistic criteria as the openness and the participatoriness of the polity, concrete performance is the most significant evaluative standard in the mind of the Hong Kong Chinese.

## Conclusion

The political ethos of the Hong Kong Chinese consists of a complex syndrome of attitudes whose nuances and inconsistencies can hardly be fully captured by the concept of political apathy, a phrase which has long been used to characterize their political orientation.

While still maintaining a largely anti-political or apolitical predisposition, the Hong Kong Chinese are somehow able, in their values, to lessen subscription to the ideas of political omnipotence, political omniscience and political omnipresence. While still recognizing the wide domain of political power, Hong Kong Chinese have, however, installed some restraints on its jurisdiction and penetration. The economic realm is basically considered as beyond political interference, so are private moral norms. Public interests are recognized, but they are no longer solely defined by the government, nor is governmental interests equated with them. Compared to traditional Chinese, the Hong Kong Chinese are more prepared to grant legitimacy to private interests and confer upon them an autonomous status, provided they are not detrimental to public interests, however defined. The social realm, in contrast, is still vulnerable to political intervention, and the government's performance in this sphere is critical to its overall appraisal by the people. At the same time, though the polity in Hong Kong is highly autonomous *vis-à-vis* society, a certain degree of social penetration into the polity is unavoidable. For example, 62 percent of respondents in the 1986 survey maintained that it was quite all right for those with status and power to take advantage of them to benefit their relatives and friends. Nevertheless, the development of the bureaucratic system of Hong Kong has largely eradicated the deleterious consequences stemming from social penetration of the polity such as corruption, nepotism and the more flagrant abuse of power by officials.

The sense of political powerlessness is still the most potent factor in perpetuating political lethargy among the Hong Kong Chinese, but they have become more aware of the multitude of means available to get access to the government, particularly those influence tactics that contain some amount of unconventionality and confrontation. Notwithstanding this, the continued preoccupation with harmony and apprehension about erosion of authority, plus the perennial lag between attitude and action, have inhibited a frequent recourse to these new tactics by the Hong Kong Chinese.

Popular acceptance of the existing political system is widespread, and the performance of the Hong Kong government is rated favorably. Most Hong Kong Chinese are prepared to trust the government, thus explaining much of the fear of 1997, when a new government is to take over the reins. Nonetheless, the less-than-given nature of the authority of the colonial government and its impersonal, faceless and secluded nature impede affective attachment to it by the ruled. Consequently, the government is respected, but not loved by the people. The strands of alienation, cynicism and suspicion toward the Hong Kong government, amid high regard for its performance, provide the context for the general ambivalence toward the government and the political system of Hong Kong.

Ambivalence toward the government and the political system, however, has not provided a fertile soil for the emergence of indigenous political leaders. Political co-option by the colonial government has pre-empted the rise of an autonomous stratum of indigenous leaders, while the government's satisfactory performance has lessened the attractions and appeals of the pressure group leaders. The pervasive sense of social complacency among the Hong Kong Chinese makes political radicalism impossible. As a result, ambivalence is generalized from the government to the budding indigenous political leaders, and pressure group leaders are not looked upon as viable alternatives to the less-than-trusted incumbent leaders.

# 4
# Legal Values

The legal system of Hong Kong is of foreign origin. English law has been either specifically imported into Hong Kong or incorporated into local ordinances. The courts of Hong Kong follow the practice and procedure of the English courts and apply English and Privy Council decisions in all areas of law.

Given the foreign origin of the common law, a certain amount of tension between it and the Chinese society is inevitable. The magnitude of the tension varies with time. It was particularly acute during the initial years of British rule, to the point that a dual system of legal rules had to be practised for a while before English laws could be accorded precedence. By legal dualism, English law was made applicable to non-Chinese residents, while Chinese people were governed according to Chinese customs and laws, which meant traditional rules and customs as they were practised in the last dynasty of China.

The tension between law and society has waned quite considerably simply because of British rule for over a century. However, a reduction in tension is one thing, an increase in affection for English law is another. The intriguing issue of the relationship among law, society and politics in Hong Kong has never been addressed by any scholar. We know practically nothing for sure about whether the legal system of Hong Kong is valued by the common people.

The issue has gained increased significance today, since Hong Kong is scheduled to be returned to China in 1997. One may suggest that the common law, as a body of rules and practices, is deeply entrenched, at least for the British-trained lawyers and judges. It is also reassuring that, according to the Joint Declaration signed by the Chinese and the British governments in 1984, "laws previously in force in Hong Kong" are to be maintained (Section 2 of Annex I), and the courts may still refer to precedents in other common law jurisdictions (Section 3 of Annex I). The trouble is that the same Declaration has called for political changes which presumably will have an impact on the legal system. In addition, social, economic and political changes of an uncertain nature have set in since the signing of the Declaration.

It seems unlikely that the legal system of Hong Kong can remain unchanged amid political transformations, at least not in the area of "the secondary rules" as defined by H.L.A. Hart.[1] That the determination what and how rules are to be introduced and applied is ultimately a political determination has been vividly demonstrated by recent discussions on the question of the applicability of Chinese laws in Hong Kong after 1997. These discussions center around the Basic Law Drafting Committee, a body established by the National People's Congress of China to formulate the fundamental law governing Hong Kong after 1997. In the Joint Declaration, with a few exceptions, Chinese laws are explicitly excluded as laws applicable in Hong Kong after 1997. Consequently, the possible relationship between Chinese laws (if introduced through the Basic Law) and common laws (if maintained) after 1997 would be a fascinating subject for legal scholars specialising in the conflict of laws. A more immediate concern is whether the common law system could be successfully maintained with the introduction of Chinese laws, even if there is no deliberate intention to qualify it with this introduction.

In the final analysis, legal development does not center upon political forces in a particular society.[2] The fate of the common law will be gloomy indeed if it is based primarily on the authority of transplanted laws and Western-trained legal practitioners alone. A broader-based support is needed for the system to weather the impending storms of uncertain changes. Hence, we feel justified in contending that politico-cultural elements are important and that what happens in the mind of individuals is of enormous moment to how the legal system will develop. In this connection, among the most pertinent issues are: Do people value the present system? Will they support it in times of difficulties? Will they, when mobilized by an appeal to nationalist symbols and sentiments, opt for the abandonment of the legal legacy? Undoubtedly, much is contingent upon the legal culture in Hong Kong.

Levine and Howe have used "legal culture" to denote the psychological world of legal practitioners.[3] In particular, it refers to the cultural environment of legal decision-making, and court opinions are claimed to be important artifacts of the legal culture. On the contrary, we are concerned with the legal culture of the common people. The study of popular legal culture has been much influenced by political cultural analyses.[4] By analogy, legal culture is here defined as the pattern of individual attitudes and beliefs, as well as cognitive and affective orientations with respect to the law and the legal institutions. We will examine the legal culture of Hong Kong in two major dimensions.

The first dimension relates to the psychological orientations of the people toward the legal system of Hong Kong. These orientations comprise the cognitive, evaluative and affective aspects. Specifically, we want to find out whether the people of Hong Kong understand the laws and the legal system, regard them as just and treat them as an integral or natural part of society and not an alien imposition. In general, it will be of great interest to know whether, and to what extent, the common people feel alienated from the common law system. In view of the symbiotic relationship between politics and law on the one hand, and the compartmentalization of politics and society in Hong Kong on the other,[5] some amount of legal alienation among the Hong Kong people is to be expected.

The second dimension deals with legal opinions. They are primarily about the role of law in society, the principle of punishment and the source of citizens' rights. There are certainly other areas about which opinions can be solicited. We have, however, focused on only three items for the sake of theoretical parsimony: the role of law, the principle of punishment and the source of citizens' rights. They constitute the three major aspects of the legal philosophy of traditional China. It is interesting to see whether these essential elements of traditional thought have undergone substantial changes as a result of modernization. As Hong Kong is a modern society with a basically educated populace, the hold of traditional modes of legal thinking presumably should have been slackened.

Finally, we will tackle the behavioral implications of these legal orientations and opinions. To stay within the psychological realm of the legal culture, we are concerned, therefore, not so much with actual legal behavior, but with the propensity to act, such as the readiness to abide by law and the predisposition to protest.

## Legal Orientations

By legal orientations, we mean the knowledge, evaluation and affection of the people toward the present legal system. These orientations are identified by a series of questions about the respondents' perceived ability to understand the law and the legal system, their judgment about judicial justice and their sentimental reaction to the foreign origin of the system. These orientations tend to form a coherent whole, as the answers to the questions are significantly correlated among themselves (at the significance level of no less than 0.005). Thus, these orientations can serve as the psychological foundation upon which the legal system of Hong Kong is received (i.e. valued) by the people.

### Perceived ability to understand the law (Legal efficacy)

In our survey, we did not test our respondents' actual knowledge of the laws and courts in Hong Kong, although this constitutes an important aspect of the cognitive dimension of legal culture. For one thing, it is difficult to test the scope of the public's knowledge of laws. Test items that are too general or closely related to a commonsense conception of morality are of little use for our purpose. For instance, it sounds both very awkward and condescending to ask whether the respondents know that murder is illegal. As law and legal institutions are complex, only specific questions can elicit reliable information about public knowledge of them. An appropriate item, for instance, would be about the maximum penalty that a district court may impose in criminal cases.

Existing literature on legal knowledge among common people is quite conclusive in establishing that, contrary to the presumption of the law (namely *Ignorantia juris neminem excusat*: everybody should know the law and ignorance of the law is no excuse), there is everywhere a widespread ignorance on the part of the public about legal matters, especially about changes in laws or laws which fail to fully correspond with social attitudes.[6] The same phenomenon is found in Hong Kong.

An exemplary case is provided by the laws against corruption. Corruption thrives upon the ambivalent or even tolerant attitudes toward it on the part of the Hong Kong Chinese. Inasmuch as this is so, it would be extremely difficult to bring it under effective control, let alone stamp it out, as that would necessitate a frontal attack on entrenched values and practices. The strenuous, but only partially successful, efforts of The Independent Commission Against Corruption (ICAC) to tackle the problem of corruption reveal the limitations of even a massive campaign to propagate legal knowledge in order to alter public attitudes; this is particularly difficult when the public does not harbor a similar sense of urgency about the issue. Thus, despite all the crackdowns on syndicated corruption and tightening up of organizational procedures and loopholes, the ignorance of the public about specific anti-corruption laws (the Prevention of Bribery Ordinance, the ICAC Ordinance, the Corrupt and Illegal Practices Ordinance) remains striking. In the mass survey conducted by ICAC in 1984 and 1986, 92.5 percent and 91.4 percent respectively of the respondents failed to name the laws enforced by the ICAC. According to the last survey mentioned, a crucial provision of the Prevention of Bribery Ordinance, Section 9, was not even known to the public,[7] despite the fact that the Section concerned was the subject of a press campaign just a few months before the survey. Upon prompting, still 90 percent of the respondents continued to report having never heard about it, while only a miniscule 7.1 percent reported otherwise.[8]

Since we are primarily concerned with the psychological distance between the self and the legal system, the sense of legal efficacy is a more appropriate concept here. By legal efficacy we mean the self-perceived ability to understand the laws and the legal system. As it requires some prior knowledge of basic legal concepts and principles in order for one to have some understanding of the laws and the legal system, we, therefore, may also be justified in saying that one's sense of legal efficacy reflects one's knowledge of the law, albeit to a less precise extent. Of even greater significance is the extent of the public's attachment to, or alienation from, the legal system. Those who perceive a low level of efficacy can thus be held to be alienated from the legal system.

The laws in Hong Kong are drafted in English. Court proceedings are likewise conducted in English; yet, the overwhelming majority of the population are Chinese. We may therefore expect that communication barriers would render the laws and court proceedings incomprehensible to the majority of our respondents. It is thus not surprising that among those respondents who gave an answer, 77.4 percent (N = 507) reported that they found it difficult to understand the law and the legal system in Hong Kong as against 22.6 percent (N = 148) who did not. Accordingly, the people of Hong Kong can be characterized as alienated, in the cognitive sense, from the common law system.

## Judgment of judicial justice (Judicial justice)

Judgment of judicial justice constitutes an important aspect of the evaluative component of legal culture. It refers to how the public evaluate court trials, the laws and the legal system as a whole. As it is often said of the rule of law, justice must be seen to have been done. The public image of justice is therefore significant for the proper functioning of the legal system. Those who believe that justice has not been done are likely to feel alienated from the legal system. If alienation is widespread, laws would not be respected and public support for law enforcement agents would decline.

Attitudes toward various aspects of the legal system usually diverge. Van Houtte and Vinke found wide divergence in the acceptance of various types of legal rules and therefore questioned whether there is a *general* sense of justice.[9] In our study, the sense of judicial justice is examined in terms of fair trial, unfair laws that concerned the respondent, unfair laws that did not concern him, and lastly the legal system as a whole.

The findings as summarized in Table 4.1 are difficult to interpret. This is due to the large discrepancy between justice in the specific sense and general justice of the overall legal system. On the one hand, it is startling to learn that as much as 73.4 percent of our respondents regarded the trials in Hong Kong as unfair. There is also a substantial proportion of people (i.e., 36.1 percent) who thought that the laws in general were not fair. The proportion of respondents who reported unfair laws that concerned them is significant too. In terms of these three areas, our citizens were clearly "alienated". It is, however, puzzling that, despite the perceived unfairness in laws and trials, an absolute majority (75.4 percent) of our respondents considered the legal system in general as just. Why should that be so? One answer may lie in the wording of the question that seems, with hindsight, to be tendentious as a result of the inclusion of the phrase "despite all the shortcomings" in the question.

TABLE 4.1
Aspects of Sense of Judicial Justice

| | Trial[1] | | Law (general)[2] | | Law (specific)[3] | | System[4] | |
|---|---|---|---|---|---|---|---|---|
| | % | (N) | % | (N) | % | (N) | % | (N) |
| Fair | 19.4 | (149) | 27.6 | (212) | 40.2 | (308) | 75.4 | (578) |
| Unfair | 73.4 | (563) | 36.1 | (277) | 30.5 | (234) | 11.0 | (84) |
| Don't know | 7.2 | (55) | 36.2 | (278) | 29.3 | (225) | 13.7 | (105) |
| Total | 100.0 | (767) | 99.9 | (767) | 100.0 | (767) | 100.1 | (767) |

The wording of the questions is:

1. Do you think that, in the courts of Hong Kong, (a) the rich are better treated than the poor; (b) all are treated equally? Or (c) you don't know?
2. Are there any unfair laws in Hong Kong that do not affect you? If yes, please specify.
3. Are there any unfair laws in Hong Kong that affect you? If yes, please specify.
4. Despite all the shortcomings, do you think that the legal system of Hong Kong, taken as a whole, is just?

Yet another and perhaps more important explanation may have to do with the personal experience of the respondents. Our reconstructions are as follows.

The legal system is, in the subjective world of the people, only marginally related to their daily living. They have no distinct knowledge about specific aspects of the system and have to rely on impressions and hearsay in order to form any opinion about it. In the final analysis, however, personal experience with the system weighs much heavier than other sources of information in determining the acceptability of the legal system as a whole to a particular individual.

As revealed by our findings, the majority of the people (56.9 percent as against 34.2 percent) did not find the laws important to their daily living. Therefore their idea of unfair laws in general must have been based on general impressions derived from dubious sources. If asked to specify those unfair laws that did not affect themselves, only about half of the respondents (135 out of 277, i.e., 48.7 percent) could give an answer. In comparison, those who reported unfair laws affecting themselves tended to be more forthcoming, as 58.1 percent of those who so reported (i.e., 136 out of 234) could make further elaborations. The sense of injustice is stronger when based on personal experience with the legal system, and since there is only a relatively small proportion of people who had found unfair laws that concerned them (30.5 percent of the total sample), the legal system of Hong Kong was, therefore, judged to be fair by a great many.

This inference can be further corroborated statistically. Evaluation of the legal system is more strongly correlated with perception of unfair laws affecting oneself than with perception of unfair trials or unfair laws affecting others. This means that those respondents who found unfair laws affecting themselves were more likely to regard the legal system as unjust than those who did not.

In order to test whether the sense of judicial justice, as reflected in the perception of unfair laws is well grounded, we asked our respondents to specify their report of unfair laws. Only those unfair laws that were seen as affecting the respondents are analysed here (unfair laws in general were in most cases identical with unfair laws affecting the respondents themselves).

Of the 234 respondents who found unfair laws that concerned themselves, 58.1 percent (N = 136) were able to elaborate on them. Among the 136 elaborations given, only 51.2 percent (N = 70) really have something to do with laws. The rest (48.8 percent or 66 cases) are concerned with public policies and their implementation or with issues in the judicial process. Among the 37 policy issues mistaken to be unfair laws are: (1) increase in prices for public services (17 cases), (2) public housing policies such as priorities in allocation of housing units (14 cases) and their implementation and (3) others such as the absence of unemployment payments (6 cases). Among the 29 judicial process issues mistaken to be unfair laws are: (1) questionable behavior of law enforcement agents, such as policemen abusing power or hawker control teams soliciting bribes (15 cases), and (2) differential treatment in the judicial process such as the rich being able to employ good lawyers and the wealthy receiving better treatment in court trials (14 cases). Among examples cited that are truly law matters, the majority (21 cases) have to do with traffic regulations such as the points system, punishment of jay walking, and so on. Next comes taxation (19 cases), such things as "the sandwiched class being taxed unfairly," presumably in comparison with the wealthy class (the highest rate for income tax in Hong Kong was 17 percent). The rest of the cases (30) touch upon a great variety of legal issues such as capital punishment, the obscene publications ordinance, the gambling law, immigration laws and so on. Given the above pattern, we may conclude that although the sense of injustice is real, it is in many cases unjustified.

**Affective reaction to the alien origin of the legal system (Sense of system foreignness)**

The legal system in Hong Kong is of foreign origin. Does that adversely affect its reception by the people of Hong Kong? Wesley-Smith argued that the common law as a body of rules and practices had been firmly established in Hong Kong.[10] At the same time, he was not hesitant to add that Hong Kong law was not an indigenous and independent system and had not been so considered, at least by lawyers and judges trained in Britain. He advocated, therefore, reconsideration and localization of law in Hong Kong. This being the case, would the present dependent legal system not appear even more starkly alien to the man in the street? It might be the case that the Chinese people's sense of historical and cultural complacency,[11] the tenacity of their antiforeignism[12] and the communication barriers between the colonial ruler and the ruled may together or separately impede the smooth reception of the common law.

Contrary to our expectations, however, our finding is that a larger proportion of people did not see the legal system as foreign. 47.6 percent of our respondents disagreed or strongly disagreed with the statement that the legal system of Hong Kong was foreign and unsuitable to Chinese society, as against 34.8 percent who agreed or strongly agreed. Nevertheless, the number of alienated citizens is still substantial.

## Correlates of the Pattern of Orientations

So far, we have studied the legal culture in Hong Kong in terms of cognitive efficacy, sense of justice and system foreignness. In view of the evidence, we may conclude that legal alienation prevails among a substantial number of people. Who are the alienated and who are not? What may be the contributing factors?

**Individual, social and economic values and legal orientations**

In various ways, perception of judicial justice by the Hong Kong Chinese is conditioned by their individual, social and political values. The thrust of all the scattered relationships is that favorable attitudes toward the individual, society and the economy are conducive to perception of judicial justice and a lower sense of legal cynicism.

Several indicators of judicial justice are particularly related to the values at hand. They are: perception of unfair laws affecting oneself, perception of unfair laws not affecting oneself, perception of the fairness of the legal system and the belief that the rich get better treated in court.

Among those respondents who were more likely to perceive unfair laws affecting themselves were, for example, those who were less satisfied with the existent Hong Kong society, those who experienced deterioration in their standard of living, those who were pessimistic about their future livelihood, those who asserted that Hong Kong society was full of problems and evil, those who considered Hong Kong as an unfair society, and those who believed that people got rich through exploitation.

Those respondents who were more disposed to perceive unfair laws not affecting themselves were, for example, those who were less satisfied with the existent Hong Kong society, those who tended to think that the economic gap between the rich and the poor was too large, those who asserted that Hong Kong was full of problems and evil and those who thought that Hong Kong was an unfair society.

Similarly, among those who were more likely to rate the legal system as fair were those who were satisfied with the existent Hong Kong society, those who were satisfied with their existent livelihood, those who considered Hong Kong as an orderly society, those who didn't think that people got rich through exploiting others, and those who believed that Hong Kong was full of opportunities.

Legal cynicism, as measured by the belief that the rich were given favorable treatment by the court, was correlated with a pessimistic view of the future conditions of the Hong Kong people, a defeatist view of long-term planning, and an inclination to adopt a passive attitude toward the future.

The instrumental conception of law as the guarantor of social order seems to have been borne out by these correlations between the perception of law and the existential socio-economic conditions of the observers concerned.

## Political attitudes and legal orientations

Law can hardly be separated from politics. Psychological orientations toward legal objects must, therefore, be influenced to a certain extent by political beliefs and attitudes. This is especially true with respect to sense of system foreignness. Table 4.2 does suggest significant relationships in the expected direction; but the associations are not particularly strong. The two strongest variables, that is, trust in the Hong Kong government and preference for democratization, explain only 3.6 and 2.9 percent respectively of the variation in sense of system foreignness.

Three sets of political attitudes, viz., political trust, governmental performance and evaluation of political system, are all weakly related to sense of system foreignness. Specifically, a sense of system foreignness is negatively related to political trust in the British and the Hong Kong governments, but positively related to trust in the Chinese government. To put it the other way round, those who are mistrustful of the Chinese government are more likely to regard the present common law system as not alien. This finding may be interpreted as a result of the 1997 issue. The prospect of transfer of sovereignty in 1997 awakened the people to the merits of the current system. Before the Sino-British negotiation over the future of Hong Kong in 1982, no one, to the best of our knowledge, had alluded to the common law as possibly the best legacy the British had bestowed upon Hong Kong. This belated appreciation was founded on the apprehensive realization of the lack of the rule of law in China in the past.[13]

The second political variable, government performance, is negatively correlated with sense of system foreignness. Those who regarded the Hong Kong government as being self-seeking also thought that the legal system was alien, whereas those who rated the government highly thought otherwise.

The relationship between attitude toward the political system and sense of system foreignness is ambiguous and insignificant. Those respondents who favored democratization and those who endorsed the present political system as the best possible under existing circumstances viewed the existing legal system as something foreign. Nevertheless, the relationship between acceptance of the political *status quo* and sense of system foreignness is so weak ($r = 0.01$ with $p = 0.01$) that we should perhaps disregard it, whereas the relationship between support for political democratization and sense of foreignness of the legal system is stronger and more significant ($r = 0.17$ with $p = 0.00$). So we may conclude that dissatisfaction with the colonial structure of government was, to a very limited extent, conducive to an unfavorable reception of the common law system.

Among all the attitudes, trust in the Hong Kong government and favorable disposition toward democratization are the most significant,

TABLE 4.2
System Foreignness and Political Attitudes (r)

| Political trust in | | | H.K. government being | | Political system | |
|---|---|---|---|---|---|---|
| U.K.[1] | H.K.[2] | P.R.C.[3] | Selfish[4] | Good[5] | Best possible[6] | Better to be democratized[7] |
| –0.141*** | –0.191**** | 0.091* | 0.121*** | –0.091* | 0.011** | 0.171**** |

* = p<0.05 ** = p<0.01 *** = p<0.005 **** = p<0.0

The questions on the political attitudes are:

A. For political trust:
   1. How much do you trust the British government?
   2. How much do you trust the Hong Kong government?
   3. How much do you trust the Chinese government?

B. For evaluation of the Hong Kong government:
   4. Do you agree that, most of the time, the Hong Kong government is defending its own interests rather than the public interest?
   5. Do you agree that the Hong Kong government is a good government?

C. For attitudes on the existing political system:
   6. Do you agree that the present political system is the best under existent circumstances, although it is not perfect?
   7. Do you agree or disagree that a government by elected politicians would be better than the present government? [At present, the government is not elected.]

though not strong, factors influencing the reception of the common law system by the people of Hong Kong.

## Legal Opinions

Hong Kong is a unique place where the East meets with the West. In the area of law, we expect to see complex interactions between Chinese and Western influences. While the modern legal system has been imposed by the British ruler, there remain two other strong influences: traditional Chinese legal thinking and, among immigrants from China (until recently the majority of the population), experiences with modern Chinese legal systems. We cannot explain what the people of Hong Kong think about law without due regard to the Chinese cultural heritage.

### The cultural heritage

Traditional China was far from being legally oriented. Rules of law had not been institutionalized. When law appeared in China, it was used neither to uphold traditional religious values, nor to protect private property. Rather, its main objective was political: it began so that tighter controls could be imposed on the disintegrating feudal society of the Zhou dynasty.[14] Despite the fact that traditional China had produced an impressive body of codified law, Vandermeersch still disputes the argument that law had really ever existed "in the sense which the term has when applied, in the Western juridical tradition, to actual positive laws." To him, Chinese law codes "have the character of administrative regulations, and not that of a corpus of legal provisions."[15]

Vandermeersch is right in one fundamental aspect: Chinese law had nothing to do with the idea of rights. It was developed purely as a coercive instrument of the ruler. Law-making power was imperial power, possessed and exercised by the emperor, and by him alone. As the Son of Heaven, he occupied a position that was supposed to mediate between heaven and man and therefore he was above the law. In other words, law was never constitutional; rather, it was overwhelmingly penal in emphasis.

In traditional Chinese political philosophy, no serious attention had been given to the possibility of conflict of interests between the ruler and the ruled. Consequently, law was never conceived of as an instrument for protecting the ruled against the government. Civil liberties were unknown, yet civil obligations were very much emphasized. Hsieh argues that Confucian ethics also underscored the freedom of the individual, but this was the freedom to choose good, not the freedom to choose evil.[16] In this sense, it can be claimed that Confucian ethics also upheld the rights of the individual. Hsieh, however, finds it necessary to insert a caveat:

> But, it was not the rights of the individual that were considered most important. Of most importance were the duties or obligations of the individual. According to Confucian ethics, in order to be a man or to be a sage, it is necessary, first, to perform one's duties, not to claim one's rights.[17]

As a penal code, traditional Chinese law was secular and secondary in nature. It was secular in the sense that it was an embodiment of the dominant ethical norms in society. It was secondary in importance to other instruments of social control, especially to *li* 禮, the rules of propriety or Confucian virtues (as the Confucians defined it). *Li* has a rich meaning that encompasses the appropriate institutions and modes of behavior in a civilized society organized as a hierarchy of unequal but harmonious relations; a society where everyone knew how to behave according to his or her assigned status in society. The teaching and practice of *li* was the cardinal principle of government, whereas law was viewed with suspicion and apprehension. The reason for such a view can be explained:

> If the people be led by laws, and uniformity sought to be given them by punishments, they will try to avoid the punishment, but have no sense of shame. If they be led by virtue, and uniformity sought to be given them by the rules of propriety, they will have the sense of shame, and moreover will become good.[18]

In conformity with this line of thinking, Confucians advocated government by moral precept and example, rather than government by law.

Law was thus used only as a last resort. When it had to be employed, it would be further diluted in two ways: by a diffusion of legal administration and Confucianization of the law.

In traditional China, law was not administered centrally. There was neither a legislature specializing in law-making, nor an independent court of justice. According to van der Sprenkel,

> . . . large areas of life, which in other societies are dealt with by specialized legal institutions, fell under the diffused jurisdiction of individual units of non-administrative social organization or were dealt with by still more informal techniques of mediation. Rules for the conduct of everyday life were formulated by the different small communities or associations to which a person belonged and were enforced by whoever exercised authority in these.[19]

Confucianization of law meant that, in the administration of justice, *li*, that is, the principles of Confucianism, was accorded more authority than law. According to Ch'u T'ung-tsu, judicial judgments based on Confucian tenets frequently went beyond the articles of the legal code.[20] This practice of *jingyi jueyu* ( 經義決獄 deciding cases according to the Confucian classics) not only occurred in ancient times but persisted well into the last dynasty of China.[21]

Confucianization of law reflects yet another characteristic of traditional Chinese attitudes toward law, that is, little concern for procedure: it was the substance that mattered. The foremost objective was protection of society from criminal acts. Determination of crime was not based on the principle of *nulla poena sine lege* (no punishment without law), but depended on whether the suspected had acted in a manner in which he should not have acted, so as to bring damage to the society. If a statute did not exist, he could still be prosecuted and punished under the principle of analogy. The idea of inadmissibility of unlawfully obtained evidence was unknown. Torture to extract confessions was permissible. The important thing was to secure punishment for the criminals, as they were people who could not be educated with Confucian virtues.

The traditional legal culture as summarized above has proved to be remarkably resilient. It survived both the revolution of 1911 and the revolution of 1949.

With the breakdown of the Chinese empire, the traditional legal system was replaced by a new one based on German and Swiss models. However, this Westernized system could not take root in Chinese soil.[22] Using data drawn from Shanghai newspapers from 1917 to 1932, Huey concludes that most people at that time were unconvinced of the wisdom and objectivity of the law. Rather,

> . . . it still appeared to most Chinese that a society which was controlled by the instruments of law—even if there were the occasional upright judges and uncorrupt policemen—was a regrettable necessity. . . . Family rules and moral censure were considered to be the more effective forms of social control. . . . Most people tried to avoid any implication with legal problems.[23]

As Cohen argues, judicial administration in contemporary China displays some striking resemblances to its predecessor under the Chinese empire, both in basic assumptions and in institutions and practices.[24]

To begin with, law continues to play a very limited role in social and economic relations. The courts in China do not do very much. The great bulk of the work of controlling deviance is handled at the small group and neighborhood level.[25] In other areas, a special kind of relationship system (*guanxi* 關係) has replaced the Confucian framework of *li* which governed the five relations in traditional China (between king and subject, father and son, husband and wife, brothers and sisters, friends) and ensured societal functioning and harmony. The *guanxi* system is based upon personal networks with power-holders as patrons. It is a dynamic organizing principle penetrating the whole of Chinese society today. Its continued existence will be hazardous to the development of a modern legal system in China.[26]

In all the constitutions promulgated by various modern Chinese governments, a catalog of civil rights was enshrined. However, they were not conceived of as rights of the citizens against the state, for the state was unable to do wrong. Rather, they were consistently regarded as a grant given by the state to the citizens, to enable them to contribute their energies to the needs of the nation.[27] In practice, citizens' rights have been wantonly encroached upon, notably during the Great Proletarian Cultural Revolution (from 1965 to 1974).[28] Although there are new departures in the Chinese constitution of 1982, the political leadership still cannot accept civil rights as safeguards against governmental abuses.[29]

It follows, then, that law is regarded purely as a political instrument. It does not enjoy any independent status. In place of the emperor of the past, the Party has become the law-maker. Law is the codification of the will of the Party. Instead of *li* or the Confucian classics, the leadership of the Party, socialism, Marxism, and Mao Zedong thought have been declared the four fundamental principles underlying the Communist state. All along, the Party has been above the law. Party cadres at various levels of government have intervened in the judicial process and passed judgments based on political considerations which went beyond legal provisions.

The penal code of today does not depart much from the past in its basic spirit. After a debate of more than 26 years, the presumption of innocence is still not acceptable.[30] Presumption of guilt lingers on, amid steps taken to tighten up the procedures of investigation. Crime is still defined in terms of the detrimental consequences of the act involved on society. Communist law is primarily concerned with substantive justice, not with due process.[31] Legal processes using the principle of analogy persist, albeit under significant constraints.

**Popular opinions about law in Hong Kong**

With reference to traditional and Communist Chinese legacies, we formulated three sets of question areas with regard to popular opinions about law: (1) the socio-political importance of law as compared with other instruments of social control, (2) the importance of punishment in dealing with crime, and (3) beliefs in civil rights.

We reported earlier that the majority of our respondents did not find law important to their daily living. When it comes to the socio-political importance of law as compared with other institutions, however, unexpected findings have been obtained.

As many as 41.0 percent of our respondents chose law as the most important instrument for social stability, as compared with *li* (15.8 percent),[32] the political system (32.3 percent), a strong leader (8.0 percent), and others (11.1 percent).

We did expect decline in the importance of Confucianism, if for no other reason than the inexorable process of modernization; yet, the extent of decline is surprising. In retrospect, we may conjecture that the exalted status of law, as a stability factor in the eyes of our respondents, may be a result of the political atmosphere prevailing at the time of the survey. Both the elites and the mass media in Hong Kong incessantly alluded to the importance of law as the foundation of prosperity and stability.

To gauge the extent to which the public did place emphasis on the penal character of law in line with traditional legal thinking, we asked our respondents to make their choices in three sets of dichotomous items on the meaning and purpose of law: (1) to have all the guilty convicted, but at the cost of accidentally convicting some of the innocent as well, or to protect all the innocent against faulty conviction but at the cost of exonerating some of the guilty; (2) to be lenient to criminals in sentencing or to mete out harsh punishment; and (3) to adopt a rehabilitative stance toward ex-convicts or to see them as beyond rehabilitation. Those who conceive of law primarily in terms of its penal aspects would naturally opt for getting all the guilty convicted, harsh sentencing and would be pessimistic about the effectiveness of rehabilitative methods.

On the first set of alternatives, opinions were equally divided. 41.6 percent insisted on convicting all the guilty as against 43.9 percent who would like to protect the innocent from faulty conviction (14.5 percent answered "don't know" or gave no answer). In regard to the second and the third sets of options, a strange picture emerged, in that, a large proportion of respondents who supported harsh punishment (as a more effective means to combat crime) paradoxically also gave equally overwhelming support for the rehabilitation of the ex-convicts. More precisely, 79.8 percent of the respondents opted for meting out harsh punishment,[33] whereas 11.3 percent supported lenient sentencing. 8.9 percent had no opinion or answer. As to dealing with the convicted, 75.1 percent believed in rehabilitation as compared with 16.3 percent who did not (8.6 percent were non-committed). The attitudes on harsh punishment and rehabilitation are moderately but significantly correlated with each other. Those who rejected harsh punishment for criminals tended to support rehabilitation for the ex-convicts. The response to the alternatives regarding convicting the innocent and the guilty is not, however, significantly correlated with the other two sets of responses.

The final measure of the degree of modernization of the legal culture is the popular attitude toward civil liberties. They constitute an area of law that defines the relationship between the state/government and the citizens. Civil liberties represents an unknown territory in traditional legal thought.

Apparently, the people of Hong Kong value the extent of the freedom they currently enjoy. This impression has been confirmed by our survey findings. A total of 68.1 percent of our respondents agreed that the protection of freedom is the major objective of law, instead of the enforcement of social morality (17.2 percent). In line with this, their support for freedom of speech was overwhelming (97.6 percent).

As immigrants, the majority of the Hong Kong people set great store by freedom. This obsession with freedom is a reaction to their experience with the past politics of China. It is interesting to note that while "protection of freedom as the purpose of law" is correlated with very few other surveyed items, it is significantly ($p < 0.05$) correlated with trust in the Chinese government. Those who were mistrustful of the Chinese government tended to support the protection of freedom as the major purpose of law.

Despite their obsession with freedom, the people of Hong Kong do not seem to have acquired the belief that freedom is a fundamental and inalienable right. The idea that there are inborn and inalienable rights, everybody is entitled to by virtue of being a human being, was unknown in traditional China. Nor has it been established in China today, despite the impressive array of civil liberties provided for in the new constitution of 1982. This idea is, however, central to the common law system as it is practised in Hong Kong. Nonetheless, the people of Hong Kong do not seem to appreciate the idea at all. When asked whether those rights they enjoy are inborn and inalienable or conferred upon them by society as a reward for their performance, only a small proportion, that is, 22.8 percent, of our respondents reported a belief in inborn and inalienable rights.

The shaky subjective foundation for civil rights and liberties is further attested to by popular beliefs about specific freedoms. Opinions were split on the right to privacy of correspondence (46.5 percent of respondents for and 53.5 percent against). As many as 77.2 percent would allow the press the right to expression only if it did not publish false news. Finally, it is evident that the people of Hong Kong were as unconcerned about judicial procedures as their forefathers in traditional China. On the question of the inadmissibility of illegally obtained evidence in a court trial, only 38.1 percent agreed to the principle, whereas 61.9 percent objected.

Legal opinions among Hong Kong people are by no means coherent. Firstly, we cannot predict support for specific liberties on the basis of a general obsession with freedom or a genuine belief in inalienable rights. These two fundamental attitudes are not significantly related to attitudes on specific liberties, except on one occasion (those who did not believe in inalienable rights tended to advocate prohibition of assembly for an unorthodox cause [$p < 0.001$]). Secondly, no significant correlations have been found among the specific liberties, except for the one between censorship of the press which publishes false news and prohibition of assembly for an unorthodox cause ($p < 0.01$).

## Behavioral Implications

So far, we have discovered a fair amount of legal alienation among our respondents. Most of them had difficulties in understanding the law, a large majority regarded court trials in Hong Kong as unfair, about one third of them were able to identify unfair laws and declared that the legal system was foreign in origin and thus unsuitable to Chinese society. Still, however, the legal system was generally regarded as just.

We have also ascertained that, on the superficial level, modern legal thinking has crept into the minds of our respondents. Law was generally rated more important than the political system, Confucian virtues, or a strong leader as the factor for social stability. Freedom was universally acclaimed. Beyond that, opinions on specific liberties were either split or conservative. No correlation has been found among the opinion items. The fundamental weakness of the legal culture in Hong Kong lies in the scanty popular support for the idea of inalienable rights, which results in the tenuous relationship between a general instrumental concern for freedom on the one hand, and its various specific manifestations on the other. Thus, support of freedom as a general principle does not necessarily entail support for particular kinds of freedom for particular individuals or groups. In short, the Hong Kong people have not yet learned to take rights seriously.

What then are the behavioral implications?

### Legal conformism or activism

The legal culture, as it stands, offers both cause for gratification and concern. What is gratifying is the degree of acceptance that the legal system seems to enjoy among the majority of people, even though injustice was still found to exist. We may, therefore, expect a fair amount of diffuse support for the system to weather whatever storm that might lie ahead. Yet concern is called for in regard to the extent of legal alienation among a substantial number of people. Will they become unscrupulous under extraordinary circumstances, say in times of economic difficulties?

The relationship between legal alienation and disobedience is complicated. Chang has suggested that, in traditional China, in response to legal alienation, people developed two distinctive behavioral syndromes—one was to rebel and defy and the other was to withdraw and obey.[34] By and large, the people of Hong Kong are law-abiding. When asked "what should we do if there is a law which we think is wrong?", 47.4 percent of the respondents agreed that "we should still obey it, since law-abiding is necessary for an orderly society." 19 percent answered that we should pretend to conform to it while breaking it in practice. 20.6 percent opted for disobedience, even if they might face prosecution and jail terms (13.1 percent gave other answers). As reported by Kaupen, 45 percent, 47 percent and 66 percent of his respondents in Poland, Holland and West Germany respectively thought that the law should always be obeyed, even if in their opinion it was wrong.[35] Legal conformism was thus less widespread in Hong Kong than in West Germany.

Podgorecki has argued that objective economic-demographic factors, judicial subcultures and personality characteristics are critical in explaining why people do respect the law.[36] In our survey, the factor of personality turns out to be an useful explanatory variable. Specifically, people who were principle-oriented tended also to be conformist. Among our respondents, conformism was correlated with support of moral principles and filial piety. More precisely, three types of respondents can be distinguished in our study. The principle-oriented people were those who held firm moral principles and were committed to them unconditionally. The instrumentalists were those who would adapt their principles to the situation in order to achieve their goals. The egocentric people believed that principles, as such, were altogether superfluous and that one should strive above all to advance one's own interests. The principle-oriented people were, more likely than the other as one would expect, the type of people to be law-abiding.

Filial piety is among the most fundamental norms in Chinese society. Despite modernization, the majority (88.9 percent) of our respondents still believed that filial piety was essential for a good society. They also agreed (79.4 percent) that the government should enact laws to penalize those who failed to take care of their parents. We think it justified to say that people who uphold filial piety are also principle-oriented. This category of people tended also to be conformist.

The second factor for conformism may lie in the general satisfaction with the socio-political regime. The relevant relations are summarized in Table 4.3.

The figures seem to suggest that a large number of people would still abide by laws that seen as unfair, provided the overall performance of the social and political system was rated as satisfactory.

TABLE 4.3
Relationships between Conformism and Socio-Political Satisfaction

| Satisfaction items | $\chi^2$ | p | d.f. |
|---|---|---|---|
| 1. Current living conditions better than 5 years ago | 10.3 | 0.04 | 4 |
| 2. Hong Kong society a stable and orderly society | 5.8 | 0.05 | 2 |
| 3. Hong Kong government a good government | 14.8 | 0.03 | 6 |
| 4. Existing political system the best possible | 10.6 | 0.02 | 4 |

The upshot of our discussion so far is this: Whether or not a citizen is conformist is not determined by his/her sense of being alienated from the legal system. It has nothing to do with an inability to understand the law, perception of the alien origin of the system, or awareness of the existence of unfair trials or unfair laws, nor does it have to do with traditional legal thinking. Rather, conformism depends more on one's moral principles and general satisfaction with the social and political system.

Conformity with an existing law that is regarded as unfair is one thing, propensity to take action to prevent an unfair law from coming into being is another. Social order will not be disrupted by people who are legally alienated and yet conformist, but it will be threatened by those who, while not alienated, are rebellious.

Let us remind ourselves that there were those younger, better educated and better employed people who felt legally efficacious about, and supportive of, the common law system. On the other hand, they were also more critical of the system, finding injustice in court trials and in the laws. In recognition of the importance of law in society, these people are likely to be active participants in the process of political development.

In response to a question about whether some course of action could be taken to prevent the government from promulgating an unfair law, 56.6 percent of our respondents answered in the negative, as against 43.5 percent who answered positively. If asked further whether he/she would actually take any action to influence the government, 45.4 percent said no, 44.2 percent answered maybe and only 10.0 percent gave a positive answer. The propensity to act is significantly related to age, education and occupation (chi square = 48.4, 41.5 and 38.4 respectively with $p < 0.0001$ for all). The younger, the more educated and the better employed were more prone to action. The pattern of responses thus indicates that civic action is a possible scenario in the future when impending legislation may be criticized.

## Litigiousness

True to the spirit of the traditional legal culture, Chinese people tried to avoid litigation as far as possible. The stress on social harmony, the preference for informal methods of conflict resolution, and the lack of confidence in the legal system combined to turn Chinese away from bringing conflicts to the courts. We have demonstrated above that most of the Hong Kong people have become aware of their rights and the importance of law in society, they must have also become more prepared to avail themselves of the service of law.

It is quite obvious that Hong Kong people today are quite litigious, although we do not know to what extent the changing legal culture has contributed to the rising level of litigiousness.

TABLE 4.4
Civil Cases in Courts of Hong Kong*
(in census/bi-census years)

| Year | Supreme Court | District Court | Total cases | Population (thousand) | Cases per population (thousand) |
|---|---|---|---|---|---|
| 1961 | 2,209 | 7,917 | 10,126 | 3,130 | 3.2 |
| 1966 | 4,396 | 14,502 | 18,898 | 3,606 | 5.2 |
| 1971 | 5,816 | 16,436 | 22,252 | 3,937 | 5.7 |
| 1976 | 6,522 | 23,390 | 29,912 | 4,403 | 6.8 |
| 1981 | 18,934 | 55,737 | 74,671 | 4,987 | 15.0 |
| 1986 | 12,434 | 50,966 | 63,400 | 5,396 | 11.7 |

* Figures are compiled from selected issues of *Hong Kong Annual Report*, published yearly by the Hong Kong Government Information Services.

As shown in the above table, the litigation rates accelerated in the late 1970s. As far back as 1971, Hong Kong already had 5.7 civil cases per 1,000 population, surpassing all countries mentioned by Ehrmann.[37] For instance, Australia and the United Kingdom, both having a larger lawyers per population ratio than Hong Kong, had only 5.3 and 3.6 cases per 1,000 population in 1969. Japan and South Korea, countries much influenced by Confucianism, lagged far being Hong Kong, with 1.2 cases (in 1970) and 0.2 cases (in 1963) respectively, thus attesting to the extent of Westernization in Hong Kong.

## Conclusion

A fair amount of legal alienation was found among our respondents: most of them had difficulties in understanding the law; a large majority regarded court trials in Hong Kong as unfair; about one third of them denounced the laws of Hong Kong as unjust and declared that the legal system was foreign in origin and thus unsuitable to Chinese society.

At the same time, there was a substantial degree of diffuse and largely instrumental support for the existent legal system. Notwithstanding all the shortcomings, the legal system of Hong Kong was generally regarded as just. A majority of people would still abide by the law even if it was considered unjust. Most people would remain inactive when faced with impending unfair legislation.

We have also ascertained that, on the superficial level, modern legal thinking has crept into the minds of our respondents. Law was generally rated more important than the political system, Confucian virtues, or a strong leader as a factor for social stability. Freedom was universally acclaimed. Unlike their forefathers, who did their best to avoid awesome court proceedings, the Hong Kong Chinese were very litigious, even when compared with the people of some Western countries.

The legal ethos of the Hong Kong Chinese is, therefore, a complex mixture of attitudes and behaviors, shaped by cultural heritage, forces of modernization, the performance of the socio-political system the good or bad, as well as, apprehensions aroused by the issue of 1997. This mixed legal culture is, however, neither coherent nor stable.

Let us recall some of the inconsistencies. There is the belief that law is unimportant to one's daily life but important for maintaining social stability. Chinese tradition still works here because law is thought of primarily as penal and therefore exists for the taming of law-breakers but not for "me." There is, as well, universal support for freedom in the general sense, but this support is, at the same time, tempered by an unequivocal denial of freedom as an inalienable human right. Therefore, support for freedom in general does not necessarily entail support for specific kinds of freedom for particular individuals or groups. Here we encounter an uneasy marriage between the modernity of civic liberties and the tradition of situational morality. The people of Hong Kong have become increasingly aware of, and concerned about, their own rights, but have not yet learnt to take the rights of the others seriously. Finally, we may mention the inconsistency between the high level of ligitiousness among Hong Kong Chinese and the low level of action propensity with regard to impending legislation which is regarded as unjust. These many inconsistencies suggest that the reception of the common law system in this rather atypical Chinese society has proceeded largely on an instrumental, utilitarian and egocentric basis, whereas the philosophical and ethical foundation on which the legal system operates still contains traces of traditional Confucian and familistic considerations.

[illegible]

[illegible] of the general sense, but this [illegible] by an [illegible] code of behaviour as [illegible] human [illegible]. [illegible] support [illegible] does not [illegible] support [illegible] of the [illegible] of [illegible] and the [illegible] and rights, but [illegible] between the high [illegible]. He [illegible] and the [illegible] with regard to [illegible] of the great [illegible]

# 5

# Socio-economic Background and Identity

The general pattern of the ethos of Hong Kong Chinese has been described in the preceding chapters without paying attention to variations among socio-economic groups and between people claiming different identities (Hongkongese or Chinese). A closer examination of inter-group variations would not only corroborate the substantial impact of modernizing influences, but might also uncover some unexpected and intriguing phenomena that would require further empirical investigation and sociological imagination for us to understand it. What this, in fact, amounts to is that some of the anticipated effects of modernization have failed to take hold, attesting, not only to the strong residual presence of tradition, but also to the molding influence of the particular Hong Kong context.

The socio-economic background factors that will be considered in this chapter include sex, age, income, occupation and education. Statistical analysis shows that they are closely inter-related, as chi-square tests have revealed that their associations are all significant at the 0.001 level of analysis. Thus, females and the older in age are more likely to have a lower income, be less educated and hold less prestigious occupations. At the same time, as we will see later, these socio-economic factors are closely related to the identity selected by Hong Kong Chinese. Hence, those who claim a Chinese identity are more likely to be those who are male, with lower income, older in age, with less prestigious occupations and less educated. Consequently, within the larger borders of the ethos of Hong Kong Chinese, two sub-cultural groups can be identified. The two sub-cultural groups differ in a wide spectrum of values, though the differences fall short of being unbridgeable. In the future, continued modernization should expand the ranks of the sub-cultural group with the Hong Kong identity. However, the scheduled return of Hong Kong to China, the ever-growing Chinese influence, the likely achievements of Chinese modernization and increasing patriotic appeals might strengthen the Chinese identity, making it no longer the preserve of those with a less desirable socio-economic background. If such is the case, the demarcation between the two sub-groups will be blurred, opening up new vistas in the analysis of value differences among Hong Kong Chinese. In the meantime, however, it is the Hongkongese/Chinese identity gap that is of enormous importance in the transitional period before 1997.

In order to avoid tedious presentation, our description of the effects of the socio-economic and identity factors will be schematic, highlighting only those findings with particular theoretical or empirical value. Therefore, unless absolutely necessary, the results of statistical tests will not be presented, nor will we make detailed analyses of specific findings that underline broad descriptive or theoretical statements.

## Sex

Among all the factors under consideration in this chapter, sex is of least significance in terms of explanatory or differentiating power. Still, the profile of females as the more traditional group as compared to males can be substantiated.

Females were generally less satisfied with Hong Kong society and tended more to lament the income disparity between the rich and the poor. They were more likely to take a negative and cynical view of Hong Kong society, for example, thinking that it was full of serious problems and evil. In addition, females were more likely to see a deterioration of their livelihood. This certainly was not conducive to a favorable image of their social environment.

The more negative image of society held by females was counterbalanced by their higher level of preoccupation with social stability. Females were more disposed to think that the basis of prosperity and stability of Hong Kong is fragile. This, coupled with their less demanding work experience, has brought them to see less exploitation in the relationship between workers and employers, despite the fact that they were more likely to say that Hong Kong was an inegalitarian society. Because the social environment was less benign and more unstable for females, they were more likely to cling tenaciously to their primary social network; thus, they were more likely to say that relatives should provide them with help when they were in difficulties.

Females had a relatively lower interest in politics. Their preoccupation with day-to-day living made them more likely to underrate the importance of the governmental system to Hong Kong. Compared to males, females adopted a more mistrustful attitude toward government, be it the Hong Kong government, the British government or the Chinese government. This more mistrustful stance, however, did not inhibit females from entrusting more interventionist functions and powers to the government. A larger proportion of women in the 1985 survey agreed or strongly agreed that the government should enact laws to punish the unfilial and that it should force the rich to donate more to charity.

Females had a greater tendency to personify government and to place more emphasis on political leaders than political systems. Somewhat surprisingly, however, a slightly smaller proportion of them (33.4 percent) than males (40.5 percent) agreed or strongly agreed that only those who held prestigious occupations and did well in them could make good political leaders. This does not necessarily mean that females were more capable of differentiating between the political and economic spheres. It might be that men, who were more involved in the world of work, had more respect for those who excelled in their vocations. Hence, they were more prone to generalize non-political capabilities to the political field.

Females were more saddled with a sense of political powerlessness. And, as shown in Table 5.1, they were more likely to prefer conventional means to influence the government.

On the whole, sex differences in legal values were minimal, except that females held a slightly more traditional and illiberal view of law and the judicial process. As an example, a larger percentage (68.1) of females agreed to the use of illegally-obtained evidence to convict a suspect, as compared to 58 percent of the males.

## Age

Age is an extremely powerful explanatory and differentiating variable in our study, because it is correlated with a vast number of normative variables in the surveys. Such well-aligned correlations testify forcefully to a generation gap among the Hong Kong Chinese. This generation gap, in turn, constitutes the cornerstone of identity differentiation. On the whole, the older generation manifested more traditional traits, but in some significant aspects they turned up unexpectedly as the more modern sub-group compared to their younger counterparts. It is these extraordinary features which demand explanation in this study.

TABLE 5.1
Sex Differences in Ways to Influence Government*
(in percent)

| Sex | Writing to/ meeting with officials | Mobilizing people | Political parties/ organizations | No way | Total (N) |
|---|---|---|---|---|---|
| Male | 21.4 | 31.7 | 21.9 | 14.8 | 89.8 (340) |
| Female | 26.1 | 34.2 | 13.5 | 18.0 | 91.8 (204) |

* Only the 4 most-picked answers are shown in the table.
$\chi^2 = 22.05$, d.f. = 6, $p<0.01$

True to the teachings of Confucius and Mencius, the older respondents in our 1985 survey were more agreeable to the statement that human nature is good. Apparently, however, a bland recognition of the intrinsic or potential goodness of human beings was far outweighed by their actual experience with other people. The older people in Hong Kong were more likely to have witnessed wars, turmoil, poverty and political repression. These unpleasant and even tormenting experiences could hardly foster a favorable view of human beings *as they really are*. Moreover, *à la* Confucianism, the older people were more tolerant of the contradictory co-existence of a view of the potential goodness of human nature and actual social inequalities. The hierarchical and authoritarian nature of the Chinese society, where many of them were socialized, was naturally not the breeding ground for a liberal predisposition toward other people. Consequently, the older in age were more likely to repudiate the notion of inborn human rights. They were more inclined to see rights as the rewards given by society in recognition of social contributions. Because of this conception of rights, the older in age were more prepared to deny the exercise of these rights by individuals or groups who disseminated heretical ideas that might be a threat to social harmony.

The older in age also had a lower sense of personal efficacy. They were more likely to inherit a numbing sense of fatalism from traditional China. The advice "let tomorrow take care of itself" was more likely to ring a believable note in their mind. They would meet the future with resignation, as they had not much confidence in the future—including the future of Hong Kong and their future livelihood—in the first place. It goes without saying that the sense of personal inefficacy among older people inevitably entailed a rejection of long-term planning as a means to structure one's life.

The older people's perception of society was deeply colored by the Chinese tradition and their lower aspirations. The latter is understandable in view of the hardships many old folks had endured in their formative years and the fact that Hong Kong's economy really took off only in the 1970s. Compared to their younger counterparts, the older people had a conception of a normal society as one immune from serious conflicts. They aspired to a harmonious society in which the spirit of filial piety would ripple throughout all social spheres and act as the underpinning of interpersonal relationships.

The older people had a more complacent view of Hong Kong society. Compared to younger people, they were more satisfied with their society and felt their livelihood had improved in the past five years. The older people were more likely to see a congruence between Hong Kong society and their ideal society, because a higher proportion of them considered Hong Kong a stable and orderly society. To the older people, collective interests took precedence over private interests. This and the notion of the societal origin of human rights made them more likely to explain the proliferation of social problems in Hong Kong as the result of too much freedom available to people.

The older people tended to set greater store by kinship relations. They lamented the erosion of kinship relations and demanded their reinvigoration, particularly in regard to mutual help among kinsmen with money problems.

The older people displayed a peculiar mixture of values in their economic orientation. Against orthodox Confucian dogma, they were more prone to insist that their most important goal in life was to make as much money as possible through licit means. However, as they were disadvantaged, not only by their age, but also by their lower socio-economic status, Hong Kong appealed less to them as a land of opportunity. In contrast with the younger ones, the older people, despite their greater materialistic emphasis, had imbibed a larger dosage of the traditional deprecatory attitude toward merchants and an intolerance of economic inequalities: they were more likely to allege that the wealthy obtained their wealth through illicit means and that a good society should be one without gross economic inequalities.

This more negative perception of the rich and of income inequalities explains why the older people were more likely to demand that the government take action to force the rich to donate more to charity. In the same vein, the older people had a more favorable view of trade unions, as a larger percentage of them agreed that trade unions in Hong Kong should be made stronger and more powerful (Table 5.2). This positive view of trade unions might also be related to the fact that a higher proportion of the older people were employed as manual workers and so had a more salient sense of class consciousness. Nevertheless, as the 1986 survey points out, they had a larger stake in their job and less opportunity for mobility, and thus they were less willing to participate in industrial actions organized by trade unions.

TABLE 5.2
Age Differences in Attitude toward Trade Unions*

| Age | Agree very much | Agree | Disagree | Disagree very much | Total (N) |
|---|---|---|---|---|---|
| 20 or below | 2.0 | 66.7 | 31.4 | 0 | 100.0 (51) |
| 21–30 | 0 | 68.2 | 30.2 | 1.7 | 100.1 (179) |
| 31–40 | 7.3 | 70.8 | 19.7 | 2.2 | 100.0 (137) |
| 41–50 | 4.2 | 77.9 | 17.9 | 0 | 100.0 (95) |
| 51–60 | 9.0 | 75.6 | 15.4 | 0 | 100.0 (78) |
| Over 60 | 5.5 | 78.1 | 15.1 | 1.4 | 100.1 (73) |

* Percentages agreeing or disagreeing with the statement "Trade unions in Hong Kong should be more powerful and influential."
$\chi^2 = 32.99$, d.f. = 15, $p<0.05$

It is the political ethos of the older people that warrants serious attention. Their overall political orientation was traditional, but, at the same time, they evinced a more sanguine view of democracy and its concomitants. This paradox might partially dissolve when three factors are analyzed. First, many of the older people had political experience either in China or in Hong Kong or in both. They had personally witnessed political ups and downs as well as the enormous impact of politics on their lives. Thus, even though they retained much of the traditional orientation toward politics, they still were able to form a view of politics that was more definite, more sensitive to the hardships spawned by political oppression and instability and more rooted in concrete personal experiences. Second, the older people were more fond of China and more distressed by the humiliation she had suffered under foreign powers. They had a more negative attitude toward colonialism and this directly affected their view of the Hong Kong government. Lastly, many of the older people fled to Hong Kong in search of political stability. In fact, to many of them, only Hong Kong could provide a stable political context wherein they and their children could develop and prosper. It was this that they very much treasured. Accordingly, they were apprehensive about any possible disruption of this stable environment. All three factors exert partly congruent and partly contradictory influences on the political ethos of the older folks in Hong Kong. The emergence of the 1997 question only exacerbates the conflicts in their political values.

We shall first of all deal with the expected, traditional elements in the political ethos of the older people, and then the puzzling issues will be taken up later in greater detail.

In general, the older in age were more prone to harbor a negative view of politics. They were more likely to say that politics was dangerous. On the other hand, they had more difficulty in differentiating the political and economic spheres: a larger percentage of them agreed or strongly agreed that managing government was akin to business management.

The older people's approach to politics was primarily instrumental in character. They were more likely to think that those who did well in their prestigious occupations should be able to make good political leaders. To engage in politics was, in their minds, to pursue self-interest, and this they felt could be generalized to others. Moreover, they thought that the form of government was immaterial provided their basic livelihood could be safeguarded.

The older people had a greater tendency to personify government and politics. They placed more value on political leadership. They were more agreeable with the statement that the emergence of a few competent leaders would be more important to Hong Kong than the search for an appropriate political system. They also thought that many problems in Hong Kong could be solved if there were upright and capable leaders. In line with this, the older people were more likely to demand that the government treat the people like a father.

Older people had a more favorable view of the political system of Hong Kong. They tended more to say that the political system of Hong Kong was good enough, and that it was the best available under existent circumstances.

Similarly, older people had a more favorable impression of the Hong Kong government. They were more willing than their younger counterparts to call the Hong Kong government a good government. Their political trust was also extended to the British and Chinese governments, as a higher proportion of them were trustful of these two governments than were younger people. It is difficult, however, to determine the basis of this higher level of trust in government on the part of the older folks. As we will discuss later, in view of their more paradoxical attitude toward government and politics, the older people *should* be more mistrustful of the three governments. An explanatory factor might be the deep-rooted proclivity to respect authority inherited from traditional China.

Older people also had a more pragmatic understanding of governmental functions. Ideological specification of governmental functions had only limited appeal to them. True to the traditional Chinese political values, older people had a more expansionist or interventionist conception of the government's role in the moral, social and economic spheres. As shown in Table 5.3, except in the area of public housing, the differences among age groups in their conception of governmental functions were statistically significant.

The development of the welfare state in modern societies and the increase in political participation among the masses are normally interwined with vociferous demands for governmental involvement in society. Therefore, modern people have a greater tendency to call for governmental actions. Traditional Chinese, on the other hand, were more concerned with warding off unnecessary governmental interference, except when it was desperately needed or when the government was judged to be benevolent. From this we see that the choice of approach or avoidance towards the government hinges upon the conditions at a particular point in time. If that is the case, the more interventionist conception of the government's role apparently does not mean that the older Hong Kong Chinese were more modern in outlook. It simply shows that when a government was perceived as more

TABLE 5.3
Age Differences in Conception of Governmental Functions
(% who agreed or agreed strongly)

| Statement | Age | | | | | | N |
|---|---|---|---|---|---|---|---|
| | 20 or below | 21–30 | 31–40 | 41–50 | 51–60 | Above 60 | |
| 1. Penalizing the unfilial.[a] | 72.6 | 70.0 | 79.5 | 88.2 | 82.8 | 88.0 | 576 |
| 2. Officials setting moral examples.[b] | 96.8 | 90.7 | 96.9 | 99.1 | 100.0 | 100.0 | 713 |
| 3. Deterring divorce.[c] | 6.6 | 17.4 | 22.2 | 31.4 | 33.0 | 46.9 | 176 |
| 4. Governmental responsibility for social problems.[d] | 21.3 | 17.2 | 34.9 | 41.3 | 47.7 | 56.8 | 225 |
| 5. Solving social problems.[e] | 81.0 | 89.3 | 95.7 | 98.3 | 96.2 | 100.0 | 684 |
| 6. Forcing the wealthy to be charitable.[f] | 17.7 | 31.1 | 40.8 | 48.2 | 51.8 | 54.6 | 295 |
| 7. Finding a job for everyone.[g] | 68.9 | 60.2 | 78.6 | 90.0 | 90.4 | 99.0 | 585 |
| 8. Providing housing for all.[h] | 91.9 | 91.2 | 95.6 | 95.1 | 94.8 | 100.0 | 713 |

a. $\chi^2 = 36.87$, d.f. = 15, $p < 0.01$
b. $\chi^2 = 35.61$, d.f. = 15, $p < 0.01$
c. $\chi^2 = 50.74$, d.f. = 15, $p < 0.01$
d. $\chi^2 = 60.85$, d.f. = 15, $p < 0.01$
e. $\chi^2 = 44.47$, d.f. = 10, $p < 0.01$
f. $\chi^2 = 51.08$, d.f. = 15, $p < 0.01$
g. $\chi^2 = 99.85$, d.f. = 15, $p < 0.01$
h. $\chi^2 = 23.85$, d.f. = 15, $p > 0.05$

or less non-oppressive, they were ready to depend on it for the satisfaction of personal or social needs, particularly when these needs were thought to be not amenable to satisfaction through private efforts. From another point of view, such an interventionist conception of the government's role was perfectly congruent with a paternalistic conception of government.

Political involvement of the older people was conspicuously lower than that of the younger ones. Older people were gripped by a stronger sense of political powerlessness and inefficacy. They were more likely to think that government and politics were complicated and difficult to understand, that they had no power to change unfair laws, that they could not change public policies and that indifference to public affairs was excusable. They were less prepared to take action to change unfair laws. They rarely discussed public affairs with friends, community leaders and the "knowledgeable." If they ever discussed them, they confined that discussion to family and kinsmen.

As presented in Table 5.4, older people were more in favor of conventional means as a more effective tactic to influence government policy. Confrontation with the government was to be shunned: older folks were more likely to agree that it was not a healthy phenomenon for an increasing number of people to use protest and demonstrations to confront the government. Their obsession with stability was crystal clear.

Older people's abhorrence of conflict, confusion and confrontation was also reflected in their attitude toward pressure groups and their leaders. While there was not much difference among age groups in their attitude toward political leaders *in general*, the older people's attitude toward pressure groups and their leaders was particularly negative. They were more likely to report that there were no trustworthy pressure group leaders; they were more prone to accuse pressure groups of endangering the prosperity and stability of Hong Kong.

There are several differences in political thinking among the age groups that come to us as a surprise, for they seem to imply that the older people were the more democratically oriented ones among the Hong Kong Chinese.

First of all, notwithstanding their favorable impression of the Hong Kong government, the older people's perception of colonial authority was suffused with a nagging ambivalence. While they were obsessed with the maintenance of strong authority as the *sine qua non* of political stability, they were less certain about the legitimacy of the authority claimed by the colonial regime. Such skepticism is reflected

TABLE 5.4
Age Differences in Ways to Influence Government Policy*
(in percent)

| Age | Writing to/ meeting with officials | Mobilizing people | Political parties/ organizations | No way | Total (N) |
|---|---|---|---|---|---|
| 20 or below | 19.0 | 37.9 | 20.7 | 8.6 | 86.2 (50) |
| 21–30 | 24.6 | 38.0 | 20.1 | 8.9 | 91.6 (164) |
| 31–40 | 17.8 | 42.2 | 20.0 | 11.9 | 91.9 (124) |
| 41–50 | 29.5 | 21.1 | 15.8 | 20.0 | 86.4 (82) |
| 51–60 | 21.5 | 21.5 | 16.5 | 31.6 | 91.1 (72) |
| Above 60 | 26.8 | 23.2 | 17.9 | 26.8 | 94.7 (53) |

* Only the 4 most-picked answers are shown in the table. The $\chi^2$ for the full table is 56.44 (d.f. = 30), which is significant at 0.01 level.

in the findings in Table 5.5, where the older respondents were more likely to agree that the erosion of the authority of the Hong Kong government was a good thing. They were also in agreement with the argument that a decline in its authority would impel the Hong Kong government to pay more attention to public opinion. They were more inclined to explain the restoration of the authority of the Hong Kong government, in the wake of the Sino-British negotiation, as the support provided to it by the Chinese government. What is the basis for this strand of cynical orientation toward the government? A clue to an answer might be that the older people did not associate the Hong Kong government with the public interest they had in mind. They were more likely to say that the government primarily catered to the interests of the wealthy and hence had forfeited its claim to represent public interests. Because of this, the older people were less likely to agree that the government should have the prerogative of forcing the people to do something against their wishes for the sake of collective benefit.

Latent anti-colonialism and nationalism might also be at work in explaining other puzzling findings. Older people were more likely to hold a positive view of political activity, as a higher percentage of them declared that it was meaningful and respectable. We have no way of telling what kinds of political activity they had in mind. Judging from the fact that they had a more favorable attitude toward certain aspects of democratic politics, we can tentatively conclude that political participation of a democratic nature would be acceptable to them. We base our conclusion on several findings.

TABLE 5.5
Age Differences in Attitude toward Erosion of Governmental Authority*

| Age | Agree very much | Agree | Disagree | Disagree very much | Total (N) |
|---|---|---|---|---|---|
| 20 or below | 5.0 | 41.7 | 53.3 | 0 | 100.0 (60) |
| 21–30 | 0.6 | 54.3 | 45.1 | 0 | 100.0 (175) |
| 31–40 | 4.4 | 54.8 | 38.5 | 2.2 | 99.9 (135) |
| 41–50 | 1.1 | 62.9 | 36.0 | 0 | 100.0 (89) |
| 51–60 | 3.8 | 63.8 | 32.5 | 0 | 100.1 (80) |
| Over 60 | 3.2 | 60.3 | 36.5 | 0 | 100.0 (63) |

* Measured by the statement: "The erosion of the authority of the Hong Kong government is good, because then it will pay more attention to public opinion in order to win the goodwill and support of the people."
$\chi^2 = 26.90$, d.f. = 15, $p<0.05$

Firstly, contrary to normal expectation, the older people were more optimistic about democratic reform in Hong Kong, as seen in Table 5.6, even though they were not informed about the content of democratic reform during the interview.

Secondly, on the controversial subject of political parties, the attitude of the older people was more positive than their younger counterparts. As shown in Table 5.7, they were more sanguine about the contributions of political parties to the existent political system. Thus, despite the ignominious connotations of the term "political party" in popular political parlance, the older in age were seemingly more prepared to accept it.

Thirdly, the older people's attitude toward elections was more positive than that of the younger ones. As Table 5.8 shows, older respondents were more confident that elected political leaders would run Hong Kong better than the incumbent government.

Lastly, we discussed the fact in Chapter 3 that there was a tendency among Hong Kong Chinese to equate democratic government

TABLE 5.6
Age Differences in Attitude toward Democratic Reform*

| Age | Agree very much | Agree | Disagree | Disagree very much | Total (N) |
|---|---|---|---|---|---|
| 20 or below | 1.8 | 73.2 | 25.0 | 0 | 100.0 (56) |
| 21–30 | 1.8 | 63.9 | 33.1 | 1.2 | 100.0 (166) |
| 31–40 | 3.3 | 77.2 | 18.7 | 0.8 | 100.0 (123) |
| 41–50 | 1.3 | 81.6 | 17.1 | 0 | 100.0 (76) |
| 51–60 | 9.5 | 76.2 | 12.7 | 1.6 | 100.0 (63) |
| Over 60 | 5.1 | 84.7 | 10.2 | 0 | 100.0 (59) |

* Percentages agreeing or disagreeing with the statement that "The chance of success for democratic reform in Hong Kong will be good."
$\chi^2 = 34.21$, d.f. = 15, $p<0.05$

TABLE 5.7
Age Differences in Attitude toward Political Parties*

| Age | Agree very much | Agree | Disagree | Disagree very much | Total (N) |
|---|---|---|---|---|---|
| 20 or below | 0 | 50.0 | 50.0 | 0 | 100.0 (50) |
| 21–30 | 0 | 43.5 | 54.5 | 1.9 | 99.9 (154) |
| 31–40 | 2.9 | 56.3 | 39.8 | 1.0 | 100.0 (103) |
| 41–50 | 0 | 48.5 | 50.0 | 1.5 | 100.0 (66) |
| 51–60 | 0 | 72.6 | 25.8 | 1.6 | 100.0 (62) |
| Over 60 | 2.0 | 73.5 | 24.5 | 0 | 100.0 (49) |

* Percentages agreeing or disagreeing with the statement that "The appearance of political parties will make the political system of Hong Kong better."
$\chi^2 = 36.42$, d.f. = 15, $p<0.05$

with consultative government. If democratic reform in the mind of the older people only means tinkering with the consultative system of Hong Kong, then the enigma of the older people appearing to be more democratically oriented will partially evaporate. However, this is

TABLE 5.8
Age Differences in Evaluation of Elected Political Leaders*

| Age | Agree very much | Agree | Disagree | Disagree very much | Total (N) |
|---|---|---|---|---|---|
| 20 or below | 1.9 | 66.7 | 31.5 | 0 | 100.1 (54) |
| 21–30 | 3.7 | 55.2 | 40.5 | 0.6 | 100.0 (163) |
| 31–40 | 5.8 | 53.7 | 40.5 | 0 | 100.0 (121) |
| 41–50 | 4.3 | 64.1 | 29.3 | 2.2 | 99.9 (92) |
| 51–60 | 2.8 | 76.4 | 20.8 | 0 | 100.0 (72) |
| Over 60 | 9.7 | 72.6 | 16.1 | 1.6 | 100.0 (62) |

* Percentages agreeing or disagreeing with the statement that "Elected political leaders will run the place better than the Hong Kong government."
$\chi^2 = 31.10$, d.f. = 15, $p<0.01$

apparently not the case. The more receptive stance of the older people toward elections and political parties should mean that they had more things in mind other than improving the consultative system. And, as shown in Table 5.9, the older in age obviously did not equate democratic government with consultative government, they even had a weaker tendency to do so in comparison with the younger respondents. What is clear in Table 5.9 is that the older people were more capable of using a more appropriate criterion—election—to define a democratic government.

On the whole, the older Hong Kong Chinese appeared to combine behavioral passivity and normative ideals in their political ethos. The younger ones had a greater, though not great enough, tendency to politically participate, but they were, at the same time, more wary of democracy and democratic reforms in Hong Kong. The older people's ideals, however, had only a remote probability of eventual realization, while the younger ones' tendency to action was suffocated by their reservations about democratic reforms. Even if the older people were to take action, in all likelihood they would immediately be restrained by their preoccupation with political harmony and their aversion to confusion. The overall picture of the political ethos of various age groups thus supplies a significant clue in understanding the general political quiescence in the Hong Kong political scene. This quiescence continued even with the surfacing of the momentous 1997

TABLE 5.9
Age Differences in Criteria of Democratic Government*
(in percent)

| Age | Consultative government | Government according to all demands | Government that can lead | Elective government | Total (N) |
|---|---|---|---|---|---|
| 20 or below | 49.2 | 1.6 | 19.0 | 28.6 | 98.4 (62) |
| 21-30 | 58.4 | 0.5 | 18.9 | 18.4 | 96.2 (183) |
| 31-40 | 57.6 | 0 | 19.9 | 20.5 | 98.0 (148) |
| 41-50 | 45.5 | 2.0 | 20.8 | 31.7 | 100.0 (101) |
| 51-60 | 41.8 | 1.1 | 16.5 | 37.4 | 96.8 (88) |
| Over 60 | 40.0 | 0 | 11.7 | 46.7 | 98.4 (59) |

* Only responses to the 4 concrete criteria are shown in the table.
$\chi^2 = 41.02$, d.f. = 25, $p < 0.05$

question and the issue of institutional reform in the greater part of the 1980s.

Age is a fairly powerful explanatory variable with regard to legal values and their behavioral implications. Age is moderately, but very significantly, correlated with sense of efficacy and sense of system foreignness, but not with the sense of judicial justice. The general pattern is that the younger one was, the more one was legally efficacious. As a group, those between 21 and 30 were most capable of comprehending the laws and the legal system. As to system foreignness, the same pattern prevails so that the legal system was more accepted by the younger generation than by the older. Although there is no significant relationship between education and sense of judicial justice in general, younger people were more likely to find unfair laws that did not affect themselves. This suggests that younger people were more critical of the laws of Hong Kong.

The difference between the older and younger people over legal opinions is clear-cut. The older people were more likely to support *li* as the most important factor for social stability, they were more favorable to the punitive emphasis of the law, less receptive of the idea of inalienable rights and more inclined toward censorship of the press that reported false news and toward prohibition of assembly for an unorthodox cause. Surprisingly again, the older generation were more concerned about due process. As seen in Table 5.10, more than half of those people over 50 years in age did not support using illegally obtained evidence against the suspect. We do not have a ready-made explanation for this finding. It, however, cannot prove that the older people had a better appreciation of the rationale of due process. It might be more reasonable to say that older people were more extreme in their moral views, and had a stronger tendency to see "right" and "wrong" as uncompromisable. That the evidence was obtained illegally might *ipso facto* be repulsive to them, impelling them to reject it as the basis for convicting a suspect.

Legal conformism is also related to age. The older generation was more conformist than the younger one. In addition, as pointed out earlier, older people were also more likely to feel alienated. Legal alienation thus presents no danger at all since it is the same kind of people who could be both alienated and conformist. This parallels the political orientation of the older people, who were both more alienated and cynical, but, at the same time, less disposed to challenge authority. To broaden the discussion a little bit, we found no statistical correlation between conformism and all other test items for the legal values under

TABLE 5.10
Age Differences in Attitude toward Illegally-obtained Evidence*

| Age | Release the suspect | Convict with the evidence | Total (N) |
|---|---|---|---|
| 20 or below | 10.3 | 89.7 | 100.0 (58) |
| 21–30 | 28.0 | 72.0 | 100.0 (168) |
| 31–40 | 33.3 | 66.7 | 100.0 (129) |
| 41–50 | 50.5 | 49.5 | 100.0 (103) |
| 51–60 | 56.6 | 43.4 | 100.0 (83) |
| Over 60 | 54.4 | 45.6 | 100.0 (68) |

* $\chi^2 = 53.94$, d.f. = 5, $p<0.01$

study, including those for legal alienation. We, therefore, cannot confirm that legal alienation necessarily breeds disobedience. It is also noteworthy that conformism is not correlated with fatalism either. As an indirect reflection of the legal conformism of the older people, they had a weaker propensity to take legal action or engage in litigious undertakings. The aphorism "you don't enter the door of the officials when you are living and you don't go to hell after death" (*sheng bu ru guanmen, si bu ru diyu* 生不入官門，死不入地獄) was still very much alive in the mind of the older Hong Kong Chinese.

## Education

As an explanatory factor with respect to the ethos of the Hong Kong Chinese, education and age are of equal importance. More or less the same puzzling findings relating to age are found in connection with education. In fact, the two factors are closely related. The smallness of the sample does not allow us to determine which factor has the greater explanatory power, but in view of the fact that age is correlated with more variables than education, age should have a slight edge over education in this respect.

Not surprisingly, the more educated had a "modernist" orientation toward society. They had experienced social progress and were optimistic that it would continue into the future. They had a stronger sense of personal efficacy, and believed much less in fatalism. They were more tolerant of social conflict, and more likely than the less educated to believe that conflict was a natural and integral part of social life. Because of this, they were more inclined to grant personal freedom to others, and less prone to blame it for the increasing social problems in Hong Kong. They were less traditional, in that they placed less emphasis on filial piety and kinship relations. They also had a less materialist outlook. A smaller proportion of them accepted the view that the primary aim in life was to make as much money as was legally possible.

The more educated were less agreeable to the notion of the social origin of individual rights. Consequently, they were more tolerant of others than their less educated counterparts. They were more likely to give freedom of speech to others, less likely to ban newspapers that published false news, and less likely to prohibit meetings for an unorthodox cause.

By and large, the economic values of the more educated do not fall outside of normal expectations. They were more likely to believe that Hong Kong was a land of opportunity, less likely to agree that economic freedom was tantamount to class exploitation and less likely to define an ideal society as an egalitarian one. It follows then that the more educated believed in competition and individual effort, and they would oppose any organizational efforts to thwart the competitive process. Therefore, they were more inclined than the less educated to disagree with the statement that trade unions should be made more powerful. At the same time, their relatively high educational status has enabled them to look beyond materialist values. Thus, they were less envious of the economically successful and less prepared to have their children emulate them.

Again, it is in the political values of the more educated, that surprises are in store, even though, in many ways, their political values are easily predictable.

The more educated had a more positive view of politics. They were less likely to agree that politics would lead to the rise of dangerous careerists, that political participation should be geared to the pursuit of self interests, that politics meant oppression, that the ignorant should be denied the right to vote or that political leaders were not trustworthy. Nevertheless, the more educated were, at the same time, more likely to say that politics was dangerous. The more educated seemed to be more bothered by a latent and diffuse fear of politics even though they were more capable of dispelling many of the traditional notions of politics that formed the basic understanding of the average Chinese.

There is no statistically significant difference between educational groups with respect to trust of the Hong Kong and British governments; but, the more educated were conspicuously less trustful of the Chinese government. Their attitude toward the political system and government of Hong Kong, however, demonstrated a higher degree of ambivalence, even though supposedly they were the major beneficiaries of the existent political order.

Table 5.11 presents the attitudes of various educational groups toward the political system. As expected, the more educated set smaller store by political leaders and were more concerned about the nature of the governmental system, but there was no difference between them and the less educated on the estimated chance of success of democratic reforms and their pace. What is astounding, however, was their less favorable attitude toward the political system and some particular kinds of changes in it. The more educated had a less favorable impression of the existing political system, tending more to say that it was not good enough. In a like manner, they were less agreeable with the judgment that the political system was already the best under existent circumstances. Furthermore, they were less enthusiastic or sanguine about democratic changes. They were more likely to disagree that political parties would improve the political system of Hong Kong or that elected leaders would perform better than the Hong Kong government. The more educated people had a larger stake in the existent social-political order. They might have set more laudable goals for the political system, but their vested interests in it also cautioned them against drastic changes. Under normal circumstances the more educated and Westernized sectors of Hong Kong should be the standard-bearers of democratization, but their special location in the society has also left in their mind serious reservations and uncertainties about political changes.

While the attitude of the more educated toward the political system was less positive than that of the less educated, the opposite was true with respect to attitude toward government. The more educated were more capable of distinguishing between political leadership and economic leadership, as a smaller percentage of them agreed that managing government was akin to managing business. Thus, politics and economics were more differentiated in their mind. They had a less paternalistic conception of government and a more idealistic expectation of its role. With regard to whether the Hong Kong government was a good government, no statistically significant difference was found between the more and the less educated. But the former

TABLE 5.11
Attitude toward Political System by Education
(% who agreed or agreed very much)

| Statement | Education | | | | | |
|---|---|---|---|---|---|---|
| | No formal education | Primary education | Lower secondary education | Upper secondary education | Post-secondary education | N |
| 1. Existing political system good enough.[a] | 76.8 | 69.8 | 62.1 | 55.3 | 27.1 | 400 |
| 2. Chance of success for democratic reform good.[b] | 82.7 | 84.0 | 76.8 | 69.7 | 71.1 | 420 |
| 3. Political parties will make things better.[c] | 66.7 | 66.3 | 51.1 | 44.0 | 48.0 | 267 |
| 4. Elected leaders will perform better than H.K. government.[d] | 84.8 | 67.9 | 67.8 | 59.1 | 55.1 | 376 |
| 5. Political reform should be gradual.[e] | 97.9 | 97.5 | 100.0 | 100.0 | 100.0 | 703 |
| 6. Better for H.K. to be governed by a few capable men.[f] | 87.5 | 78.7 | 65.9 | 59.4 | 45.6 | 451 |
| 7. Kind of government immaterial.[g] | 81.1 | 77.0 | 63.4 | 51.2 | 22.2 | 466 |
| 8. Political system already best.[h] | 83.0 | 86.7 | 85.5 | 77.3 | 63.7 | 569 |

a. $\chi^2 = 53.52$, d.f. = 12, $p<0.0001$
b. $\chi^2 = 18.48$, d.f. = 12, $p>0.05$
c. $\chi^2 = 23.30$, d.f. = 12, $p<0.05$
d. $\chi^2 = 26.13$, d.f. = 12, $p<0.05$
e. $\chi^2 = 11.58$, d.f. = 8, $p>0.05$
f. $\chi^2 = 54.45$, d.f. = 12, $p<0.0001$
g. $\chi^2 = 107.79$, d.f. = 12, $p<0.0001$
h. $\chi^2 = 20.65$, d.f. = 8, $p<0.01$

were less likely to agree that the government primarily catered to its own interests or that it took care solely of the interests of the wealthy. Compared to the less educated, they were more aware of the intimate relationship between government and daily living.

The more educated people's skepticism about elections or drastic political change can be gleaned from Table 5.12. The more educated were more likely to choose the less democratic definition of democratic government as consultative government and less disposed to define it as elective government. It goes without saying that the more educated would, in reality, adopt a gradual, incremental and *status quo*-oriented posture toward political reform in Hong Kong.

The conception of governmental functions or the jurisdiction of political power by the more educated was, in large measure, a relatively liberal one. A limited government was more to their liking. In this respect the doctrine of "positive non-interventionism" should appeal to them. As shown in Table 5.13, the more educated were, across the board, less supportive of an interventionist government or the expansive role of politics, particularly in areas pertaining to private moralities and economic freedom. They were less averse to a more active governmental role in social welfare and social problems. But what is most astonishing is that an overwhelming proportion of the more educated also demanded a moralizing role for officials, thus testifying to the continued hold of traditional norms.

While it is true to say that the more educated Hong Kong Chinese were more liberal in outlook than their less educated counterparts, the figures in Table 5.13 also provide abundant evidence that, compared to the more educated in Western countries, the more educated in Hong Kong were supportive of a more active moral and social role, but a less active economic role, for the government. In other words, contrary to traditional thinking, the more educated Hong Kong Chinese had, in their mind, autonomized the economic sector from political power, but their conception of the relationship between political power on one side and morality and society on the other still retained many of the trappings of tradition.

As expected, the more educated manifested a higher level of political interests and political involvement than the less educated. We must be aware, however, that even the more educated were afflicted by severe political powerlessness and political inefficacy. All the same, in the 1985 survey, the more educated were found to be more likely to endorse political involvement, to be active in political participation, to be more political efficacious, to discuss public affairs

TABLE 5.12
Criteria of Democratic Government by Education*
(in percent)

| Education | Consultative government | Government acceding to all demands | Government that can lead | Elected government | Total (N) |
|---|---|---|---|---|---|
| No formal education | 37.8 | 0 | 24.4 | 37.8 | 100.0 (82) |
| Primary education | 47.9 | 0.9 | 16.3 | 33.0 | 98.1 (211) |
| Lower secondary education | 58.1 | 0 | 17.1 | 23.3 | 98.5 (127) |
| Upper secondary education | 60.8 | 1.8 | 16.9 | 17.5 | 97.0 (161) |
| Post-secondary education | 42.9 | 0 | 23.8 | 27.0 | 93.7 (61) |

$\chi^2 = 48.91$, d.f. = 20, $p < 0.001$

* Only responses to the 4 concrete criteria are shown in the table.

TABLE 5.13

Attitude toward Governmental Functions by Education
(% who agreed or agreed very much)

| Statement | Education | | | | | N |
|---|---|---|---|---|---|---|
| | No formal education | Primary education | Lower secondary education | Upper secondary education | Post-secondary education | |
| 1. Penalizing the unfilial.[a] | 89.2 | 82.6 | 87.3 | 69.1 | 59.0 | 575 |
| 2. Officials setting moral examples.[b] | 100.0 | 98.8 | 97.1 | 94.6 | 84.6 | 712 |
| 3. Deterring divorce.[c] | 35.3 | 31.6 | 24.4 | 15.0 | 16.1 | 176 |
| 4. Governmental responsibility for social problems.[d] | 54.1 | 41.8 | 29.0 | 22.8 | 14.8 | 225 |
| 5. Solving social problems.[e] | 98.2 | 97.2 | 91.9 | 88.9 | 89.1 | 683 |
| 6. Forcing the wealthy to be charitable.[f] | 55.2 | 45.7 | 40.6 | 26.7 | 33.9 | 295 |
| 7. Finding a job for everyone.[g] | 95.9 | 88.0 | 77.4 | 62.2 | 63.5 | 584 |
| 8. Providing housing for all.[h] | 97.6 | 97.7 | 93.3 | 91.7 | 86.2 | 711 |

a. $\chi^2 = 55.70$, d.f. = 12, $p<0.0001$
b. $\chi^2 = 45.59$, d.f. = 12, $p<0.0001$
c. $\chi^2 = 32.06$, d.f. = 12, $p<0.01$
d. $\chi^2 = 55.29$, d.f. = 12, $p<0.0001$
e. $\chi^2 = 25.32$, d.f. = 8, $p<0.01$
f. $\chi^2 = 35.22$, d.f. = 12, $p<0.001$
g. $\chi^2 = 92.88$, d.f. = 12, $p<0.0001$
h. $\chi^2 = 28.21$, d.f. = 12, $p<0.01$

with family, friends, the knowledgeable, and community leaders and to expect fair treatment by officials. Interestingly, as shown in Table 5.14, despite their less enthusiastic reception of elective government and democratic changes, the more educated placed greater stress on group-based methods as the most effective way to influence government. This might be the result of their relatively lower trust in the government and a more rational or instrumental approach to influence tactics. In view of their basic conservatism with regard to the *status quo*, it was unlikely that they conceived of these less conventional tactics as the gateway to fundamental changes in the political system.

With respect to political leadership, it is interesting to find that the more educated had a more favorable attitude toward Hong Kong's political leaders, but, at the same time, placed less emphasis on the importance of leaders in politics (see Table 5.15). It follows that the more educated had a more institutional, and less personalistic, conception of the political system. Furthermore, they were also more capable of treating political leadership as a profession in its own right instead of just an extension of economic leadership. Be that as it may, in general, the more educated did not differ significantly (in the statistical sense) from the less educated in their attitude toward, and trust in, political leaders. The most that can be said in our study is that the more educated were much less likely to criticize pressure groups as a menace to prosperity and stability; at the same time, they refrained from actively embracing them.

Education is perhaps the most important explanatory variable with respect to legal values. Educational achievement is the most important background variable affecting all aspects of legal orientations under study. The more educated were more likely to be able to understand the laws, to experience a stronger sense of judicial justice, and to accept the present legal system as suitable for Chinese society.

Education is also the most important factor shaping people's legal opinion. There was less support among the more educated for *li* as the most important factor for social stability, less support for the penal emphasis of the law, more acceptance of the idea of inborn and inalienable right, more tolerance of freedom for the dishonest press and of assembly for an unorthodox cause. Surprisingly, however, the less educated were more likely to be against the admission of illegally obtained evidence against defendants. The percentages of those who agreed to the use of illegally obtained evidence to convict were 51.1 for those without formal education, 54.3 for those with primary education, 63.7 for those with lower secondary education, 74.1 for those

TABLE 5.14
Ways to Influence Government Policy by Education*
(in percent)

| Education | Writing to/ meeting with officials | Mobilizing people | Political parties/ organizations | No way | Total (N) |
|---|---|---|---|---|---|
| No formal education | 17.9 | 29.5 | 7.7 | 35.9 | 91.0 (71) |
| Primary education | 24.0 | 27.0 | 15.8 | 18.4 | 85.2 (167) |
| Lower secondary education | 25.9 | 26.8 | 26.8 | 13.4 | 92.9 (104) |
| Upper secondary education | 23.2 | 40.0 | 21.9 | 8.4 | 93.5 (145) |
| Post-secondary education | 20.0 | 48.3 | 20.0 | 6.7 | 95.0 (57) |

* Only the 4 most-picked answers are shown in the table. The $\chi^2$ for the full table is 69.25 (d.f. = 24), which is significant at 0.0001 level.

TABLE 5.15
Attitude toward Political Leaders by Education
(% who agreed or agreed very much)

| Statement | Education | | | | | N |
|---|---|---|---|---|---|---|
| | No formal education | Primary education | Lower secondary education | Upper secondary education | Post-secondary education | |
| 1. Most leaders have engaged in illicit activities.[a] | 43.6 | 39.0 | 41.4 | 37.7 | 45.5 | 219 |
| 2. Political activities respectable and meaningful.[b] | 76.7 | 73.0 | 54.5 | 49.1 | 37.1 | 350 |
| 3. Upright and competent leaders can resolve problems.[c] | 84.7 | 83.2 | 69.9 | 66.7 | 45.8 | 486 |
| 4. Those excelling in prestigeous occupation make good leaders.[d] | 57.1 | 49.3 | 27.7 | 26.9 | 21.0 | 248 |

a. $\chi^2 = 12.91$, d.f. = 12, $p > 0.05$
b. $\chi^2 = 45.69$, d.f. = 12, $p < 0.0001$
c. $\chi^2 = 50.31$, d.f. = 12, $p < 0.0001$
d. $\chi^2 = 67.24$, d.f. = 12, $p < 0.0001$

with upper secondary education and 73.1 for those with post-secondary education. This seems to show that the more educated were more likely to adopt a more instrumental or less principled approach to law. If this is really the case, it is a source of concern.

The influence of education on legal conformism is less straightforward. In general, the less educated were more likely to be conformist. At the same time, the less educated were also more likely to be rebellious. On the other hand, the more educated were more inclined to pretend to abide by unfair laws but actually to breach them in practice. This result-oriented attitude toward law echoed their legal instrumentalism touched upon above.

The propensity to take legal action is significantly related to education. The more educated were more prone to action. As the average level of education in Hong Kong improves, litigiousness among the Hong Kong Chinese will inexorably rise.

## Occupation and Income

The factors of occupation and (monthly) income are discussed together in this section because income is a relatively unimportant explanatory variable in our study and because the two factors are intimately correlated.

There is no statistically significant difference among occupational groups in terms of a conception of human nature. Those higher in the occupational hierarchy, however, had a greater sense of personal efficacy and were less given to fatalistic resignation. They were less materialist in their definition of life-goals. They were more tolerant of the exercise of personal freedom by others and took a more libertarian stance toward individual rights. Though they were less likely to endorse the idea of the social origin of individual rights, still 66.3 percent of professionals and 60.4 percent of clerical workers agreed or strongly agreed that individual rights were not natural or inborn but were withdrawable awards from society. What is puzzling, but by no means incomprehensible, is that the better employed were more likely to agree to forbid the ignorant from making known their opinions. This anti-libertarian attitude on the part of the better employed most probably was derived from their inordinate emphasis on knowledge and expertise, which were integral parts of their occupational success and which were then generalized to the domain of civil liberties. They were more intolerant of those without the necessary objective knowledge laying a preposterous claim to their right of expression. Fortunately, this understanding has not been carried over by the better educated to the point of equating business management with governance or preferring that political leaders come from the ranks of the professionally successful.

Those higher in the occupational ladder were more satisfied with their living condition in the past and were optimistic about it in the future. They subscribed less to a traditional orientation toward society by agreeing less with the view that conflict should have no place in a normal society. Their attitude toward Hong Kong society was one of complacence. They were less likely to think that the basis of prosperity and stability of Hong Kong was shaky, and a smaller proportion of them agreed that Hong Kong was an unfair society. Being firmer believers in individual striving, they were more likely to take issue with the view that a good society was one where there was income equality among people. Traditional virtues such as filial piety occupied a less central position in their hierarchy of values.

The better employed had a less instrumental view of politics. They were *in general* less worried about the detrimental consequences of democracy. They were more likely to be concerned with the institutional aspects of the polity and less enamored of its personalistic dimensions. They were less prone to confuse political and economic talents, and they had a less paternalistic conception of the government's role. Political pragmatism appealed less to them than to those lower in the occupational ladder.

While those on the higher and lower rungs of the occupational ladder did not differ much in their trust in the Hong Kong government, the former were more likely to disagree with the comment that it primarily took care of the interests of the rich.

Ironically, the better employed had a slightly poorer evaluation of the existent political system of Hong Kong, and they were more likely to say that the erosion of the authority of the Hong Kong government was a good thing. This does not mean that they would contemplate large-scale political changes. On the contrary, they were more apprehensive about drastic reforms. They were, in fact, less certain that elected leaders would perform better than the incumbent government, and they were less optimistic about the development of democracy in Hong Kong. Thus, despite their reservations about the political system of Hong Kong, their vested interests in it cautioned them against drastic changes. In fact, because the Hong Kong government by and large underwrote their well-being, they would even go to the extent of endorsing some authoritarian move by the government. Thus, they were more likely to agree with the statement that for the sake of public interest the government had occasionally to force people to act against their wishes.

On the whole, the better employed had a more restrictive definition of governmental functions: they would support a higher level of socio-cultural and economic autonomy.

The better employed also distinguished themselves by their greater mistrust of the Chinese government, in spite of their overall higher level of political interest, political and administrative efficacy and political involvement. They were more fearful that their interests and life-style would be jeopardized under direct or indirect Communist rule.

Just as the more educated did, those higher up on the occupational ladder were more likely to see group-based methods as the most effective means to influence the government (see Table 5.16), but it was quite unlikely that they would make frequent resort to these methods or to employ them to restructure the existent system.

TABLE 5.16
Ways to Influence Government Policy by Occupation*
(in percent)

| Occupation | Writing to/ meeting with officials | Mobilizing people | Political parties/ organizations | No way | Total (N) |
|---|---|---|---|---|---|
| Professional | 27.3 | 42.9 | 19.5 | 6.5 | 96.2 (74) |
| Clerical | 20.8 | 42.7 | 22.9 | 8.3 | 94.7 (91) |
| Skilled | 26.0 | 26.5 | 18.8 | 17.1 | 88.4 (160) |
| Unskilled | 12.5 | 16.7 | 33.3 | 31.3 | 93.8 (45) |
| Housewife | 22.1 | 28.6 | 13.0 | 28.6 | 92.3 (71) |
| Unemployed | 18.1 | 34.7 | 12.5 | 18.1 | 83.4 (44) |

* Only the 4 most-picked answers are shown in the table. The $\chi^2$ for the full table is 82.34 (d.f. = 36), which is significant at 0.0001 level.

There was, overall, not much difference between those with more and those with less prestigious occupations in attitude toward political leaders. But the former were less given to the omnipotent view of political leadership. Nor would they simplistically equate competent political leadership with leadership in other fields (see Table 5.17). What is most surprising is that the better employed were more likely to look down upon the value of political activities, and this was particularly so in the case of the professionals. This finding might provide *prima facie* support for a view that in modernized Hong Kong the non-political spheres of activity have matured to such a point that politics, as a profession, is unable to enjoy a superior status among the more educated. This contrasts sharply with the situation in underdeveloped countries.

> Politics will in fact remain a major alternative open to the intellectuals for achievement and for absorption into a wider, no longer primordial collectivity as long as the underdeveloped societies remain underdeveloped. Only when they have become more differentiated occupationally, and when they have developed a sufficiently large and self-esteeming corps of professional intellectuals, carrying on the specifically intellectual professions with their own corporate traditions and corporate forms of organization, will the passionate sentiment and energy flow into channels other than the political.[1]

What is ironical about the situation in Hong Kong is that the differentiation of politics as one among many lines of activity is achieved not because Hong Kong has already had an autonomous political institution manned by career political professionals. The unattractiveness of politics to professionals, unfortunately, is due to the inaccessibility of meaningful political power, as they reckon it, both before and after 1997.

The attitude of the better employed toward pressure groups and their leaders was in the main no different from others except that they were less likely to see them as a threat to prosperity and stability. They were, however, as ready as the others to withhold support from them.

The relationship of occupation to legal orientations is complex. Occupation is strongly correlated with the sense of legal efficacy, only weakly with the sense of system foreignness, and not at all significantly related to sense of judicial justice. The better employed one was, the more legally efficacious one became. Professionals and white-collar workers fared better than blue-collar (skilled and unskilled) workers; housewives were the least legally efficacious. The same pattern holds with respect to sense of system foreignness, with

TABLE 5.17
Attitude toward Political Leaders by Occupation
(% who agreed or agreed very much)

| Statement | Occupation | | | | | | N |
|---|---|---|---|---|---|---|---|
| | Professional | Clerical | Skilled | Unskilled | Housewife | Unemployed | |
| 1. Most leaders have engaged in illicit activities.[a] | 61.4 | 66.7 | 63.8 | 65.3 | 47.5 | 56.1 | 303 |
| 2. Political activities respectable and meaningful.[b] | 42.1 | 50.0 | 57.9 | 75.0 | 78.9 | 76.0 | 326 |
| 3. Upright and competent leaders can resolve problems.[c] | 57.5 | 67.7 | 78.7 | 77.2 | 82.0 | 81.9 | 457 |
| 4. Those excelling in prestigeous occupation make good leaders.[d] | 29.1 | 23.8 | 38.5 | 45.7 | 41.3 | 59.4 | 96 |

a. $\chi^2 = 19.28$, d.f. = 18, $p > 0.05$
b. $\chi^2 = 53.02$, d.f. = 18, $p < 0.0001$
c. $\chi^2 = 50.00$, d.f. = 18, $p < 0.001$
d. $\chi^2 = 60.93$, d.f. = 18, $p < 0.0001$

the better employed more attached to the present legal system. Although no significant relationship was found between occupational status and sense of judicial justice in general, it is not the case when we go back to individual questions. There is some weak, but significant association between occupation on the one hand and views on fair trials and fair laws affecting oneself on the other. The better employed were more likely to find court trials and laws to be fair.

All in all, our examination of the socio-economic variables suggests that both generation (age) and class (occupation) in the weak sense did play a role in shaping the Hong Kong Chinese legal orientations. The younger generation, who were more likely to be locally born and better educated (and educated in a modern way), were less alienated from the imported legal system in cognitive, evaluative, and affective terms. Their parents, who were likely to be immigrants and less educated (and perhaps educated in the traditional way), tended to go to the other direction due to different socialization experiences.

The class factor should be interpreted with extra caution. It is a controversial topic as to whether there are subjectively conceived classes in Hong Kong at all. In our 1985 survey, the belief that the rich were better treated in judicial proceedings was widespread (73.4 percent of respondents). The difference between the white-collar/professional group and the blue-collar group in this respect was only about 10 percent. More significant was personal experience with the law. There were substantially more complaints from the blue-collar workers than from the while-collar/professional group. 52.1 percent of the former found unfair laws affecting themselves, as against only 36.1 percent of the latter group. Why? Is it possible that the better employed were beneficiaries of the law while their less fortunate brethren were not only less protected by the law, but also more likely to be the target of law enforcement agents? Unfortunately we cannot provide any answer at this stage.

Next to education, occupational status is also an important factor shaping people's legal opinions. As compared with white-collar workers, blue-collar workers were slightly more likely to favor *li* as the most important factor for social stability, more inclined toward the penal emphasis of the law, less supportive of the idea of inalienable right, and less tolerant of dishonest and unorthodox exercises of freedom of expression. Again surprisingly, it was the blue-collar workers who cared more about due process. Half of the unskilled workers (50 percent) who answered spoke against the admissibility of illegally obtained evidence, as compared to only 36.6 percent of professionals and 31.9 percent of clerical workers. All in all, it appears that those who were older, less educated and lower in occupational status tended to take a more rigid, black-and-white moral view, and the illegality of the evidence ran against the grain of their moral values.

The relationship between the ethos of the Hong Kong Chinese and income largely parallels that between it and occupation, though income in this connection is a less powerful explanatory variable.

There is a general understanding in the literature that the poor are somewhat more likely than the well-to-do to support economic changes in the redistributive direction but are more likely to be illiberal in their orientation toward politics. Lipset has put it eloquently,

> [t]he poorer strata everywhere are more liberal or leftist on economic issues; they favor more welfare state measures, higher wages, graduated income taxes, support of trade-unions, and so forth. But when liberalism is defined in non-economic terms—as support of civil liberties, internationalism, etc.—the correlation is reversed. The more well-to-do are more liberal, the poorer are more intolerant.[2]

The description of the political tendency of the poor in a Mexican city is a good example of this theory.

> [T]he lower class for rather obvious reasons has least allegiance both to the economic system and to conventional democratic rhetoric. Neither has served its members particularly well, and it is not inconsistent that although fearing some changes, they also at times articulate positions that imply other changes—especially those of obvious and immediate personal benefit.[3]

In Hong Kong, the contention that those with lower income are more redistributively oriented is basically true, though the orientation is far from very strong. The assertion that they are more politically illiberal is, according to the data available, far from an accurate observation.

In our 1985 survey, those with lower income were more likely to agree that a good society was one marked by economic egalitarianism. With this understanding, they were more likely to castigate the rich for using illicit means to make money; they tended more to call Hong Kong an inegalitarian society. Their more unfavorable image of the rich apparently also prompted them to urge the government to compel the rich to donate more to charity. Moreover, they were more likely to agree that the government should provide housing for all.

With regard to political attitude the findings are fascinating. On most of the items related to political values, there is no statistically significant difference between income groups. Those items that show differences, however, would make those with lower income look more politically liberal. Those lower in income were more likely to disagree that politics was dangerous, to disagree that political parties would make the existent political system better, to agree that elected leaders would perform better than the incumbent government, to regard political activities as meaningful and respectable. Probably because of their less favorable image of the Hong Kong government, they were less willing to allow the government to force people to do things against their wishes on the pretext of public interest. Ironically, however, their attitude toward the pressure groups was more negative than those with higher income. More of them regarded the pressure groups as a menace to the prosperity and stability of Hong Kong. The latter finding seems to confirm a similar observation in a Mexican city,

> [o]rdinary citizens withhold energy and resources, remaining at the periphery of politics and public affairs, while viewing ''agitators'' with substantial hostility because they are likely to disrupt the smooth flow of public life.[4]

## Hong Kong vs. Chinese Identities

In the beginning of Chapter 1, we mentioned that when asked to select their primary identity, 59.5 percent of the respondents identified themselves as Hongkongese, 36.2 percent as Chinese. The proportion of those opting for a Hong Kong identity is indeed striking, but an even larger percentage (67.9) agreed or strongly agreed with this statement: ''Hongkongese have a lot of common characteristics, these make it difficult for them to get along with the Chinese on the Mainland.'' Further, 86 percent of them agreed or strongly agreed that since they shared the same fate with their fellow Hongkongese, if others did not do well, neither would they. Last, but not least, 23.7 percent of respondents declared that they had a very strong, and 55.8 percent a strong, sense of belonging to Hong Kong. Overall, the sense of attachment to Hong Kong is tremendous among our respondents.

Those who claimed the Hong Kong identity were more likely to find it difficult to get along with the Mainland Chinese. We also found in our survey that 44.6 percent of respondents admitted that they would emigrate if they had the opportunity, while 48.5 percent would not do so. Ironically, it was those who claimed the Hong Kong identity who were more prepared to emigrate (52 percent) as compared to their Chinese counterparts (40.9 percent). This held too for those who professed not much or very little sense of belonging to Hong Kong (27.9 percent in contrast to 6.2 percent for those with the sense of belonging). Therefore, claiming a Hong Kong identity was not tantamount to having a strong sense of belonging to Hong Kong, and so it was not a powerful factor dampening the desire for emigration. To go a little bit further, what is startlingly absent in the Hong Kong identity is affective attachment to Hong Kong society. In a previous study one of us carried out, Hong Kong Chinese were found to regard their society instrumentally as a place to make a living or prosper.[5] This observation seemingly still stood as late as 1985, after all the political ordeals the Hong Kong Chinese had undergone in the intervening years.

Another issue involved in the Hong Kong/Chinese identities is the degree of identification with China in different senses. Table 5.18 provides some data for the discussion.

It can be gathered from Table 5.18 that in the ethno-cultural sense there was a strong sense of identification with China. It goes without saying that many of those who claimed a Hong Kong identity were also imbued with ethnic and cultural pride. Thus, 60.8 percent of respondents agreed or strongly agreed that Chinese culture was the finest culture on earth, and 78.6 percent felt proud to be Chinese. When attention was shifted to identification with the People's Republic and the Mainland Chinese, however, the level of identification dropped. Less than half of respondents (42.5 percent) were proud of the achievements of the People's Republic of China in the past several decades. Only slightly more than half (52.5 percent) of them felt close to the Chinese on the Mainland.

The 1997 shock has driven many Hong Kong Chinese to obtain foreign passports or the right of abode in foreign countries. Nevertheless, a substantial number of these people preferred to continue to stay and work in Hong Kong. It would be interesting to learn about the Hong Kong Chinese perception of their qualification to be the future political leaders of Hong Kong. In view of the queer mixture of ethnocentrism and anti-(Chinese) communism among the Hong Kong

TABLE 5.18
Identification with China
(in percent)

| Statement | Agree very much | Agree | Disagree | Disagree very much | Don't know/ No answer |
|---|---|---|---|---|---|
| 1. Chinese culture is the finest culture on earth. | 4.8 | 55.7 | 23.1 | 0.1 | 16.3 |
| 2. I am proud to be Chinese. | 6.5 | 72.1 | 12.8 | 0 | 8.6 |
| 3. I am proud of the achievements of the People's Republic of China in the past several decades. | 1.8 | 40.7 | 38.1 | 4.3 | 15.1 |
| 4. I feel close to the Chinese on the Mainland. | 2.2 | 50.3 | 37.4 | 2.7 | 7.2 |
| 5. Those holding foreign passports should not be the future political leaders of Hong Kong. | 4.2 | 36.0 | 38.6 | 1.7 | 19.6 |

Chinese, how would they react to those who apparently had "deserted" Hong Kong but whose rationale for doing so was also sympathetically understood? As seen in Table 5.18, the respondents were equally split on this issue. 40.2 percent agreed or strongly agreed that foreign passport holders should not be allowed to become Hong Kong's future political leaders, while 40.3 percent took the opposite view. It is noteworthy that 19.6 percent failed to give definite answers, thus attesting to the ambiguous and controversial nature of this newly-arisen issue. It is difficult to predict at the present moment in which direction public opinion will tip in the future, it is quite likely that the strengthening of local sentiments and the emergence of interest conflicts later on will engender more negative sentiments against foreign passport holders in Hong Kong.

In general, those claiming the Hongkongese identity were more disinclined to identify with China. They were less likely to be proud of being Chinese, to be proud of the achievements of the PRC, or to be affectively related to the Mainland Chinese.

The factor of identity is correlated with the socio-economic factors we have examined above, and age is the most relevant variable in this respect. The socialization process the older people have undergone has instilled in them stronger nationalistic feelings toward their motherland. This is amply demonstrated in Table 5.19.

The older people were less likely to consider themselves as Hongkongese, less likely to think that it would be difficult for Hongkongese to get along with the Mainland Chinese, more likely to agree that the fate of Hongkongese and Chinese was the same and less likely to take advantage of opportunities to emigrate. All the same, there is no statistically significant difference between age groups with respect to a sense of belonging to Hong Kong. Having a Chinese identity, therefore, is not incongruent with feeling a sense of belonging to Hong Kong.

The older people also more strongly identified with China. As can be seen in Table 5.20, they were more likely to be proud to be Chinese, to take pride in the achievements of the PRC, to feel close to the Mainland Chinese and to deny foreign passport holders the privilege of being Hong Kong's future political leaders. Nevertheless, there is no statistically significant difference between age groups with respect to the evaluation of Chinese culture.

Educational achievement is also closely related to identity. The more educated were more likely to claim a Hongkongese identity.

TABLE 5.19
Age Differences in Chinese/Hong Kong Identity
(in percent)

| Identity | Age | | | | | | N |
|---|---|---|---|---|---|---|---|
| | 20 or below | 21-30 | 31-40 | 41-50 | 51-60 | Above 60 | |
| 1. Considering oneself Hongkongese.[a] | 75.4 | 85.9 | 64.2 | 46.2 | 45.3 | 40.6 | 456 |
| 2. Thinking that it would be difficult for Hongkongese and Mainland Chinese to get along.*,[b] | 74.2 | 82.1 | 79.2 | 58.6 | 71.1 | 58.6 | 521 |
| 3. Agreeing that the fate of Hongkongese and Chinese is the same.[c] | 56.9 | 81.2 | 84.4 | 83.0 | 84.9 | 86.9 | 583 |
| 4. Saying that one will emigrate if there's the opportunity.[d] | 52.5 | 58.1 | 55.7 | 47.9 | 32.7 | 29.3 | 342 |
| 5. Feeling a sense of belonging to Hong Kong.[e] | 75.4 | 82.7 | 85.5 | 83.1 | 89.2 | 84.3 | 610 |

* % of those who agreed or agreed very much with the statement.
a. $\chi^2 = 95.20$, d.f. = 5, $p<0.01$
b. $\chi^2 = 44.04$, d.f. = 15, $p<0.01$
c. $\chi^2 = 38.64$, d.f. = 15, $p<0.01$
d. $\chi^2 = 34.43$, d.f. = 5, $p<0.01$
e. $\chi^2 = 15.90$, d.f. = 15, $p>0.05$

TABLE 5.20
Identification with China by Age
(in percent)

| Statement | Age | | | | | | N |
|---|---|---|---|---|---|---|---|
| | 20 or below | 21–30 | 31–40 | 41–50 | 51–60 | Above 60 | |
| 1. Agreeing that Chinese culture is finest.*,[a] | 72.9 | 71.1 | 74.1 | 71.3 | 74.7 | 70.1 | 464 |
| 2. Proud to be a Chinese.*,[b] | 82.7 | 78.2 | 90.2 | 86.4 | 90.4 | 91.0 | 603 |
| 3. Proud of the achievements of the PRC*,[c] | 32.7 | 29.1 | 51.7 | 66.0 | 61.9 | 72.6 | 326 |
| 4. Feeling close to the Mainland Chinese.*,[d] | 38.3 | 34.0 | 53.7 | 70.7 | 75.7 | 81.1 | 404 |
| 5. Denying foreign passport holders future political leadership.*,[e] | 36.7 | 48.9 | 50.4 | 53.9 | 59.2 | 46.7 | 308 |

* Combining those who agreed or agreed very much with the statement.
a. $\chi^2 = 6.72$, d.f. = 9, $p > 0.05$
b. $\chi^2 = 20.70$, d.f. = 10, $p < 0.05$
c. $\chi^2 = 86.86$, d.f. = 15, $p < 0.01$
d. $\chi^2 = 108.52$, d.f. = 15, $p < 0.01$
e. $\chi^2 = 31.58$, d.f. = 15, $p < 0.01$

They were more likely to emigrate if there was the opportunity, and had a weaker sense of belonging to Hong Kong.

As expected, the more educated people had a lower level of identification with China. They were less likely to be proud of being Chinese, less likely to be proud of the achievements of the PRC, and less likely to have affective attachment to the Mainland Chinese.

By the same token, the Hongkongese identity was adopted by a larger proportion of those with higher occupational status. They were also slightly less prone to think that they shared the same fate with others in Hong Kong. Moreover, they were more prepared to emigrate given the opportunity.

Those with higher occupational status also had less conspicuous identification with China. They were less likely to be proud of the achievements of the PRC, or to feel close to the Mainland Chinese.

In a similar vein, those with higher income were more likely to claim the Hongkongese identity, or to emigrate if given the opportunity.

Gender is also of importance in identity orientation. 67.3 percent of females called themselves Hongkongese, while only 58.8 percent of males did so.

As an explanatory variable, the factor of identity is by and large irrelevant in personal, social, economic and legal values. But it is of enormous importance in political values. Graphically put, the factor of identity acts like a wedge dividing the Hong Kong Chinese clearly into two groups with different political sub-cultures. This is captured in Table 5.21.

As those who claimed a Hong Kong identity were younger in age, more educated and higher in occupational status, it was quite natural for them to show a more modern political outlook. On balance, they had a less instrumental conception of government. They were more trustful of the Hong Kong government and less so for the Chinese government. They had a less interventionist view of governmental functions, particularly in the realms of public and private moralities. They were less likely to blame the government for social problems and were slightly more inclined to lay the responsibility for their solution on society itself. They showed greater political interests and a higher level of political involvement. The differences between those with the Hong Kong identity and those with the Chinese one, however, were not so great as to produce two conflicting sub-cultures in Hong Kong. It is quite likely that, in the long run, the more modern outlook will prevail over the less modern one as the older generation

TABLE 5.21
Correlates of Hong Kong/China Identity
(in percent)

| Statement | Identity: Hong Kong | China | $\chi^2$ | d.f. | p |
|---|---|---|---|---|---|
| 1. Managing government same as managing a business.[1] | 41.3 | 51.7 | 9.64 | 3 | 0.02 |
| 2. Government should be pragmatic rather than idealistic.[1] | 77.3 | 86.0 | 10.06 | 3 | 0.02 |
| 3. Government cares solely for the rich.[1] | 45.7 | 58.0 | 9.75 | 3 | 0.02 |
| 4. Great or very great trust in Hong Kong government. | 87.1 | 78.9 | 10.09 | 3 | 0.02 |
| 5. Great or very great trust in Chinese government. | 32.4 | 57.3 | 35.02 | 3 | 0.00 |
| 6. Government should punish the unfilial.[1] | 76.6 | 83.8 | 8.32 | 3 | 0.04 |
| 7. Government should deter divorce.[1] | 21.4 | 33.7 | 13.02 | 3 | 0.00 |
| 8. Social problems caused by the fault of government.[1] | 28.5 | 42.6 | 14.70 | 3 | 0.00 |
| 9. Government primarily responsible for solving social problems.[1] | 92.1 | 96.6 | 13.18 | 2 | 0.00 |
| 10. Government should force the rich to donate to charity.[1] | 37.6 | 47.3 | 13.76 | 3 | 0.00 |
| 11. Government should find jobs for everyone.[1] | 75.6 | 85.2 | 10.34 | 3 | 0.02 |
| 12. Defining democratic government as consultative government.[2] | 55.1 | 44.6 | 14.26 | 5 | 0.01 |
| 13. PRC will allow the people of Hong Kong to govern Hong Kong. | 25.9 | 48.0 | 23.45 | 1 | 0.00 |
| 14. Often or very often discuss public affairs with friends. | 50.1 | 32.0 | 24.30 | 3 | 0.00 |

TABLE 5.21 (Continued)

| Statement | Identity: Hong Kong | China | $\chi^2$ | d.f. | p |
|---|---|---|---|---|---|
| 15. Often or very often discuss public affairs with the knowledgeable. | 39.7 | 31.2 | 11.81 | 3 | 0.01 |
| 16. Officials take my view seriously.[3] | 9.4 | 14.9 | 7.61 | 2 | 0.02 |
| 17. Expect fair treatment from government. | 71.7 | 62.3 | 4.93 | 1 | 0.02 |

1. Percentage agreeing or strongly agreeing.
2. The percentages of respondents claiming Hong Kong or Chinese identities who defined democratic government as elective government are 22.3 and 35.7 respectively.
3. The percentages of respondents claiming Hong Kong or Chinese identities who said that he/she would be ignored by officials are 20.1 and 25.1 respectively.

passes away, though it is not certain whether popular trust in the Chinese government will deteriorate.

There are, however, two seemingly peculiar findings. A larger proportion of those claiming the Hong Kong identity (55.1 percent) defined democratic government as consultative government than those claiming the Chinese identity (44.6 percent). This might be due to the more "anti-colonial" and nationalistic orientation of the older in age and the *status quo* orientation of the more educated.

Though Hong Kong Chinese as a whole did not expect officials to consider their views seriously, those with the Chinese identity were more likely to have this expectation. The only explanation we can come up with, and we think it is plausible, is that the older people, who were also less educated, had lower expectations in their encounters with officials and thus they could be satisfied with less difficulty.

## Conclusion

In this chapter we have examined the way different socio-economic groups differ in their ethos. The fact that these differences are manifest and in many cases statistically significant indicates the rapidity of social change in Hong Kong in the post-war era. New values had made their entry, but without tremendously displacing old values. Consequently, the old and the new not only found a place in different groups, but also co-existed within these groups or even within individuals. The salience of the demarcation between "Hongkongese" and "Chinese" also attests to the rise of localism or provincialism among an increasing number of Hong Kong Chinese. The increasing contacts between China and Hong Kong and the 1997 question have ineluctably intensified, and will continue to intensify, this identity differentiation. As identity is particularly pertinent to political values, it will inevitably have significant reverberations for future political changes in Hong Kong.

# 6

# Conclusion

Colonial rule, the self-select character of the Chinese immigrants, modernization and separation from mainstream development on the Mainland have together molded a distinctive ethos among the Hong Kong Chinese. This ethos represents a constellation of elements with disparate origins: Chinese tradition, Western modernizing influences and local developments. The abstinence from "thought engineering" on the part of the colonial government as well as its lack of capability to do so, mean that value changes in Hong Kong are essentially spontaneous. What is more significant is that some of the changes that have come about have not been undergirded by supportive institutional changes, but are largely the product of changing conventions or practices.

Simply put, the authoritarian social-political order of Hong Kong differs from its more extreme counterpart in China in several respects:

(1) There is a higher level of social or interpersonal trust in the general sense in Hong Kong. More emphasis is placed on personal freedom and civil liberties. A somewhat higher level of social and political tolerance is also evident.

(2) Though social harmony is still highly cherished, Hong Kong Chinese are more tolerant of social conflict. Attachment to traditional ties is weaker, so are feelings of fatalism. There is less emphasis on social egalitarianism, and, correspondingly, demands for social levelling are faint. Overall, the Hong Kong Chinese take an optimistic view of social development, even though this has been qualified by their pessimistic reception of the 1997 challenge.

(3) In the economic sphere, Hong Kong Chinese have fully endorsed the capitalist system with its trappings of market superiority, individual competition, sacredness of private property and "positive non-interventionism." In their mind, the economy is clearly differentiated from the polity. Economic inegalitarianism is accepted as the natural state of affairs, and political power is not supposed to interfere with it. This contrasts starkly with the subordination of economics to politics in China, and the economy's endemic vulnerability to the harassment of political imperatives.

(4) Perhaps the most significant finding in our study is the changed conception of politics and government by the Hong Kong Chinese. Many of the traditional political values have been retained, such as the hierarchical ordering of political roles, the primordial function of political authority to maintain social order and dependence on governmental authority for both public and private problem-solving. However, the less-than-given authority of the colonial regime, its limited functions and the changing political experience of the Hong Kong Chinese have jointly worked to produce changes in these traditional political values. Admittedly, political interests and political involvement are still low, and the sense of political powerlessness is strong, but Hong Kong Chinese are now less fearful of the government and even expect fair treatment from it. There is not much affective feeling for the colonial regime, but it is not mistrusted either. In fact, the hitherto good performance of the government has not failed to impress the Hong Kong Chinese. Compared to both traditional and modern Chinese, the political experience of the Hong Kong Chinese must be more gratifying, as they now hold more favorable attitudes toward politics in general, and political leaders in particular.

All these changes are significant in their own right, but what is most "revolutionary" is the changed conception of state (government)-society relationships. In China, state and society are rigidly defined and separated and the political power wielded by the state is not subject to societal constraints. In other words, the jurisdiction or scope of political action is unlimited, and societal forces are not powerful enough to withstand the arbitrary encroachment of the government. In the authoritarian social-political order of Hong Kong, there is no institutional structure to safeguard social autonomy or to bring the state under social control. Theoretically speaking, the only autonomous institution in Hong Kong is the colonial government, whose monopolization of unchecked political power should enable it to subjugate all social sectors. In reality, however, the limited political power at the disposal of the government, its profession of limited governance, the less-than-given nature of its authority, and the need to depend on the initiative of the people to develop Hong Kong both economically and socially caution it against involvement in social and economic affairs. The *de facto* restriction of the scope and functions of political power has enabled the Hong Kong Chinese to enjoy and exercise an amount of social-economic freedom unheard of for Chinese in traditional or modern China.

Though the limited government of Hong Kong is more the result of ruling ideology and habitual practice than the product of constitutional or institutional prescriptions, the fact that it has been in existence for such a long time is enough to mold popular expectations. Accordingly, a constellation of proto-democratic values can be found in the ethos of the Hong Kong Chinese. As Hong Kong has been, and still is, a minimally-integrated social-political system, the thrust of these values is not to integrate polity and society by instituting a socially-dominated political order in which society dominates the polity through democratic reforms and the ''capturing'' of the state by the people's elected representatives. If control of the government by the people represents a ''positive'' democratic value, then the proto-democratic values of the Hong Kong Chinese tend toward the negative direction. Instead of trying to subjugate the polity by society, they aim at circumscribing the jurisdiction of political power so that social and economic autonomy can result. The government is allowed to dominate the political field, and is expected to intervene in the sphere of public morality with the consent of the governed. Private moralities, the economy and the legal system should not be subject to political manipulation or intrusion. Such constriction of the jurisdiction of the polity also requires a changed understanding of the relationship between public interest and the state; the alien nature of the colonial regime in fact facilitates this change. By disentangling the colonial government from public interest, the distinction between the public and the private becomes blurred. As such, public interests can be served both by the government and private groups or individuals, while the government itself also pursues its own self-interests. Through such a twist in thinking, the legitimacy of the government as the only custodian of public good suffers. However, the legitimacy of private interests is given a boost. Because the state cannot claim omnipotence, and omnipresence, based on its ostensible claim as the only representative of public interest, the circumscription of the jurisdiction and power of the polity can be legitimated. Nevertheless, since the Hong Kong Chinese still expect the government to act as the guardian of public moral virtues, the intervention of the state in the social sector is less resisted than in the economy, the legal system and the realm of private moralities.

(5) The highly autonomous judiciary of Hong Kong and the central role of the legal system in society have, to a fairly large extent, endeared the law to the Hong Kong Chinese. They have learnt to substantially differentiate the legal system from the political system and to respect the integrity and value of law. Nevertheless, many of the Hong Kong Chinese still approach law in an instrumental manner, placing more stress on its regulative and stabilizing functions than on its role in upholding justice, the latter term being not quite well-understood. An emphasis on the utility of law inevitably makes its reception by the people contingent upon its performance: positive judgment of the legal system by the Hong Kong Chinese is closely related to satisfaction with one's life, with society and with the government. Thus, there is a limit to the autonomy of the law in the ethos of the Hong Kong Chinese.

It is quite common for mass belief systems to have embedded in them contradictions that would, under certain conditions and in certain times, become uncontainable. In the United States, for example, the largely dormant contradiction between the values of political equality (democracy) and economic inequality (justified by liberalism and capitalism) is a case in point. Recently, this contradiction has become sufficiently manifest so as to threaten the legitimacy of the American democracy.[1] On the whole, at least on the level of values, contradictions in the ethos of the Hong Kong Chinese are minimal. Up to the present moment, relationships within the political, economic and social sectors are all conceived hierarchically. Inegalitarianism is treated as natural, and there are only faint calls for social, economic or political equality. The inaccessibility of ultimate political power arguably creates a status inconsistency between political status on the one hand, and social-economic status on the other. Localization of the civil service, and the preparedness of the colonial government to consult public opinion, have mitigated the frustrations thus generated and moderately assuaged hurt political feelings. The success attained by the consultative process can be evidenced by the general tendency of the governed to equate consultative government with democratic government and their reluctance to contemplate drastic political changes.

Political scientists in the West have long been intrigued by the lack of correlation between economic development and political participation (or democratization) in the Four Little Tigers in East Asia. The experience of these four newly industrializing countries (although Hong Kong is by no means a country) has even forced them to revise their accustomed understanding of the relationship between economic and political development. Myron Weiner, for example, expressed this new-found revision in the following terms:

> The denial of opportunities for popular political participation has, surprisingly, been less a source of political instability than one might have expected. The proposition that modernization would lead to increased demands for political participation that, if repressed and blocked, would lead to large-scale opposition, extremist movements, and revolutionary upheavals has not been proven by events of the last two decades. Indeed, one of the surprising developments in East Asia is that such high levels of modernization have taken place with relatively low levels of mass political participation.[2]

Another student of development, Peter Berger, even phrased the following law-like proposition: "The East Asian evidence provides weak support for the thesis that successful capitalist development generates pressures toward democracy."[3] Arguably, later developments might render these observations anachronistic, but, as of now, they apparently are not vulnerable to refutation.

Political stability in Hong Kong and the other Little Tigers has so far been maintained by authoritarian governments, and it is of essential importance to their success in industrialization. Coercion is not alone responsible for political stability and weak demands for political change. In Hong Kong, the tranquillity of the political scene is owing to many idiosyncratic factors specific to Hong Kong,[4] but the nature of the ethos of the people obviously plays a crucial part. The "negative" proto-democratic values of the Hong Kong Chinese, which set out to distance the polity from society instead of calling for control of the polity by society through democratic participation, function, in fact, to dampen political aspirations and to depoliticize society. That these values present serious obstacles to those who campaign for democracy can be evidenced by the inability of the 1997-induced democratic movement in Hong Kong to grow beyond the fledging stage.

The advocacy of paternalistic state intervention in the realm of public morality and the obligatory welfare functions of the government, both conspicuous features in the ethos of the Hong Kong Chinese, are in latent contradiction to the intolerance of economic intervention by the state. The contradiction has remained latent heretofore because of continued economic prosperity and the resilience of the family and kinship systems of the Hong Kong Chinese. Inevitably, however, the contradiction will become more explicit with a decline in Hong Kong's economic fortunes, incessantly rising aspirations of the people, increased political participation, an increase in "class awareness" and further erosion of the primary groups. By then the Hong Kong Chinese will be confronted with a very difficult choice between a paternalistic interventionist government and the preservation of an economy basically free from state interference.

This brings us to a more taxing issue. Relatively speaking, the legal system's autonomy from the state has been institutionally secured, but that cannot be said for the autonomy of the social and economic systems. The widespread apprehension stemming from the 1997 question owes its origin primarily to the popularly perceived vulnerability of the social and economic spheres to political intrusion, and, to a lesser extent, this applies to the legal system despite all the institutional guarantees already in place. The modest appeal of the democratic movement is, to a certain extent, also rooted in this gap between the values of the Hong Kong Chinese and the existent institutional structure. The Basic Law, the mini-constitution of post-1997 Hong Kong to be promulgated by China in 1990, seeks to enshrine the autonomy of the legal, social and economic institutions in constitutional provisions. Nevertheless, as ultimate political power in Hong Kong resides in the hands of China, which has the right to interpret and revise the Basic Law, these constitutional guarantees can only be partial and their effectiveness inevitably varies with the trustworthiness of the Chinese government in the eyes of the Hong Kong Chinese.

It is always hazardous to venture into predicting future developments. Within the next decade, the numerical dominance of those who identify with Hong Kong will be complete, unless increasing contacts between Hong Kong and China and the latter's patriotic appeal can manage to turn back the tide. The impact of this trend on the relationship between the state and other sectors hinges upon two conflicting effects. On the one hand, more Hong Kong Chinese will take a restrictive, and hence less interventionist view, of government. This trend might be reinforced by their aversion to Communist China's proclivity towards subjecting almost everything to political domination. Accordingly, they would increasingly espouse autonomy for the legal, social and economic spheres. On the other hand, there is an unstoppable tendency for a modern government to be more active socially and economically, which would definitely weaken the autonomy of the economy. In the case of the social sphere, the persistent paternalistic appeals even from the "modern" Hongkongese, if extended, would also weaken their will to resist intervention from the state. On balance, it should be reasonable to expect more integration of the political and socio-economic sectors. If this is the inevitable scenario, the "negative" proto-democratic precepts of the Hong Kong Chinese might become increasingly irrelevant. A more "positive" proto-democratic stance has to be adopted to seek a higher level of democratic control of the government.

# Notes to Chapter 1

1. For a detailed description of the 1985 and 1986 questionnaire surveys, see Appendix. Unless otherwise noted, the data and findings presented in the book are based on the 1985 survey.
2. Donald J. Munro, *The Concept of Man in Early China* (Stanford: Stanford University Press, 1969), p. 23.
3. Tang Tsou, "Twentieth-Century Chinese Politics and Western Political Science," *Political Science*, Vol. XX, No. 2 (Spring 1987), p. 328.
4. John C. H. Wu, "Chinese Legal and Political Philosophy," in *The Chinese Mind*, Charles A. Moore, ed. (Honolulu: University of Hawaii Press, 1968), p. 213.
5. Andrew J. Nathan, *Chinese Democracy* (Berkeley: University of California Press, 1985), p. 114.
6. When a society develops through assimilation and outside influence is always subordinated to existing values and myths, unity is not *achieved*. Rather, it is assumed as a natural state that can be only temporarily interrupted by conflict. Since unity is natural rather than contrived, it reconstitutes itself upon cessation of hostilities whether or not basic issues are resolved. It can even result from the outward denial that any conflict exists, as when disputes are ended through conciliation (forgiving) rather than a rationally negotiated settlement. See J. Victor Koschmann, "Soft Rule and Expressive Protest," in *Authority and the Individual in Japan*, J. Victor Koschmann, ed. (Tokyo: University of Tokyo Press, 1978), p. 5 and pp. 14-15.

   Even though China had experienced a "feudal" age before being unified into a centralized bureaucratic empire under the Qin dynasty, "feudal China" was more politically centralized than is generally understood. See Herrlee G. Creel, *The Origins of Statecraft in China*, Vol. I (Chicago: University of Chicago Press, 1970).
7. See, for example, Hsiao Kung-chuan, *Rural China: Imperial Control in the Nineteenth Century* (Seattle: University of Washington Press, 1960).
8. Joseph Fewsmith, *Party, State, and Local Elites in Republican China: Merchant Organizations and Politics in Shanghai, 1890-1930* (Honolulu: University of Hawaii Press, 1985), pp. 19-20. See also his "From Guild to Interest Group: The Transformation of Public and Private in Late Qing China," *Comparative Studies in Society and History*, Vol. 25, No. 4 (October 1983), pp. 617-40.
9. Fewsmith, "From Guild to Interest Group," p. 626.
10. Jack Gray, "China: Communism and Confucianism," in *Political Culture and Political Change in Communist States*, Archie Brown and Jack Gray, eds. (London: Macmillan, 1979), pp. 202-203.
11. Simon de Beaufort, *Yellow Earth, Green Jade: Constants in Chinese Political*

*Mores* (Cambridge, Mass.: Center for International Affairs, Harvard University, 1978), pp. 19-20.

12. Lucian Pye, *Asian Power and Politics: The Cultural Dimensions of Authority* (Cambridge, Mass.: Harvard University Press, 1985), pp. 27-28. As a matter of fact, in most Asian cultures leaders are expected to be nurturing, benevolent, kind, and sympathetic figures who inspire commitment and dedication.
13. See Lucian W. Pye, *The Spirit of Chinese Politics: A Psychocultural Study of the Authority Crisis in Political Development* (Cambridge, Mass.: M.I.T. Press, 1968); and Richard H. Solomon, *Mao's Revolution and the Chinese Political Culture* (Berkeley: University of California Press, 1971).
14. Francis L. K. Hsu, *Americans and Chinese: Passage to Differences*, 3rd ed. (Honolulu: The University Press of Hawaii, 1981), p. 205.
15. Wang Liu Hui-chen, *The Traditional Chinese Clan Rules* (New York: J. J. Augustin, 1959).
16. Maurice Freedman, *Lineage Organization in Southeastern China* (London: University of London Press, 1958), p. 125.
17. See, for example, Chang Chung-li, *The Chinese Gentry* (Seattle: University of Washington Press, 1955), Fei Hsiao-tung, *China's Gentry* (Chicago: University of Chicago Press, 1953), and Hosea B. Morse, *The Gilds of China* (London: Longman's, 1909).
18. Charles O. Hucker, *The Censorial System of Ming China* (Stanford: Stanford University Press, 1966), and Ch'ien Mu, *Traditional Government in Imperial China* (Hong Kong: The Chinese University Press, 1982).
19. Hsu, *Americans and Chinese*, p. 226.
20. Harry Eckstein, *Divison and Cohesion in Democracy: A Study of Norway* (Princeton: Princeton University Press, 1966), p. 134.
21. Koschmann, "Soft Rule and Expressive Protest," pp. 6-7.
22. Robert J. Smith, *Japanese Society: Tradition, Self and the Social Order* (Cambridge: Cambridge University Press, 1983), pp. 12-13.
23. Hsu, *Americans and Chinese*, p. 234.
24. The conditional legitimacy of authority was well expressed in Mencius' theory of the importance of the people (*min gui lun* 民貴論). Mencius believed that the ultimate sovereignty lay with the people. Therefore, the people could indicate the choice of a successor by resisting or accepting him, not solely in times of dynastic changeover, but also in ordinary times, the major policies of government should reflect popular opinion. In addition, Mencius, in placing authority with the people, thereby recognized that the government had the absolute duty of nourishing the people and maintaining peace and stability, while the people did not have any absolute duty of obedience to the government. If the government should fail in its responsibilities, then the people need not be loyal to it. See Hsiao Kung-chuan, *A History of Chinese Political Thought* (Princeton: Princeton University Press, 1979), Vol. 1, pp. 158-59.
25. See S. van der Sprenkel, *Legal Institutions in Manchu China: A Sociological Analysis* (London: Athlone Press 1977), pp. 66-79; and Derk Bodde and Clarence

Morris, *Law in Imperial China* (Philadelphia: University of Pennsylvania Press, 1967).

26. *Cf.* Bong Duck Chun *et al.*, *Traditional Korean Legal Attitudes* (Berkeley: Institute of East Asian Studies, University of California, 1980), and William Shaw, *Legal Norms in a Confucian State* (Berkeley: Institute of East Asian Studies, University of California, 1981).
27. In the Confucian tradition, morality was particularistic. One's moral obligations to others were defined by their positions within one's network of personal affiliations. The moral duties and obligations of a particular individual depended on the situation at hand, which would determine the particular set of social relationships in which that individual was enmeshed. The concept of generalized universal moral duties based on the equality of man was poorly developed in traditional China, and in other Confucian societies, for example, Japan. See Smith, *Japanese Society*, pp. 47-49 and Frank K. Upham, *Law and Social Change in Postwar Japan* (Cambridge: Harvard University Press, 1987), pp. 16-27.
28. See Mark Elvin, *The Pattern of the Chinese Past* (London: Eyre Methuen, 1973), pp. 268-316; *Zhongguo ziben zhuyi de mengya* 中國資本主義的萌芽 (The sprouting of Chinese capitalism), Xu Dixin and Wu Chengming, eds. (Beijing: Renmin chubanshe, 1985); Yu Yingshi (Yu Ying-shih), *Zhongguo jinshi zongjiao lunli yu shangren jingshen* 中國近世宗教倫理與商人精神 (Religion, ethics and the spirit of the merchants in late imperial China) (Taibei: Lianjing chuban shiye gongsi, 1987), and Thomas A. Metzger, "The State and Commerce in Imperial China," *Asian and African Studies*, Vol. 6 (1970), pp. 23-46.
29. Gilbert Rozman *et al.*, *The Modernization of China* (New York: The Free Press, 1981), pp. 107-108.
30. *Ibid*, p. 139.
31. George M. Foster, "Peasant Society and the Image of Limited Good," in *Peasant Society: A Reader*, Jack M. Potter *et al.*, eds. (Boston: Little, Brown and Co., 1967), pp. 300-23; Edward C. Banfield, *The Moral Basis of a Backward Society* (New York: The Free Press, 1958); and James C. Scott, *The Moral Economy of the Peasant: Rebellion and Subsistence in Southeast Asia* (New Haven: Yale University Press, 1976).
32. Pye, *Asian Power and Politics*, p. 49.
33. Hsiao, *A History of Chinese Political Thought*, p. 109.
34. See Fu Zhufu, *Zhongguo jingjishi luncong* 中國經濟史論叢 (Discussions on Chinese economic history) (Beijing: Remin chubanshe, 1985); and Zeng Zhaoxiang, *Zhongguo fengjian shehui de qingshang zhengce he yishang zhengce* 中國封建社會的輕商政策和抑商政策 (Policies to disparage and harness merchants in Chinese feudal society) (Beijing: Zhongguo shangye chubanshe, 1983).
35. See for example John K. Fairbank, *The Great Chinese Revolution: 1800-1985* (New York: Harper and Row, 1986).
36. Lau Siu-kai, *Society and Politics in Hong Kong* (Hong Kong: The Chinese University Press, 1982); "Social Change, Bureaucratic Rule, and Emergent Issues in Hong Kong," *World Politics*, Vol. XXXV, No. 4 (July 1983), pp. 544-62; *Decolonization Without Independence: The Unfinished Political Reforms of the*

*Hong Kong Government* (Hong Kong: Centre for Hong Kong Studies, The Chinese University of Hong Kong, 1987); and Lau Siu-kai and Kuan Hsin-chi, "Hong Kong After the Sino-British Agreement: The Limits to Change," *Pacific Affairs*, Vol. 59, No. 2 (Summer 1986), pp. 214-36.

37. Brian Hook, "The Government of Hong Kong: Change Within Tradition," *The China Quarterly*, No. 95 (September 1983), pp. 491-511.
38. Lau, *Society and Politics*, pp. 157-82.
39. *Ibid.*, pp. 121-56.
40. Lau Siu-kai, "The Government, Intermediate Organizations, and Grassroots Politics in Hong Kong," *Asian Survey*, Vol. 21, No.8 (August 1981), pp. 865-84; and Lau, "Social Change, Bureaucratic Rule," pp. 544-62
41. Leung Sai-wing, *Perception of Political Authority by the Hong Kong Chinese* (Hong Kong: Centre for Hong Kong Studies, The Chinese University of Hong Kong, 1986).
42. Alexander Gerschenkron, *Economic Backwardness in Historical Perspective* (New York: Frederick A. Praeger, 1962), pp. 5-33.
43. For example, in 1977 the government formed the Hong Kong Industrial Estates Corporation to develop unused properties and supply infrastructure to investing businesses that met certain criteria. The establishment of the Hong Kong Productivity Centre in 1967 was designed to supply a "one-stop" service for both local and foreign investors. In 1980 an industrial development board was formed to coordinate industrial policies. In the mid-1980s, there was increased regulation of the banking sector and the financial markets. In order to maintain confidence in Hong Kong as a financial center, the government was even forced to take over several bankrupt banks.
44. Stephen Haggard and Cheng Tun-jen, "State and Foreign Capital in the East Asian NICs," in *The Political Economy of the New Asian Industrialism*, Frederic C. Deyo, ed. (Ithaca: Cornell University Press, 1987), p. 107.
45. *Ibid.*, pp. 107-108
46. Frederic C. Deyo, "State and Labor: Modes of Political Exclusion in East Asian Development," in *The Political Economy*, p. 187.
47. *Ibid.*, p. 195.
48. *Hong Kong Annual Digest of Statistics: 1986 Edition* (Hong Kong: Census and Statistics Department, 1986), p. 32.
49. Carl J. Friedrich, Constitutional Government and Democracy, 4th ed. (Calcutta: Oxford & IBH Publishing Co., 1968), p. 105.
50. *Ibid.*, p. 110
51. *Ibid.*, p. 111-12.
52. John Griffiths, "The Constitution of Hong Kong: The Hub of the Wheel of State," in *Hong Kong 1983* (Hong Kong: Government Information Services, 1983), p. 8.
53. *Ibid.*, pp. 8-9.
54. Rupert Emerson, *From Empire to Nation: The Rise to Self-Assertion of Asian and African Peoples* (Cambridge, Mass.: Harvard University Press, 1960), p. 230.
55. See Lau Siu-kai and Kuan Hsin-chi, "Hong Kong After the Sino-British

Agreement''; and Lau Siu-kai, *Decolonization Without Independence.*
56. Emerson, *From Empire to Nation*, p. 235.
57. See for example Alex Inkeles and David H. Smith, *Becoming Modern: Individual Change in Six Developing Countries* (Cambridge, Mass.: Harvard University Press, 1974), and Alex Inkeles, *Exploring Individual Modernity* (New York: Columbia University Press, 1983).
58. Lau Siu-kai, *Society and Politics in Hong Kong*, pp. 174-76.
59. Carl T. Smith, *Chinese Christians: Elites, Middlemen, and the Church in Hong Kong* (Hong Kong: Oxford University Press, 1985), p. 10.
60. Lucy Cheung Tsui-ping, *The Opium Monopoly in Hong Kong 1844-1887* (Unpublished M. Phil. Thesis, University of Hong Kong, 1986).
61. Smith, *Chinese Christians*, p. 139.
62. Richard E. Barrett and Soomi Chin, ''Export-oriented Industrializing States in the Capitalist World System: Similarities and Differences,'' in *The Political Economy of the New Asian Industrialism*, p. 29.
63. Irving L. Horowitz, ''Personality and Structural Dimensions in Comparative International Development,'' *Social Science Quarterly*, Vol. 51, No. 3 (1970), pp. 494-513.
64. Lau Siu-kai, ''Social Change, Bureaucratic Rule, and Emergent Political Issues in Hong Kong."
65. Lau Siu-kai and Kuan Hsin-chi, ''The Changing Political Culture of the Hong Kong Chinese,'' in *Hong Kong in Transition*, Joseph Y. S. Cheng, ed. (Hong Kong: Oxford University Press, 1986), pp. 26-51.
66. Richard Hughes, *Borrowed Place, Borrowed Time: Hong Kong and Its Many Faces* (London: Andre Deutsch, 1976).

# Notes to Chapter 2

1. Steven Lukes, *Individualism* (Oxford: Basil Blackwell, 1973), and Nicholas Abercrombie *et al.*, *Sovereign Individuals of Capitalism* (London: Allen & Unwin, 1986), pp. 80-83.
2. Abercrombie *et al.*, *Sovereign Individuals*, p. 78.
3. *Ibid.*, pp. 50-51.
4. George M. Foster, "Peasant Society and the Image of Limited Good," in *Peasant Society: A Reader*, Jack M. Potter, *et al.* eds. (Boston: Little, Brown and Co., 1967), pp. 300-23; James C. Scott, *Political Ideology in Malaysia: Reality and the Beliefs of an Elite* (New Haven: Yale University Press, 1968), pp. 91-117, and *The Moral Economy of the Peasant: Rebellion and Subsistence in Southeast Asia* (New Haven: Yale University Press, 1976); and Edward C. Banfield, *The Moral Basis of a Backward Society* (New York: The Free Press, 1958).
5. See, for example, Hu Hsien-chin, *The Common Descent Group in China and Its Functions* (New York: Viking, 1948); Marion J. Levy, Jr., *The Family Revolution in Modern China* (Cambridge, Mass.: Harvard University Press, 1949); Arthur H. Smith, *Village Life in China* (Boston: Little, Brown and Co., 1970) and *Chinese Characteristics* (Singapore: Graham Brash, 1986).
6. Compared to other non-industrial societies, traditional China was more "advanced." Traditional Chinese hence had more exposure to outsiders as the market town was an integral part of rural life in the more developed areas of China. See G. William Skinner, "Marketing and Social Structure in Rural China," *Journal of Asian Studies*, Vol. 24 (1964-65), pp. 3-43.
7. Donald J. Munro, *The Concept of Man in Early China*, p. 12.
8. *Ibid.*, p. 15.
9. Alex Inkeles and David H. Smith, *Becoming Modern: Individual Change in Six Developing Countries* , p. 23.
10. Gabriel A. Almond and Sidney Verba, *The Civic Culture: Political Attitudes and Democracy in Five Nations* (Princeton: Princeton University Press, 1963), p. 267.
11. Hsieh Yu-wei, "The Status of the Individual in Chinese Ethics," in *The Chinese Mind*, Charles A. Moore, ed. (Honolulu: The University Press of Hawaii, 1968), p. 310.
12. Munro, *The Concept of Man in Early China*, p. 48.
13. In the West, particularly in the Atlantic community, the idea of freedom is intimately related to the idea of the rights of individual persons. In its fully developed forms this process comprehended three kinds of rights: freedom of the spirit, which included the right to hold and communicate beliefs and opinions; material liberties, which included rights of free economic initiative and exchange, of social mobility and juridical security; and, finally, the broad distribution of

political powers which conferred control over public institutions upon representative sections of the governed. The lasting social achievement of nineteenth century Europe was the reorganization of law and politics which produced in public institutions an operative respect for the rights of individual persons. (See Leonard Krieger, *The German Idea of Freedom: History of a Political Tradition* [Chicago: University of Chicago Press, 1957], p. 3.) The idea of freedom was poorly developed in traditional and even in modern China. What little knowledge we have about freedom in China seems to indicate an idea of freedom in the negative sense of "freedom" from political (governmental) control, harassment or persecution. The idea of freedom, moreover, is rarely associated with the idea of individual or personal rights, which, again, are underdeveloped concepts in China.

14. Richard Madsen, *Morality and Power in a Chinese Village* (Berkeley: University of California Press, 1984), pp. 54-55.
15. *Ibid.*, p. 57.
16. John C. H. Wu (Wu Jingxiong), *Falü zhexue yanjiu* 法律哲學研究 (Research on legal philosophy) (Shanghai: Huiwentang shuju, 1937), p. 45.
17. Andrew J. Nathan, *Chinese Democracy*, p. 107.
18. *Ibid.*, p. 127.
19. Hsieh Yu-wei, "The Status of the Individual in Chinese Ethics," p. 314.
20. Herbert McClosky and Alida Brill, *Dimensions of Tolerance: What Americans Believe About Civil Liberties* (New York: Russell Sage Foundation, 1983), p. 92.
21. *Ibid.*, p. 125.
22. *Ibid.*, p. 241.
23. *Ibid.*, pp. 125-26.
24. See, for example, Herbert P. Phillips, *Thai Peasant Personality* (Berkeley: University of California Press, 1966), pp. 143-99.
25. R. H. Tawney, *Land and Labor in China* (Boston: Beacon Press, 1966).
26. Lau Siu-kai, *Society and Politics in Hong Kong*, pp. 100-101.
27. *Ibid.*, pp. 70-71.
28. Lau Siu-kai, "Chinese Familism in an Urban-Industrial Setting: The Case of Hong Kong," *Journal of Marriage and the Family*, Vol. 43, No. 4 (November 1981), pp. 977-92.
29. Lau Siu-kai, "Social Change, Bureaucratic Rule, and Emergent Political Issues in Hong Kong," *World Politics*, Vol. XXXV, No. 4 (July 1983), p. 562.
30. Lucian W. Pye, *The Spirit of Chinese Politics*; Richard H. Solomon, *Mao's Revolution and the Chinese Political Culture* (Berkeley: University of California Press, 1971).
31. Zheng Shoupeng, *Zhongguo gudai de zhidao* 中國古代的治道 (The ancient Chinese way to rule) (Taibei: Shangwu yinshuguan, 1972).
32. Sidney Verba and Gary R. Orren, *Equality in America: The View From the Top* (Cambridge, Mass.: Harvard University Press, 1985), p. 180.
33. Jennifer L. Hochschild, *What's Fair? American Beliefs about Distributive Justice* (Cambridge, Mass.: Harvard University Press, 1981), p. 44.
34. Hsieh Yu-wei, "Filial Piety and Chinese Society," in *The Chinese Mind*, Charles

A. Moore, ed. (Honolulu: University of Hawaii Press, 1968), pp. 167-87.
35. *Ibid.*, p. 171.
36. Sidney Verba, "The Parochial and the Polity," in *The Citizen and Politics: A Comparative Perspective*, Sidney Verba and Lucien W. Pye, eds. (Stamford: Greylock Publishers, 1978), p.18.
37. *Ibid.*, p. 19.
38. Lau, *Society and Politics in Hong Kong*, pp. 88-89.
39. *Ibid.*, p. 98.
40. Lau Siu-kai and Ho Kam-fai, "Social Accommodation of Politics: The Case of the Young Hong Kong Workers," *Journal of Commonwealth and Comparative Politics*, Vol. 20, No. 2 (July 1982), pp. 172-88.
41. Lau, *Society and Politics in Hong Kong*, p. 99; for a study of the privatized worker, see David Lockwood, "Sources of Variation in Working-Class Images of Society," in *Working-Class Images of Society*, Martin Bulmer, ed. (London: Routledge and Kegan Paul, 1975), pp. 16-31.

# Notes to Chapter 3

1. For a discussion of the parochial-subject culture, see Garbriel A. Almond and Sidney Verba, *The Civic Culture: Political Attitudes and Democracy in Five Nations* (Princeton: Princeton University Press, 1963), pp. 23-24.
2. See for example Philip E. Converse, "The Nature of Belief Systems in Mass Publics," in *Ideology and Discontent*, David Apter, ed. (New York: Free Press, 1964), pp. 206-61.
3. According to Lucian W. Pye, *Asian Power and Politics: The Cultural Dimensions of Authority*, in Asian cultures "people tend to see power as status, a tendency which even today many Asian rulers nostalgically wish to preserve. For when power implies the security of status there can be no political process. Contention and strife cease. All are expected to devote themselves to displaying the proper respect and honor for others, according to their station. Any criticism of leaders becomes an attack upon the social system. Hence to criticize is to display bad taste, to be less than worthy." (p. 22)
4. Bradley M. Richardson, *The Political Culture of Japan* (Berkeley: University of California Press, 1974), pp. 46-47.
5. *Ibid.*, pp. 60-61.
6. Lau Siu-kai and Kuan Hsin-chi, "The Changing Political Culture of the Hong Kong Chinese," pp. 30-35. In our 1985 survey, 74.3 percent of respondents agreed and 4 percent strongly agreed with the statement that the work of the government had intimate relationship to their daily living.
7. *Ibid.*, p. 29.
8. Chang Wei-jen, "Traditional Chinese Attitudes Toward Law and Authority," pp. 26-31.
9. Hsiao Kung-chuan, *A History of Chinese Political Thought*, Vol. 1 (Princeton: Princeton University Press, 1979), p. 123.
10. *Ibid.*, p. 123.
11. *Ibid.*, p. 124.
12. See Ssu-yu Teng, "Chinese Influence on the Western Examination System," in *Studies of Governmental Institutions in Chinese History*, John L. Bishop, ed. (Cambridge, Mass.: Harvard University Press, 1968), pp. 197-242.
13. See Lau Siu-kai, "Local Leaders and Local Politics in Hong Kong," in *Family and Community Changes in East Asia*, A. Aoi *et al.*, eds. (Tokyo: Japan Sociological Society, 1985), pp. 374-96.
14. Richardson, *The Political Culture of Japan*, pp. 67-68.
15. Lau and Kuan, "The Changing Political Culture," p. 29.
16. Sidney Verba, "The Parochial and the Polity," in *The Citizen and Politics: A*

*Comparative Perspective*, Sidney Verba and Lucian W. Pye, eds. (Stamford: Greylock Publishers, 1978), p. 26.

17. Lau and Kuan, "The Changing Political Culture," p. 31 and p. 34.
18. A comparable case of the inability to relate social problems to governmental responsibility can be found in the study of a Mexico city. "The local agenda is singlemindedly focused on economic and service deficiencies to the almost complete exclusion of structural and political problems. It is an agenda of people who live in a well managed political environment—one in which conflict is limited to occasional tax and service issues that get out of hand. Above all, it is the agenda of a citizenry that has not made the connection between private troubles and public objects except to identify government as responsible for helping out. Missing is a sense that the political process could be other than it is, that politics might be part of the problem, or that change in the basic economic situation implies change in the political system as well. Although visions of a city in which the economic situation is not so harsh and services of all kinds are more plentiful are clearly implied by the agenda, no such image of either the possibility or the necessity of an improved political process is suggested. It is an agenda to warm the heart of the most complacent public official, for nowhere therein would he find the germ of a challenge to business-as-usual in party, bureaucracy, or government." Richard R. Fagen and William S. Tuohy, *Politics and Privilege in a Mexican City* (Stanford: Stanford University Press, 1972), pp. 73-74.
19. West Germany presents a case of low political efficacy but high subject (administrative) efficacy. Judging from the democratic experience, subject competence (efficacy) is instrumental to the development of democratic ethos and can partially substitute for political participation in democratic socialization. The quasi-democratic and idealistic elements in the political ethos of the Hong Kong Chinese might have relation to this sense of administrative competence. In Germany, "[w]hile in the nineteenth century the German middle class accepted the law and the order of the German *Reichtsstaat*, under which it might prosper but have no political influence. Power over governmental decisions was left in the hands of competent government officials; it was not distributed among the populace. But though the German was not a competent citizen, he remained a competent subject. His rights under the law were clearly defined and carefully protected by a system of courts and administration free from political influences. In contrast with Britain, then, the belief in one's political competence has not taken a firm root among the population. If in the United States the competent citizen tends to replace the competent subject, and if in Britain the two tend to coexist in harmony, in Germany the competent subject remains the dominant form of competence." (Almond and Verba, *The Civic Culture*, p. 227.) For a discussion of the development of German political culture, see, for example, David P. Conradt, "Changing German Political Culture," in *The Civic Culture Revisited*, Garbriel A. Almond and Sidney Verba, eds. (Boston: Little, Brown & Co., 1980), pp. 212-72; and Kendall L. Baker *et al.*, *Germany Transformed: Political Culture and the New Politics* (Cambridge, Mass.: Harvard University Press, 1981).

20. *South China Morning Post*, December 1, 1986, p. 1.
21. Lau Siu-kai, *Society and Politics in Hong Kong*, pp. 105-109.
22. Lau and Kuan, "The Changing Political Culture," p. 36.
23. *Ibid.*, p. 34 and p. 36.
24. Sidney Verba, Norman H. Nie and Jae-on Kim, *Participation and Political Equality: A Seven-Nation Comparison* (Cambridge: Cambridge University Press, 1978), p. 54.
25. Verba, "The Parochial and the Polity," p. 5.
26. *Ibid.*, p. 25.
27. *Ibid.*, pp. 25-26.
28. Verba, Nie and Kim, *Participation and Political Equality*, pp. 58-59.
29. Lau and Kuan, "The Changing Political Culture," p. 41.
30. *Ibid.*, pp. 36-37 and p. 41.
31. Samuel J. Eldersveld and Bashiruddin Ahmed, *Citizens and Politics: Mass Political Behavior in India* (Chicago: University of Chicago Press, 1977), pp. 214-15.
32. Lau, *Society and Politics in Hong Kong*, pp. 121-55.
33. Lau Siu-kai, Kuan Hsin-chi, and Ho Kam-fai, "Leaders, Officials, and Citizens in Urban Service Delivery: A Comparative Study of Four Localities in Hong Kong," in *Community Participation in Delivering Urban Services in Asia*, Y. M. Yeung and T. G. McGee, eds. (Ottawa: International Development Research Centre, 1986), p. 251.
34. Mistrust of incumbent political elites oftentimes makes trust of "counter-elites" difficult. For example, in the city of Jalapa, Mexico, economic difficulties engendered even more intense negative feelings toward radicals. In brief, "ordinary citizens withhold energy and resources, remaining at the periphery of politics and public affairs, while viewing 'agitators' with substantial hostility because they are likely to disrupt the smooth flow of public life." Fagen and Tuohy, *Politics and Privilege*, p. 142.

# Notes to Chapter 4

1. H.L.A. Hart, *The Concept of Law* (London: Oxford University Press, 1969), Ch. 5.
2. Eugene Ehrlich, *Fundamental Principles of the Sociology of Law*, Walter L. Moll, trans. (Cambridge, Mass.: Harvard University Press, 1936), *passim.*
3. Murrary Levine and Barbara Howe, "The Penetration of Social Science in Legal Culture," *Law and Policy*, Vol. 7, No. 2 (1985), pp. 173-98.
4. Leon Friedman, "Legal Culture and Social Development," *Law and Society Review*, Vol. 6, No. 1 (1969), pp. 19-46; also Henry W. Ehrmann, *Comparative Legal Cultures* (Englewood Cliffs: Prentice Hall, 1976), pp. 6-11.
5. Lau Siu-kai, *Society and Politics in Hong Kong*, pp. 157-82.
6. C. E. Maloney Banks and H. D. Willcock, "Public Attitudes to Crime and the Penal System," *British Journal of Criminology*, Vol. 15, No. 2 (1975), pp. 228-40; B. Kutchinsky, "The Legal Consciousness: A Survey of Research of Knowledge and Opinion About Law," in *Knowledge and Opinion About Law*, C. M. Campbell *et al.*, eds. (London: Martin Robertson, 1973), pp. 101-38.
7. Section 9 deals with the unauthorized acceptance of advantage in the private sector.
8. *ICAC Mass Survey 1986* (Hong Kong: Community Research Unit, Independent Commission Against Corruption), p. 5-3.
9. J. van Houtte and P. Winke, "Attitudes Governing the Acceptance of Legislation Among Various Social Groups," in *Knowledge and Opinion About Law*, C. M. Campbell *et al.*, eds. (London: Martin Robertson, 1973), pp. 13-42.
10. Peter Wesley-Smith, "The Reception of English Law in Hong Kong," Paper presented to the Conference on the Common Law in Asia held at the University of Hong Kong on December 15-17, 1986.
11. W. Lucian Pye, *The Spirit of Chinese Politics*, esp. Ch. 4.
12. Liao Kuang-sheng, *Antiforeignism and Modernization in China, 1860-1980* (Hong Kong: The Chinese University Press, 1984), *passim.*
13. Parallel to the correlation between trust in the Chinese government and sense of system foreignness found in our study, we also find, in a Social Indicator Survey of Kwun Tong conducted in summer 1986 by Lau Siu-kai and Law Wan Po-san, a negative relationship between trust in the Chinese government and trust in the laws of Hong Kong ($\chi^2 = 24.9$, d.f. = 9, $p < 0.005$). Trust in the laws of Hong Kong is also related to a fear of the reduction in civil liberties and deterioration in the judiciary after 1997 ($\chi^2 = 20.4$ and 19.6 respectively, both with d.f. of 9 and $p < 0.05$). It is interesting to know that in that study, a majority of the respondents (78.7 percent) reported trust or great trust in the laws of Hong Kong, while only 9.3 percent did not.

14. Derk Bodde and Clarence Morris, *Law in Imperial China: Exemplified by 190 Ch'ing Dynasty Cases* (Philadelphia: University of Pennsylvania Press, 1967), p. 11.
15. Leon Vandermeersch, "An Enquiry into the Chinese Conception of the Law," in *The Scope of State Power in China*, Stuart R. Schram, ed. (London: School of Oriental and African Studies, University of London; Hong Kong: Chinese University Press, 1985), p. 3.
16. Hsieh Yu-wei, "The Status of the Individual in Chinese Ethics," in *The Status of the Individual in East and West*, Charles A. Moore, ed. (Honolulu: University of Hawaii Press, 1968), pp. 274-76.
17. *Ibid.*, p. 277.
18. *The Four Books: Confucian Analects, The Great Learning, The Doctrine of the Mean, and the Works of Mencius*, James Legge, trans. (New York: Paragon Books, 1966), p. 13.
19. Sybille van der Sprenkel, *Legal Institutions in Manchu China: A Sociological Analysis* (London: Athlone Press, 1977), p. 124.
20. Ch'u T'ung-tsu, *Law and Society in Traditional China* (Paris: Mouton & Co., 1965), pp. 275-76.
21. Chang Wei-jen, "Traditional Chinese Attitudes Toward Law and Authority," Paper presented to the Symposium on Chinese and European Concepts of Law held in Hong Kong on March 20-25, 1986, p. 7.
22. Victor H. Li, *Law Without Lawyers: A Comparative View of Law in China and the United States* (Boulder: Westview Press, 1978), p. 20.
23. Herbert Huey, "Law and Social Attitudes in 1920s Shanghai," *Hong Kong Law Journal*, Vol. 14, No. 3 (1984), pp. 306-22.
24. Jerome A. Cohen, "Introduction," in *Essays on China's Legal Tradition*, J. A. Cohen, R. R. Edwards and F.M.C. Chen, eds. (Princeton: Princeton University Press, 1980), p. 4.
25. Li, *Law Without Lawyers*, p. 67-73.
26. D. J. Lewis, "The *Guanxi* System: An Inquiry into Chinese Conservatism in the Face of Legal and Ideological Reform," Paper presented to the 7th Annual Conference of the Chinese Law Program at The Chinese University of Hong Kong, November 1986.
27. Andrew J. Nathan, *Chinese Democracy* (Berkeley: University of California Press, 1985), p. 107.
28. Yen Jia-qi and Kau Hau, *A Ten-Year History of the Great Cultural Revolution in China* (Hong Kong: Ta Kung Pao, 1986), *passim.*
29. Kuan Hsin-chi, "New Departures in China's Constitution," *Studies in Comparative Communism*, Vol. 17, No. 1 (1984), pp. 53-68.
30. G. V. Thieme, "The Debate of the Presumption of Innocence in the People's Republic of China," *Review of Socialist Law*, Vol. 10, No. 4 (1984), pp. 277-90.
31. Richard M. Pfeffer, "Crime and Punishment: China and the United States," in *Contemporary Chinese Law: Research Problems and Perspectives*, Jerome A. Cohen, ed. (Cambridge, Mass.: Harvard University Press, 1970), p. 280; William C. Jones, "Due Process in China: The Trial of Wei Jinsheng," in *Review of*

*Socialist Law*, Vol. 1, No. 1 (1983), pp. 55-59.

32. The actual term used in the question was *li, yi, lian, chi* (rules of propriety, righteousness, modesty and sense of shame). *Li, yi, lian, chi* was used instead of *li* alone for fear that among the common people of Hong Kong, *li* may be understood in a narrow sense, i.e., social etiquette. Together with *yi, lian, chi, li* acquires its broader meaning and has direct relevance to the overall socio-political order. According to a common saying, *li, yi, lian, chi* are the four fundamental principles of the Chinese nation.
33. A related question was asked about popular support for capital punishment, which is provided for on the books, but has not been carried out since 1966, as the Governor of Hong Kong invariably pardons those sentenced to the death penalty in conformity with the law of England. Over the past few years, there have been campaigns for the actual administration of the death penalty. Widespread support for the proposition is well known. The question was, therefore, asked for the sake of confirmation only.
34. Chang Wei-jen, "Traditional Chinese Attitudes Toward Law and Authority," pp. 26-31.
35. Wolfgang Kaupen, "Public Opinion of the Law in a Democratic Society," in *Knowledge and Opinion About Law*, C. M. Campbell *et al.*, eds. (London: Martin Robertson, 1973), pp. 43-64.
36. A. Podgorecki, *Law and Society* (London: Routledge & Kegan Paul, 1974), pp. 65-100.
37. Ehrmann, *Comparative Legal Cultures*, p. 84.

# Notes to Chapter 5

1. Edward Shils, "The Intellectuals in the Political Development of the New States," *World Politics*, Vol. 12 (1960), p. 342.
2. Seymour Martin Lipset, *Political Man* (Garden City: Doubleday & Co., Inc., 1960), pp. 101-102.
3. Richard R. Fagen and William S. Touhy, *Politics and Privilege in a Mexican City*, p. 127. See also Charles A. Valentine, *Culture and Poverty: Critique and Counter-Proposals* (Chicago: The University of Chicago Press, 1968), and Eleanor B. Leacock, ed., *The Culture of Poverty: A Critique* (New York: Touchstone Book, 1971).
4. Fagen and Touhy, *Politics and Privilege in a Mexican City*, p. 142.
5. Lau Siu-kai, *Society and Politics in Hong Kong* , pp. 74-75.

# Notes to Chapter 6

1. See Herbert McClosky and John Zaller, *The American Ethos: Public Attitudes toward Capitalism and Democracy* (Cambridge, Mass.: Harvard University Press, 1984), Chapter 6; Jennifer L. Hochschild, *What's Fair? American Beliefs about Distributive Justice* (Cambridge, Mass.: Harvard University Press, 1981); and Alan Wolfe, *The Limits of Legitimacy: Political Contradictions of Contemporary Capitalism* (New York: The Free Press, 1977).
2. ''Political Change: Asia, Africa, and the Middle East,'' in *Understanding Political Development*, Myron Weiner and Samuel P. Huntington, eds. (Boston: Little, Brown and Co., 1987), p. 45.
3. Peter L. Berger, *The Capitalist Revolution: Fifty Propositions about Prosperity, Equality, and Liberty* (Hants: Wildwood House, 1987), p. 161.
4. Lau Siu-kai, *Decolonization Without Independence: The Unfinished Political Reforms of the Hong Kong Government*.

# Appendix

# The 1985 and 1986 Surveys

A survey was conducted in the summer and autumn of 1985 in Kwun Tong. The district of Kwun Tong was selected as the research site because, as a heterogeneous industrial-cum-residential community, it was most representative of Hong Kong as a whole. The sampling frame used was based on a 2 percent sample of the complete household list prepared by the Census and Statistics Department for the 1981 Census. The size of the systematic sample was 1,687. In all, 792 interviews had been successfully completed, yielding a response rate of 46.9 percent. This rate can be considered fairly satisfactory, as it is increasingly difficult to get access to respondents lately. This is because the people of Hong Kong have been, in recent years, bombarded by a huge number of polls conducted by the government, pressure groups, political organizations, marketing research firms, not to mention academic institutions. Consequently, there is a pervasive phenomenon of "interviewee fatigue" among the people of Hong Kong. The diminishing interest in interviewing on the part of college students also explains the lowered response rate in recent years. Surveys have become such a common phenomenon in Hong Kong that it is becoming quite difficult to call on the enthusiasm of college students, who provide the manpower for survey research by academic institutions; besides, the relatively low pay for interviewers fails to attract college students who have become more affluent since late 1970s.

Residents living in private apartments and those belonging to a higher social strata are particularly difficult to get access to. This is almost a universal phenomenon in developing societies. As a result, the sample is biased in the sense that the higher strata in society are less represented. In the end, after further checking, 767 relatively error-free cases were found as usable for quantitative analysis.

The locale of the second survey is also Kwun Tong, thus allowing more valid comparisons between the findings of the two surveys. It was implemented in the summer and autumn of 1986. The sampling frame was furnished by the Census and Statistics Department in April 1986, and consisted of 175,138 households. The final systematic sample was composed of 800 households. At the end of the exercise, 539 completed interviews were obtained.

In both surveys, only persons 18 years old or over were interviewed. In the 1985 survey, they were the heads of the household or their spouses when the former could not be reached. In the 1986 survey, a person over 18 years old was randomly selected for interview from each household in the sample.

On the whole, the socio-demographic profile of the respondents in the two samples does not depart too much from that of the population of Hong Kong as a whole. In comparison with the population of Hong Kong (as of 1986) as a whole, the 1985 sample contains a slightly larger percentage of people aged 40 and over, a larger percentage of males, a slightly larger percentage of persons who are married. It is difficult to make a comparison in terms of income as only the respondent's personal income was asked about in the survey while it is the household income which is the standard item in the published statistics released by the Hong Kong government.

The profile of the respondents in the 1986 survey bears a striking similarity to the profile of the population of Hong Kong as a whole. Therefore, the "representativeness" of the 1986 sample is slightly higher than that of the 1985 sample.

# Index